THE LEGACY OF BOADICEA

Where had the English nation come from?
What were its roots in antiquity?
And what kind of foundation would native antiquity provide
for modern nation-building and nationalist self-celebration?

The Legacy of Boadicea explores the construction of personal and national identities in early modern England, highlighting problems and anxieties attendant on historicist projects of national identity in a nation with no native classical past.

Pre-eminent among these anxieties was the fear of a savage femininity at the very origins of the nation. Boadicea, the ancient warrior queen, epitomised early modern beliefs in the inevitable excess and failure of female rule.

Written in an accessible style, *The Legacy of Boadicea*:

- offers powerful new readings of the ancient British past in Shakespeare's *King Lear* and *Cymbeline*
- links early modern concerns about native origins with Hobbes's articulation of the state of nature in the *Leviathan*
- persuasively illuminates a 'Boadicean' heritage in royal iconography, drama, and the social symptoms of religious dissent
- articulates parallels between the eventual domestication of Britain's warrior queen in Restoration drama, and the social, political, and legal decline in the status of women.

Jodi Mikalachki is Associate Professor of English at Wellesley College.

THE LEGACY OF BOADICEA

Gender and Nation in
Early Modern England

Jodi Mikalachki

London and New York

First published 1998
by Routledge
11 New Fetter Lane, London EC4P 4EE

Simultaneously published in the USA and Canada
by Routledge
29 West 35th Street, New York, NY 10001

© 1998 Jodi Mikalachki

Typeset in Goudy by
Ponting-Green Publishing Services,
Chesham, Buckinghamshire
Printed and bound in Great Britain by
Biddles Ltd, Guildford and King's Lynn

British Library Cataloguing in Publication Data
A catalogue record for this book is available
from the British Library

Library of Congress Cataloging in Publication Data
A catalogue record for this book has been requested

ISBN 0–415–18263–8 (hbk)
ISBN 0–415–18264–6 (pbk)

To my parents
Dorothy Martin Mikalachki
and Alexander Mikalachki

CONTENTS

PLATES

ACKNOWLEDGEMENTS

I would like to thank the many people who generously offered their support and expertise while I was writing and revising this book. Frances E. Dolan, Heather Dubrow, Katharine Park, Mary Beth Rose, and Linda Woodbridge all read the full manuscript and made many useful comments and suggestions. Jean E. Howard also offered crucial advice and encouragement. My colleagues in the Wellesley English Department were engaged readers and interlocutors; I would particularly like to thank Philip J. Finkelpearl, Kathryn L. Lynch, and Luther Terrell Tyler for their thoughtful responses to work in progress, as well as Margaret D. Carroll and Alice T. Friedman of the Wellesley Art Department. Anita Leah Pettway, Amanda Clay Powers, and Sarah E. Wall provided excellent research assistance at different stages in the project. Wellesley Shakespeare students listened to work in progress, asked good questions, and participated in precociously nuanced discussions of *King Lear*, *Cymbeline*, and the staging of native origins. When I first set out to recover the poetics of Renaissance English antiquarianism, I had the good fortune to work under the direction of Thomas M. Greene, G. K. Hunter, and David E. Underdown. To them, and to Susan Dwyer Amussen, I am grateful for early guidance and encouragement.

I am also grateful for the support of friends and family. Margaret Cezair-Thompson, Richard G. French, and Marilyn Sides encouraged me by word and example. Members of St James's Episcopal Church took a lively interest in my work and made many contributions to my spiritual well-being while I was completing it. My family have been engaged participants from the beginning. More than anything else, the lifetime of love and support I have received from my parents, Dorothy and Al Mikalachki, has made this book possible. I dedicate it to them.

I am grateful to Wellesley College for an early leave grant and for other research support. I have also drawn on doctoral research I did with the financial support of The Mrs Giles E. Whiting Foundation and the

Social Sciences and Humanities Research Council of the Canada Council. An earlier version of Chapter 3 was published in *Shakespeare Quarterly* 46 (1995) under the title "The Masculine Romance of Roman Britain: *Cymbeline* and Early Modern English Nationalism." It is reprinted here by permission of *Shakespeare Quarterly*. The illustrations are reproduced by permission of the following: the frontispiece to Christopher Saxton's [*Atlas of England and Wales*] (1579) (C.3.bb.5) and both images from Maurice Bouguereau's *Le Théâtre François* (1594) (C.7.c.22) by permission of the British Library; the "Ditchley" portrait of Elizabeth I by courtesy of the National Portrait Gallery, London; the map of Elizabeth I as Europa by permission of the Ashmolean Museum of Art and Archaeology; the frontispiece and engraved map of Warwickshire from Drayton's *Poly-Olbion* (1612) by courtesy of Special Collections, Wellesley College Library; the frontispiece to John Speed's *Theatre of the Empire of Great Britain* (1612) by permission of the Yale Center for British Art; the frontispieces to Hobbes's *Leviathan* (1651) and to Case's *Sphaera Civitatis* (1588), as well as the woodcuts of Voadicia and Cordeilla from Holinshed's *Chronicles* (1577), by permission of the Houghton Library, Harvard University; the frontispiece portrait from the Duchess of Newcastle's *Plays* (1668) (HEW 7.10.19) by permission of the Harry Elkins Widener Collection, Houghton Library, Harvard University; and the "Rainbow" portrait of Elizabeth I by courtesy of the Marquess of Salisbury. I am grateful to them all.

NOTE ON CITATIONS

Spelling is modernized throughout, with the exception of the works of Spenser, Drayton, and Hobbes, whose original spelling is maintained in modern critical editions. For ease of reference to other editions, I note the part and chapter numbers in citations of Hobbes's *Leviathan*, followed by the page number in the Penguin edition. I draw extensively on two early modern works whose composition, revision, expansion, and translation involved multiple authors: Raphael Holinshed's *The Chronicles of England, Scotland and Ireland* (1587), and William Camden's *Britannia* (1610). Recognizing the complex production of these works, I nevertheless refer to "Holinshed" and "Camden" for ease of reference, noting the contributions of other authors, translators, or editors where relevant. Unless otherwise indicated, all references to Holinshed are to the 1587 edition of the *Chronicles*. Because of the complicated pagination of the 1587 edition, I include the name of any section other than "The History of England" in citations. Unless otherwise indicated, all references to Camden are to the 1610 English translation of the *Britannia*, which I cite by its Latin title, rather than the English translation *Britain*.

I frequently invoke the rather unwieldy terms "historiography" and "historiographical" in describing texts and projects of national recovery. I do so in order to distinguish between history and the historical in their broader senses, and the particular focus *on* history of works such as the *Britannia* and Holinshed's *Chronicles*. Anything written in early modern England might now be described as historical; early modern texts that involve the study and recovery of earlier periods are historiographical.

I consider the year to begin on 1 January in all date references.

INTRODUCTION

The birth of the English nation was not the birth of a nation; it was the birth of the nations, the birth of nationalism.
    Liah Greenfeld, *Nationalism: Five Roads to Modernity*

Nations [...] have no clearly identifiable births.
    Benedict Anderson, *Imagined Communities*

We all need to know where we come from. During the intense period of scholarly, artistic, religious, and political innovation we call the English Renaissance, questions of provenance and identity took on a national dimension. Where had the English nation come from? What were its roots in antiquity? And what kind of foundation would native antiquity provide for modern nation-building and nationalist self-celebration? By the last decades of the sixteenth century, the historiographical recovery of ancient Britain had emerged as one of the central concerns of English cultural production. From scholars and theorists to epic poets, dramatists, and visual artists, those concerned with the articulation of national identity turned their attention to the nation's origins in antiquity. I explore their attempts to define a beginning or place of origins for the nation – a birth or *natio* – and the particular set of problems that plagued them in the late sixteenth and seventeenth centuries.

All terminology derived from *natio* has a doubleness in early modern England, invoking both contemporary efforts to define and represent the nation, and also the recovery of the nation's birth or origins in antiquity. I use the term "native" rather than "national" when referring to the earliest known inhabitants of the island of Great Britain and to the period of antiquity before other peoples intervened in their history. Hence, it generally appears in conjunction with the word "origins" in my work, most often in the phrase "the recovery of native origins." When I use the terms "nation," "national," "nationalist," and "nationalism," they refer to early modern representations, definitions, and understandings. Yet both "native" and "nation" are derived from the Latin *natio*, and it would be artificial and misleading to suggest any absolute distinction between the two, especially in reference to a period when origins were still regarded as definitive rather than as an evolutionary starting point. The identity of the nation with its nativity was a commonplace of Renaissance historiography. Yet because they were disturbed by much of what they recovered about British antiquity, early modern English nationalists devoted considerable energy and ingenuity to distancing the modern nation from its native origins. Their struggles to reconceive British antiquity in ways that would provide a civilized historical foundation for the nation are the theme and focus of my book.

The epigraphs to this chapter indicate some of the complexity – indeed, the contradictions – that persists in late twentieth-century studies of nationalism. The first introduces Liah Greenfeld's account of early modern England as the world's first nation. Assuming the causal primacy of ideas, Greenfeld claims that the idea of the nation is the constitutive element of modernity. The second epigraph virtually concludes the last "appendix" to Benedict Anderson's influential *Imagined Communities*, a work that famously rejects ideological definitions of nationalism. Considering nationalism alongside anthropological topoi such as kinship or religion, Anderson posits its emergence in the eighteenth-century Americas. Both Anderson and Greenfeld participate in the new social, political and historical interest in nationalism that developed during the 1980s, just as its subject seemed about to become historically obsolete.[1] I juxtapose them not simply to illustrate the divergence of scholarly and theoretical opinion in the study of nationalism, but also to suggest the persistent doubleness of terminology derived from *natio*. In her insistence on English priority, Greenfeld refers to the births of the nation as a political entity and of nationalism as a political ideology in sixteenth-century England. In contrast, Anderson invokes the (usually imagined to be) ancient birth of something that will later become a nation – what I call native origins. Any discussion of early modern English nationalism must address the historical and theoretical concerns of both writers. The origins of the English nation and English nationalism in the early modern period cannot be recovered without considering early modern England's own recovery of its native origins in antiquity. Shaped by the humanist historiographical revolution and by medieval and Renaissance conceptions of origins as definitive, early modern English nationalism was inevitably affected by attitudes to British antiquity.[2]

Apprehending native antiquity – in both senses of "capturing" and "learning" it – was in many ways a fearful undertaking for early modern English scholars. The historical status accorded the *Aeneid* as a record of the Trojan founding of Rome, along with the humanist veneration of classical historians, had allowed Renaissance Italian nationalists to integrate their work on Roman topography and monuments with nationalist mythology and the glories of the ancient republic and empire.[3] English scholars who adopted similar principles of historical investigation were faced with two problems. The first was the lack of any native records of antiquity, an absence that forced them to search for textual evidence of native origins in the records of their Roman conquerors. The second and more serious problem was that when they examined these records, they found a race of barbarians more like the American "savages" and "wild Irish" of their budding colonial ventures than the civilized and powerful people of ancient Rome. At the same time, historical evidence for the ennobling Trojan founding of Britain and the chivalric materials of Arthurian romance was found to date from no earlier than Geoffrey of Monmouth's twelfth-century *Historia Regum Britanniae*, a work whose historiographical authority was all but destroyed by the Italian humanist Polydore Vergil during his tenure as historian to the courts of Henry VII and Henry VIII.[4]

In seeking to document their native origins, the English were thus confounded by what Arthur B. Ferguson has called the "utter antiquity" of their nation's prehistory. Ferguson uses the term "prehistory" in its conventional modern sense of the undocumentable past, citing the importance of antiquity to early modern historiographers as they "sought the logical vanishing point for the perspective of history they were coming more and more to consider essential, not only to the completion of their picture of universal history but to their own orientation in an age of ever more evident change" (1993: 1). In our own attempts to orient ourselves in an age of receding modernism and advancing postmodernism, we have reconceived the Renaissance itself as a prehistory, the "early modern" precursor to fully developed modernity. While I would not reduce this rich period to a trial run at a set of problems only resolved in succeeding centuries, I do find it useful to consider the early modern as a broader field including viable alternatives to the naturalized constructs that came to dominate modernity, from nationalism to individualism or sexual identity.[5] The development of early modern English nationalism inevitably engages questions of "prehistory," both in its central concern with recovering national prehistory or native origins, and in its own historical status as the precursor to modern nationalism.[6] In studying these related phenomena, I give as much attention to what disappeared over the course of the seventeenth century as I do to what prefigured or anticipated more modern constructs of national identity and historiography.

THE RECOVERY OF NATIVE ORIGINS

Elizabethan nationalism has traditionally been studied as a straightforward celebration of native history, topography, and legends that brought

England out of the cultural insecurity of the early sixteenth century by constructing a stable, historically based national identity.[7] While not denying the primarily celebratory quality of nationalist projects in this period, I emphasize the anxieties and tensions inherent in national self-definition and representation. Chief among these was the absence of a native classical past on which to found the glories of the early modern nation. As much as English historiographers sought to recover their nation's unrecorded prehistory, they also recoiled from the evidence of native barbarism in the only reliable written records of British antiquity, namely, the histories of the island's Roman conquerors. Early modern English nationalism was shaped by this central contradiction between a longing on the one hand to establish historical precedent and continuity, and an equally powerful drive on the other to exorcise primitive savagery from national history and identity. The tensions between these two imperatives inform virtually all articulations of the nation in this period – from literary evocations and reconstructions of British antiquity, to scholarly and theoretical treatises, visual representations including maps and allegorical portraits, and popular rituals, local history, and legends.

In developing my analyses of these materials, I consider how certain literary and artistic forms – the dramatic genres of tragedy and romance; the topographical epic; the allegorical frontispiece – focused the tensions inherent in projects of national representation. At times these works reveal the mutually untenable nature of English desires both to recover native origins and to establish a civilized foundation for the early modern nation. I read *King Lear*, for instance, as a nationalist tragedy, a play in which all the tools of national recovery – from chronicle history to cartography to local description – fail to deliver the king and his subjects from the self-destructive savagery of ancient Britain. In other plays, however, dramatic form offers an artistic solution to intractable historiographical problems. Shakespeare's use of the romance genre to dramatize the reign of Cymbeline allows for the resolution of the purely British tragedy that imprisoned Lear. Set in Roman Britain, *Cymbeline* is a romance precisely because it incorporates Rome, both in the resolution of the political issue of tribute in the play's long last scene, and in the personal engagement of Imogen/Fidele as a page to the honorable Roman Lucius. Reintegrating Britain with honor into the civilized world of empire, the romance conclusion of *Cymbeline* "romanizes" and ennobles British antiquity.

As I pursue these literary readings, I also consider how the problems of historically based nationalism intersected with broader social concerns about order in the period, concerns that manifested themselves most acutely in formulations of the family and its status as a model for the larger order of the state. I have found Anderson's anthropological sense of nationalism as analogous to kinship or religion especially useful in this regard, particularly given the centrality of the family and religion to articulations of the nation in the period. His understanding of nationalism as aligned "not with self-consciously held political ideologies, but with the large cultural systems that preceded it, out of which – as well as against which – it came into being" (1992: 12) informs my own approach to the phenomenon in early modern England, and guides my consideration of how perceptions of native origins reflected and shaped conceptions of the nation. Early modern anxieties about native origins predictably reflect English concerns about contemporary social and political issues, particularly those related to familial roles and gender relations. Drawing on feminist political theory and history of the family, I pursue the connections between the resolution of certain intellectual problems of nationalism and redefinitions of the state and the family in the seventeenth century.

If Anderson's cultural anthropology informs my theoretical understanding of nationalism, Greenfeld's intellectual history illuminates some of the issues of definition in the period. Citing the work of Guido Zernatto on the European derivation of "nation" from the classical Latin *natio*, she bases her argument for English priority as a nation in part on the adaptation of the language of *natio* to the whole people in sixteenth-century England (1992: 6–7). The earliest classical and medieval uses of *natio* designate a group of foreigners united by place of origin. When the university emerged as the dominant intellectual institution of medieval Europe, *natio* was used in reference to groups of students attending universities outside their native region. In this context, it began to develop the connotations of a community of opinion and purpose as well as origin. This shared identity only held while the students remained abroad, however, losing its meaning once they returned to their region of origin (Zernatto 1944: 352–6). This derivation of "nation" from what was originally a group designation for foreigners indicates the complexity of the term's medieval heritage. National community, in the sense of a shared identity based on a shared place of origin, seems to have emerged in medieval Europe as a function of foreignness or estrangement from the defining place of origin. Only in evidence outside this place of origin, the *natio* depended on the necessary precondition of alienation. Its primary context was the unilingual intellectual and theological institution of the university, itself a product of the spiritual universalism of western Christendom. These medieval "nations" thus had meaning only in the context of a universalism to which their members paid tribute even as they defined a distinct (if temporary) status within it.

The influence of medieval senses of *natio* is evident in a number of ways in early modern English nationalism. As a community formed in alienation from its place and culture of origin, the medieval *natio* also anticipated the central contradiction of early modern England's need to estrange itself from the very historical origins that defined its national identity. Richard Helgerson conceives of English national identity in this period as rooted in self-estrangement and doubleness: "sixteenth-century national self-articulation began with a sense of national barbarism, with a recognition of the self as the despised other, and then moved to repair that damaged self-image with the aid of forms taken from a past that was now understood as both different from the present and internally divided" (1992: 22). Helgerson's account recalls the original derogatory sense of *natio* to designate those of foreign birth. This archaic sense of the term was preserved in early modern biblical translations of "gentiles" as "the nations." Identifying with the people of Israel, however, English translators used "nation" at least as often to translate self-defining terms for the people, polity, and territory of Israel. Greenfeld distinguishes English translations from their contemporary European counterparts and the Vulgate in this regard, arguing strongly for a peculiarly English emphasis on political self-definition in biblical references (51–9).[8] Both self-defining and self-alienating, the idea of the nation thus emerged with a complex and contradictory set of associations in early modern England.

The adaptability of this medieval construction of *natio* to the conflicts inherent in early modern English projects of national recovery may be one of the factors responsible for the early articulation of modern nationalism in England. It is not the only example of English priority in this regard. Beginning in the late thirteenth century, university delegations to church councils also adopted the term *natio* (Zernatto 1944: 361–3). Representing secular and religious leaders as well as the universities, they generated an understanding of the *natio* more broadly as "cultural and political authority, or a political, cultural, and then social *elite*" (Greenfeld 1992: 5). This sense of the nation as the governing elite rather than the whole body of the people was still evident in eighteenth- and nineteenth-century continental theory of the state, as in Montesquieu's assertion, "Sous les deux premières races on assembla souvent *la nation, c'est à dire, les seigneurs et les évêques*; il n'était point des communes" [my emphasis].[9] Greenfeld rests her argument for England's inauguration of modern nationalism on the adaptation of this concept of the *natio* as governing elite to the whole people as nation: "At a certain point in history – to be precise, in early sixteenth-century England – the word 'nation' in its conciliar meaning of 'an elite' was applied to the population of the country and made synonymous with the word 'people'" (6).

Greenfeld's ascription of elite status to the whole people of early six-teenth-century England strikes me as premature, invoking a concept of popular sovereignty that I do not find in evidence until a century later. But her sense of the nation as an elite body does resonate with the development of English nationalism throughout this period. The loss of the historical status of the Trojan founding, with its extension of elite status to the race of Brute, was one of the most difficult intellectual adjustments for English scholars and artists. Even historians committed to Roman records and principles of historiography were loath to give up this legendary material, especially given its barbarous alternative in Roman histories. William Camden, author of the definitive reconstruction of Roman British topography and history, protested in an address to the readers of the first English edition of his *Britannia* that "I have done dishonor to no nation, have descanted upon no man's name, I have impaired no man's reputation, I have impeached no man's credit, no not Geoffrey of Monmouth whose history (which I would gladly support) is held suspected among the judicious" (1610: π5r).

The intellectual difficulties of scholars such as Camden – as well as their intellectual debts to medieval concepts of *natio* – had wider cultural resonance in early modern England. Greenfeld asserts that intellectuals have played the leading role in the development of modern nationalism generally, both articulating and popularizing emerging concepts of the national community (22). While I give serious attention to the social and cultural contexts shaping elite and popular conceptions of national identity in early modern England, I would agree that historically minded intellectuals – scholars, poets, and visual artists – did indeed take the lead in developing the narratives and icons of early modern English nationalism. In doing so, they put the intellectual problems of native origins at the center of attempts to define the early modern English nation. Historiographical dismissals of the legendary matter of Britain restricted nationalist scholars to the new canons of historical evidence, from classical texts to monuments, artifacts, and native topography. Hampered by the paucity of written records and monumental remains from antiquity, as well as by the difficulty of identifying ancient sites mentioned in surviving records, these scholars conceived of their project as fraught with uncertainty and even danger. Invoking a common antiquarian trope in terms that also point to contemporary naval exploration in the search for new territory and trade routes, Camden complained in the *Britannia*, "who is so skillful as in this dark ocean of antiquity to struggle with time without splitting on the rocks" (1610: π5v).

Camden's vivid sense of physical danger indicates the degree of cultural anxiety provoked by the recovery of native origins. Shipwreck was commonly used as a metaphor in early modern definitions of this enterprise, partly to indicate the fragmentary quality of most ancient remains, but also to suggest the virtually irrecoverable loss of the ancient past. Francis Bacon placed the imperfect recovery of the ancient past, or "antiquities," between memoirs and "perfect history" in his tripartite division of civil history in *The Advancement of Learning*, calling antiquities "the wrecks of history […] by which means something is recovered from the deluge of time." Acknowledging the laboriousness of collecting and interpreting these fragments, he nevertheless commended the project as work "that deserves to come in the place of those fabulous and fictitious origins of nations we abound with" (1900: 53).[10] The prevalence of watery images of loss and destruction in describing antiquarian projects indicates how far they were from providing the historiographical security that might replace the fabulous and fictitious origins of nations. Rather than grounding a clear, united vision of the nation as transcending the vicissitudes of time, attempts to recover native origins consistently provoked images of obscurity and fragmentation, the watery loss of definition, and the scattering of evidence over the deluge of history.[11]

Struggling to repair the double loss of the ancient past and those fabulous and fictitious origins of nations discredited by humanist historiography, Camden and other scholars turned to classical records of the people encountered by Julius Caesar, Agricola, and other Roman generals during their conquest of the island. Relying on these records for the ancient history of Britain, Camden privileged the period of Roman Britain as the only firm ground in the watery abyss of native antiquity:

> I am not ignorant that the first originals of nations are obscure by reason of their profound antiquity, as things which are seen very deep and far remote: like as the courses, the reaches, the confluents, and the outlets of great rivers are well known, yet their first fountains and heads lie commonly unknown. I have succinctly run over the Roman's government in Britain, and the inundation of foreign people thereinto, what they were, and from whence they came.
>
> (1610: π4r)

Camden's analogy, in which the watery source of native origins is unknowable in its fluid obscurity, contrasts that period with the "succinct" running over provided by the firm rock of the recorded Roman presence in Britain. The succeeding "inundation" of foreign peoples submerges this rock of certainty, re-engulfing Britain in that dark ocean of antiquity on which scholars were wrecked.

Raphael Holinshed makes a similar distinction between Roman Britain and the unverifiable legends of British prehistory: "I have thought good both to show what I find in our histories and likewise in the foreign writers, to the which we think (namely in this behalf, whilst the Romans governed there) we may safely give most credit, do we otherwise never so much content ourselves with other vain and fond conceits" (1587: 51).[12] If Roman history of ancient Britain provided the only firm ground in the dark ocean of native antiquity, however, it was also the rock on which scholarly hopes for a civilized point of origins were dashed. One of the principles governing early modern efforts to recover native antiquity was the classical premise that a nation that did not know its own origins was barbarous. Yet when English historians of the late sixteenth century consulted Roman records as the first contemporary accounts of their ancestors, they found the ancient Britons depicted as just such an ignorant race. Tacitus was the most explicit in this regard, introducing his description of the ancient Britons in the *Agricola* with the following dismissal of their barbarous obscurity: "what race of mortal birth inhabited Britain originally, whether native to the soil or later comers, is a question which, as one would expect among barbarous people, has never received attention" (1932: 11).[13]

The double-bind of native origins – barbarous if unknown and barbarous when found – produced complicated and at times alienating versions of nationalism in early modern England, requiring both affirmation and denial of the "native" in projects of national recovery. One of the effects of this conflicted nationalism was the consistent preference for Roman over pre-Roman Britain in nationalist histories of the period, with their almost axiomatic response to the period of Roman conquest as the first great moment in British history. Julius Caesar in particular was formative in English knowledge of native antiquity. His early place in the grammar school curriculum guaranteed that any English schoolboy who had attempted Latin composition had done so with the model of his ancient forebears as half-naked savages who stained their bodies with woad and committed human sacrifices.[14] Legends of Caesar's conquest were also preserved among the uneducated in plant and place names and in the many architectural remains ascribed to him (Nearing 1949a, 1949b). For people at all levels of society, from those with a knowledge of local nomenclature and topography to boys learning the rudiments of Latin composition to the masculine scholarly elite, Caesar's invasions and the eventual Roman conquest of Britain represented an important and indeed founding moment in national history.

Britain's ancient vassal status in the Roman Empire left no mark upon popular evocations of the Roman presence in Britain. Indeed, the name of Caesar seems to have ennobled native antiquity, associating local place names, ruins and even vegetation with the elite culture and history of empire. This incorporation of the Roman conquest – its intertwining of the history of empire with the material reality of native topography and monuments – is one of the hallmarks of early modern English nationalism. In one way or another, I explore it in all the chapters of this book, from the visual personifications of Britannia in Chapter 1, to the "topo-historiographical" tragedy of British antiquity enacted in *Lear* in Chapter 2, to the romance conclusion of the Roman-British drama *Cymbeline* in Chapter 3, to the anti-Roman uprising of the British queen Boadicea in Chapter 4. Just as the medieval concept of *natio* took shape in the context of the transcendent universalism of western Christendom, so early modern English nationalism took its most confident definition from the historical period when Britannia was a province of Rome.

The rejection of a purely native antiquity has analogues in the later history of Britain's own colonial empire. One of the curious intersections between Anderson's work (which denies any pre-eighteenth-century European nationalism) and my own is the striking adaptability of his discussion of "last wave" nationalism to early modern England. Considering the emergence of non-European nationalisms under colonialism in the nineteenth and twentieth centuries, Anderson notes their absorption of the imperial terminology of the "native" as both inferior and "belonging here" (122). His account of changes in the vocabulary of space and community in early twentieth-century Siam parallels Greenfeld's similar study of the vocabulary of the polis in early modern England, especially in their shared emphasis on a shift from religious or dynastic terminology to terms indicating bounded, territorial space (Greenfeld 1992: 31–42). Indeed, Anderson attributes the rapid standardization of Siamese national iconography to the colonial introduction of printed texts and maps – precisely the objects most responsible for rapid transformations of early modern national consciousness. And just as the intellectual work of English antiquarians was central to the formation of national identity in early modern England, so twentieth-century Siamese nationalists drew on the work of colonial archaeologists. Like the antiquarians who attributed such monuments as the Tower of London and Stonehenge to the genius of the Roman conquerors, so too did archaeologists reconstructing the history of ancient Siamese monuments insist that their builders were foreign conquerors, now departed, and not the ancestors of Siamese "natives."[15]

One should not discount the central role of colonial records in shaping this account of Siamese nationalism and its emergence in the early twentieth century. Similarly, the importance of Roman records and Rome itself in the historiography of ancient Britain accounts to some extent for the oddly colonized quality of historically based nationalism in early modern England. It may be, however, that some concept of empire, some larger external order within which the nation both pays tribute and rebels, is endemic to the articulation of nationalism in any period. In the remainder of this chapter, I consider an incident in the historiography of Roman Britain that illustrates the complex negotiations of tribute and rebellion informing the recovery of native origins in early modern England. While I save the full elaboration of the uprising in which it figures for Chapters 3 and 4, I would like to examine this striking incident now as a way of introducing the issues of gender that were central to the recovery of native origins in early modern England, and hence, to my analysis.

THE LEGACY OF BOADICEA

One of the most disturbing aspects of British antiquity as documented by the Romans was the Britons' apparent indifference to the masculinist principle of gender hierarchy. Tacitus described them as making no distinction of sex in government, and Dio Cassius compounded this evidence of female autonomy with the assertion that British wives were held in common (Tacitus 1932: 16.2–3; Cassius 1925: LXII.6.3). Insubordinate and unchaste, ancient British females violated both halves of the golden rule of early modern womanhood, with its insistence on feminine subordination and chastity. Powerful females loom large in early modern visions of native origins, from the universal gendering of the topographical and historical "Britannia" as feminine to the troubling eruptions of ancient queens in the process of civilization by Rome. Like the unruly women who challenged the patriarchal order of early modern England, these powerful and rebellious females in native historiography threatened the establishment of a stable, masculine identity for the early modern English nation.

Early modern historiographers gave disproportionate attention to examples of female authority in accounts of ancient Britain, from the establishment of the nation's first "gunarchie" under Queen Cordeilla, to the invocation of native goddesses and the political and military responses of British queens to Roman rule. British queens who exercised independent authority were especially liable to editorial condemnation and moralizing. Represented as violating all principles of feminine subordination and social order, particularly in their betrayal of male relatives and allies, they inevitably plunged their families and subjects into ruin.

Queen Cartismandua, who handed over the British hero Caractacus to the Romans, exemplified the early modern expectation of social ruin as the consequence of female rule. In Camden's account, her monetary reward for betraying Caractacus led directly to the downfall of the ruling house. From her favor to the Romans, he writes, "ensued wealth: of wealth and prosperity riotous and incontinent life: in so much, that casting off Venusius her husband, and intercepting his kinsfolk, she joined herself in marriage with Vellocatus his harness-bearer, and crowned him King: which foul fact was the overthrow immediately of her house" (1610: 53). Once given power, the ancient queen immediately indulged her basest appetites, throwing off the proper authority of her husband and promoting a social inferior to his place, thus subverting class and gender hierarchies to the ruin of her house.

Disrupting social hierarchies, resisting civility and dragging the native race into ruin, the savagery of ancient British women consistently thwarted early modern attempts to merge national history with the masculine order of Rome. One woman in particular threatened this foundation of the modern nation on Roman Britain. Unrelenting in her violent resistance to Rome, she began her uprising with the undeniably legitimate grievances of her own shameful flogging, the rape of her royal daughters, and the despoiling of her people by Roman soldiers. Her patriotic orations appear prominently in classical and early modern accounts, invoking all the topoi of sixteenth-century nationalism, from the natural glories of the island to the noble heritage of its freedom-loving people. In scope, ferocity, and duration, the uprising she led was the most significant challenge to Roman rule in ancient Britain. And yet as a martial and outspoken woman, exercising independent female sovereignty even as she threatened Britain's ancient membership in the Roman Empire, she was not easily incorporated into nationalist historiography by those seeking to establish a civilized, masculine foundation for the early modern nation.

Boadicea re-entered British historiography in the early sixteenth century, recovered with other disturbing examples of native savagery and resistance to Roman rule. A British queen of the Iceni tribe who led a widespread revolt against Claudian rule in the mid first century, she was acknowledged in classical sources as having very nearly driven the Romans out of Britain. Her revolt eventually failed when she suffered defeat by Suetonius, and her own life ended shortly thereafter, either from grief and illness or suicide. A complicated figure in early modern accounts, she became emblematic of that period's belief in savage excess as the inevitable consequence of female rule. Boadicea's treatment in reconstructions of Roman Britain is the best single example of the intersection of early modern misogyny with anxiety about savage native origins. In their concern to recover a civil period of native antiquity, early modern historians projected ancient British savagery onto Boadicea and other ancient queens. Redefining the national problem of ancient savagery as an issue of female insubordination, they sought to isolate a complementary tradition of native masculine civility. Far from containing their anxieties about ancient Britain, however, their emphasis on the savagery of ancient queens raised the even more disturbing possibility that native origins were to be understood entirely in terms of female excess. Savage, rebellious, and self-destructive, ancient Britain as a whole became analogous in their accounts to early modern constructions of insubordinate womanhood.

Holinshed's presentation of Boadicea exemplifies this historiographical strategy. Throughout his account of her uprising, he emphasizes female excess, from the omnipresence of British women in battle, fighting audaciously and delivering frenzied prophecies of victory, to the military leadership and oratory of Boadicea herself, culminating in pagan prognostication and an ecstatic prayer to the goddess Adraste (1587: 42–6). British men figure only in general terms in this account, invoked incidentally in descriptions of their women's like audacity in war, or appealed to by Boadicea as she raises her army. In his description of the final battle, Holinshed notes "the shrill and vain menacing threats of the Britons, since there was among them more women than men, they having no skill in warlike discipline" (45). Holinshed's Romans, on the other hand, are resolutely male, from the Emperor Claudius and his named officers in Britain, to the disciplined and heavily outnumbered Roman troops whose manhood Suetonius invokes before defeating the British forces and ending the uprising. Culminating in this description of the Britons' defeat, Boadicea's revolt in Holinshed becomes a narrative of gender conflict rather than native resistance to empire. Thus recasting the difficult national issues of rebellion against Rome in gendered terms, Holinshed resolves the conflict by superimposing a masculinist gender hierarchy on the two armies.

What he sacrifices in doing so is any independent native masculinity. The whole British polis figures as feminine in Holinshed's account. A widowed mother of two daughters, Boadicea presides over an exclusively female royal family. She leads a predominantly female army into battle, and invokes the goddess Adraste as "thou woman of women," celebrating the fact that it is "a goddess which governest the Britons" (44).[16] If her defeat by Suetonius is the ultimate verdict on the inability of women to exercise sovereignty, Boadicea's conduct of the revolt is the strongest evidence of her savage female excess. Holinshed emphasizes the Britons' cruelty in killing captives of all ages and sexes. His condemnation of the lack of discipline and savage violence of the troops under Boadicea's command culminates in an atrocity story that places grotesque emphasis on the overwhelmingly female nature of the rebellion:

> They spared neither age nor sex: women of great nobility and worthy fame, they took and hanged up naked, and cutting off their paps, sewed them to their mouths, that they might seem as if they sucked and fed on them, and some of their bodies they stretched out in length, and thrust them on sharp stakes.
>
> (45)

This grotesque expression of ancient British savagery points to early modern anxiety about the overwhelming femininity of native origins. The terminology of *natio* foregrounds birth, and with it, issues of maternity and early nurture. Similarly, the terrible parody of maternal nurture in this atrocity story invokes the question of origins in its mockery of the earliest stage of human development. The addition of these mutilated women to the all-female cast of Boadicea's revolt suggests something of the smothering weight of femininity in early modern investigations of native origins. Savage, self-sustaining, and deadly, this gendered atrocity embodies the inward-turning isolationism of Boadicea's female resistance to Rome.

And yet, far from consigning British native origins to savage isolation from civilization, this violent parody of maternal nurture has a historiographical parallel in Roman iconography. The masculine empire of Rome also had a savage female breast at its origin. Romulus, the legendary founder of Rome, along with his twin brother Remus, was suckled by a she-wolf after the murder of their mother. Their family drama was as savage and self-destructive as any episode in the chronicles of British antiquity. The twins' grandfather, the last of the legendary Alban kings directly descended from Aeneas, was ousted by his brother, who forced the future mother of the twins to become a vestal virgin in order to end the direct royal line. Impregnated by Mars nevertheless, she gave birth to the twins and was thrown with them into the Tiber. The twins were washed ashore, where they were nursed by the she-wolf until taken in by a herdsman and his wife, who raised them to adulthood. Eventually restoring their grandfather to his rightful throne, the twins founded a new settlement in the place on the banks of the Tiber where they had been rescued by the she-wolf. Taking its name from Romulus, the new city of Rome developed this foundation myth into a civic icon of the nursing she-wolf and her foster sons.

During the Italian Renaissance, Roman antiquarians recovered this classical icon of the founding of Rome. In 1471, an antique bronze she-wolf was donated by the pope to the city of Rome, to be displayed on the Capitoline as a public image of the civic founding. Installed with Renaissance casts of the nursing twins beneath, the Capitoline Wolf became one of the most common images of the Roman founding, widely disseminated in drawings, paintings, and sculpture. Renaissance adaptations of the classical grouping foregrounded the act of suckling, making maternal nurture a visually explicit element of its iconography.[17] Their emphasis on the nursing twins indicates the importance of rechannelling the savage female nurture of the she-wolf. Unlike the mutilated British captives, the she-wolf did not suck her own breasts; rather, she suckled Romulus and Remus, descendants of Aeneas and progenitors of the Roman race. Her savagery was thus naturalized as an emblem of native vigor imbibed from the natural world. Rechannelled into the male line of Romulus, this native femininity was properly subordinated, issuing eventually in the masculine empire of Rome.[18]

In contrast to the Roman icon of contained and rechannelled savagery, the Boadicean atrocity story offers no masculine afterlife of order and civility. Forced to suck their own breasts in a grotesque parody of maternal nurture, Boadicea's female victims can neither exercise their true maternal function nor escape from the enclosed circle of femininity imposed on them by the British queen. The nature of Boadicea's own maternity is inevitably called into question by this atrocity. Beginning her revolt to avenge herself, her daughters and her people after Roman violation, Boadicea assumed the queenly role of a mother to her people, leading them against foreign aggressors.[19] As her revolt progressed, however, she yielded to the undisciplined cruelty and lust for plunder of her savage female nature. Holinshed does not indicate whether her mutilated captives were Roman women or Britons who supported Rome. The gruesome parody of maternal nurture visited on the bodies of these "women of great nobility and worthy fame" stands as an emblem of Boadicea's own monstrous reversal of the role of maternal leadership and protection she claimed at the beginning of her revolt. Far from approximating the savage nurture of the she-wolf whose native milk invigorated the masculine race of Rome, the breasts Boadicea mutilates bring nothing but humiliation and death to her people.

The parodic violence of this atrocity story also reflects Boadicea's inward-turning patriotism, that radical isolationism that threatened to leave ancient Britain with nothing but the breast of its own savage origins to feed on. The fear of collapsing into such grotesquely feminized savagery is Boadicea's legacy to early modern English nationalism. Emblematic of the ancient female savagery haunting native origins, her uprising represented the rejection of everything masculine, civilized, and Roman that the English sought to integrate into national history. In the following chapters, I suggest how a variety of masculine bonds were substituted for the self-contained and self-destructive femininity of Boadicea's legacy. From the masculine embrace of empire that crowns dramatizations of Roman Britain, to the articulation of the nation as a set of ascriptive bonds between men in Hobbes's social contract theory, early modern visions of the nation were centrally concerned with exorcising the savage femininity so vividly apprehended in native origins.

In Chapter 1, "From Mater Terra to the Artificial Man," I discuss how early modern responses to ancient British femininity influenced the gendering of national iconography and the development of Hobbes's theory of the state of nature. My complementary readings of the tragedy of *King Lear* and the romance of *Cymbeline* in Chapters 2 and 3 suggest how anxieties about ancient British queens intersected with concern about unruly women in early modern English drama. Emphasizing the collapse of all social structures in *Lear*, from the family to the nation, I read it as a tragedy of native origins, relentless in its terrible revelation of ancient British isolation and barbarity. Turning to *Cymbeline*, I trace the rejection of this purely native antiquity in favor of what I call "the masculine embrace of Roman Britain," a complex resolution of the play's issues of gender, sexuality, and national identity. I return to the historiography of Boadicea in Chapter 4, considering how negative examples of ancient female sovereignty affected Elizabeth's self-representations as a regnant queen and symbol of native resistance to foreign empire. In this last chapter, I also situate issues of gender, native origins, and national identity in the context of early modern attitudes to motherhood, drawing parallels between the containment and appropriation of maternal authority in the seventeenth century, and the domestication of Boadicea in Restoration drama, which prepared the way for her resurrection as a national heroine in the eighteenth century.

I conclude with a speculative essay surveying English articulations of universal human nature and corporate identity in the quarter century following the publication of Hobbes's *Leviathan* in 1651. This final chapter points to ways in which peculiarly English issues of national self-definition – the gendering of native origins and national iconography; associations of nationalism with female savagery; the role of the maternal breast in the construction of public masculine identity – are reconstituted in universal terms by writers ranging from Thomas Browne to John Milton and John Bunyan. These authors seem (and perhaps seek) to transcend the nationalism that animated earlier literary and historical projects in the period. And yet rather than turning away from these earlier projects of national self-definition, they effectively naturalized the concerns of early modern English nationalism. Responding to anxieties about native origins, and drawing on a century's literary and historiographical efforts to resolve them, these mid to late seventeenth-century writers reintegrated the issues of English nationalism into a context of spiritual universalism similar to the one in which the medieval *natio* emerged. Embedding specifically English concerns in universalist narratives of human spirituality, they produced some of the most enduring examples of English cultural normativity on the eve of the full development of modern nationalism and English colonial imperialism.

1

FROM MATER TERRA TO THE ARTIFICIAL MAN

> At the beginning of modern moral and political philosophy stands
> a powerful metaphor: the "state of nature." This metaphor is at
> times said to be fact.
>
> Seyla Benhabib, *Situating the Self*

The founding text of the modern philosophical tradition described above
is Hobbes's *Leviathan*, composed during its author's royalist exile in Paris
in the late 1640s and first published in 1651. Hobbes's (in)famous articulation of "the life of man" in the state of nature – "solitary, poore, nasty,
brutish, and short" – owes much to the English civil wars of the mid
seventeenth century and the political chaos of national government before Cromwell established his republican sovereignty in the 1650s. In the
new political "science" of the *Leviathan*, Hobbes developed a theoretical
analysis of the crisis of national government in England (and other western European nations) in the seventeenth century. At the same time, in
his founding metaphor of the state of nature as one of unmitigated savagery and conflict, Hobbes wrote into his theoretical apparatus the anxieties
about native origins that had so exercised an earlier generation of nationalist English writers. The metaphor of the state of nature that stands at
the beginning of modern moral and political philosophy is thus arguably
derived from the historiographical "fact" of early modern English anxiety
about native origins.

This chapter moves toward a sustained reading of the *Leviathan*'s two
formative metaphors – the state of nature and the titular Leviathan or
"Artificial Man" – as theoretical responses to the preceding century's
historiographical recovery of native origins in England. To frame this
reading, I juxtapose Hobbes's "Artificial Man" with an earlier figure I
call "Mater Terra" – a composite of various feminine icons of the nation,
ranging from portraits of Elizabeth I to topographical allegories and maps.
Over the first half of the seventeenth century, the predominantly feminine iconography of Elizabeth's reign was first effaced and then replaced

by masculinist theory and imagery of the state. Foregrounding the category of gender, I survey the shift in national iconography from the feminine images of Elizabeth's reign to the bearded king of Hobbes's title page. Both recalling and supplanting the earlier images, Hobbes's "Artificial Man" represents the early modern state as fully and exclusively masculine.

My literary and iconographical reading of the *Leviathan* complements reassessments of Hobbes and social contract theory by feminist political theorists. Just as women or feminine allegories disappear from national iconography during the first half of the seventeenth century, so women's experience drops out of articulations of political theory. These parallel effacements of the feminine go beyond the conventional subordination of women to men. As Seyla Benhabib (whom I quote in the epigraph to this chapter) argues, "It is not the misogynist prejudices of early modern moral and political theory alone that lead to women's exclusion. It is the very constitution of a sphere of discourse which bans the female from history to the realm of nature (1992: 157). In the "visual discourse" of national iconography, and in the overwhelming rhetorical bias of the *Leviathan*, both "the female" and "the realm of nature" lose their pre-eminence in English national iconography. My reading of the images, and my consideration of Hobbes's metaphors, explore the trajectory and the means of this effacement; i.e., the cultural history of how the conventional femininity of national iconography was replaced by the masculinist imagery and rhetoric of the state in the *Leviathan*.

Other historicist accounts of Elizabethan nationalism have also taken the mid seventeenth century as their horizon. Arguing for the development of a non-dynastic vision of the nation in maps, topographical allegories, and even some royal portraits, these accounts draw a direct line from what they perceive as an iconographical struggle between crown and people to the civil wars of the mid seventeenth century. Both the reductive "crown/country" dichotomy and the historiographical determinism that inform these readings have undergone serious challenges and qualifications in the last two decades. In developing my own narrative of cultural change in this period, I emphasize the continuity of certain conflicts and anxieties inherent in the materials of English national recovery and self-representation. The trajectory I trace from Elizabethan nationalism to Hobbes is both political and cultural. It begins with a reassessment of Elizabeth's "authorship" of the first English county atlas, develops into a critical reading of authority and gender in Hobbes's political science, and concludes with the imaginary world of Margaret Cavendish, the first science fiction author.

TWO MONARCHS' BODIES

As has been frequently noted, Saxton's county atlas bore neither title nor author's name at its 1579 publication. Rather, it was introduced by an engraving of Elizabeth, crowned and enthroned, bearing scepter and orb, and flanked by figures of cosmography and geography (Figure 1). Her place on the title page of the county atlas has generally been taken as a sign of her authority over the administrative units represented within it. The most elaborate treatment of the title page, Richard Helgerson's "The Land Speaks: Cartography, Chorography, and Subversion in Renaissance England," extends this thesis to give Elizabeth ultimate "authorship" of the atlas, as head of the chain of patronage that hired Saxton and produced the maps. Helgerson compares the county atlas title page with the Ditchley portrait of Elizabeth by Marcus Gheeraerts the Younger, where the queen stands on a map modeled on Saxton's composite of England and Wales (Figure 2). In company with most readers of the images, he takes both portraits as deliberate and insistent statements of royal power over the land represented. Helgerson regards the Ditchley portrait as a more fixed and unchallengeable version of that power. Noting the gradual exclusion of the royal arms from reprints of Saxton's maps and later versions of the county atlas, he posits a progressive marginalization of royal and dynastic claims in favor of a land-based model of national identity. Helgerson locates the agency of this shift in what he calls the "built-in bias" of the map as a form of representation, where such surrounding symbols of royal control as arms and insignia are made to look marginal and merely decorative, as against the intrinsic features of the land itself (1992: 51–85).[1]

This large claim for cartography as the originator and primary agent of national transformation has a number of problems. First, it is by no means clear, as Helgerson claims, that "there is really no way to overcome" the built-in cartographical bias as he defines it. The royal presence need not be relegated to the margins of a map, as indeed it is not in a 1598 Dutch engraving of Europe as Elizabeth I, where the queen's left arm forms England and Scotland, her right, Italy, and her body, the mass of the continent (Figure 3). Neither need one designate the framing material of an image as less "intrinsic" than what it contains and to some measure defines. Still less should that image be taken in isolation as the origin and cause of the kind of massive shift in national identity Helgerson ascribes to it. In his confessedly Whiggish reading of chorographic developments, Helgerson sees cartographic representation as having increased both local and national identity at the expense of dynastic loyalty. "Maps thus opened a conceptual gap between the land and its ruler," he concludes, "a gap that would eventually span battlefields" (114).

1. Frontispiece to Christopher Saxton's [*Atlas of England and Wales*] (1579) (C.3.bb.5), by permission of the British Library.

2. "Ditchley" portrait of Elizabeth I, attr. Marcus Gheeraerts the Younger (1592?), courtesy of the National Portrait Gallery, London.

3. Map of Elizabeth I as Europa (1598), by permission of the Ashmolean Museum of Art and Archaeology.

The Whig model of an inexorable movement toward the civil wars of the mid seventeenth century has been largely discredited by social and administrative historians of early modern England.[2] Even if one were to accept it provisionally, Helgerson's location of the agency of this drive in a claimed imperative of cartographical representation would still need qualification. In his claim that maps "opened a conceptual gap between the land and its ruler," Helgerson assumes a split between the land and the monarch, in which these two embodiments of the nation are engaged in a struggle for mastery over its representation. His premise is that once the land is stripped of encroaching royal symbols and presented in its "naked" state, then the rival figure of the monarch will be banished as the constitutive body of the nation. And yet, if one takes seriously the identification of Elizabeth's body with the land, an identification that is a necessary prelude to Helgerson's imagined gap, the figure of the queen can be taken as present in any representation of the land.[3]

Helgerson remarks of the Ditchley portrait in passing, "After all, by putting the queen *on* the map the Ditchley artist had hidden what most people bought an atlas to see – a representation of the land itself" (112). And yet the land "itself" as represented by the Ditchley artist seems to be precisely a version of the queen's body, the flat representation of what she in her three-dimensional majesty embodies: the nation. One might read the county atlas title page in the same way; the image of the monarch, herself the embodiment of the nation, introduces the maps that will follow. The cartouche beneath her feet bears the Latin inscription "*Clemens et Regni moderatrix iusta Britanni / Hac forma insigni conspicienda nitet*," a crude English rendering of which would be "The merciful and just ruler of the Kingdom of Britain / Shines in this notable image, worthy of being seen." "*Hac forma*," this figure, shape or image, presumably refers to the frontispiece – i.e., the figure of the queen – and yet its representational insistence on likeness and outline might apply as easily to the maps, equally notable and worthy of being seen. This conflation of the figure of the queen and the figures of the maps suggests not so much an imposition of royal authority on the otherwise neutral or subversive map, but rather a construction of mutual identity out of the interplay of the queen's body and the land.

The importance of this interplay, and its distinctiveness to Elizabeth, emerges more fully through comparison to a contemporary topographical work dedicated to another monarch and representing another kingdom. Maurice Bouguereau's *Le Théâtre François, où sont comprises les chartes générales et particulières de la France*, was prepared and presented to Henri IV in 1594 to commemorate the king's retaking of Paris after the revolt of 1589–94. It is the first atlas of France, and was explicitly designed as a symbol of national unity under one monarch.[4] The atlas opens with a description of its contents, an advertisement for subscribers, and a chronology of the kings of France from the legendary Pharamond to Henri IV. The second leaf presents the standard topographical title page, with the full title framed by a classical arch. On its verso is a half-page portrait bust of Henri IV in armor, flanked by female personifications of France and Navarre (Figure 4a). French verses in a cartouche praise Henri for his military victories and his clemency. On the lower half of the page is an acrostic sonnet to Henry Bourbon by Bouguereau (π2v).

In many ways, this page recalls the title page of Saxton's atlas. Both monarchs are framed by personifications and celebrated in verses on their glory and clemency. Each seems to stand as an emblem or embodiment of the nation represented cartographically in the atlas. The emblems differ slightly in that Elizabeth's whole body performs this function, whereas Henri's head and torso alone appear. They are also placed differently. Elizabeth's portrait is the first page of Saxton's atlas, and her name appears nowhere on it, as though her *forma* alone introduces and authorizes the atlas. In contrast, Henri's portrait appears on the verso of Bouguereau's second leaf, after the title page and other written preliminaries. The king's image is almost obsessively supplemented by the written characters of his name, in the frame surrounding the portrait, the verses in the cartouche, and the acrostic sonnet to Henry de Bourbon. One last feature of Henri's portrait reveals the most important difference between the representational properties of these two royal bodies.

The half-page portrait of Henri IV is in fact an addition to the printed title page of Bouguereau's atlas. Glued along its top edge only, it folds up to reveal a map of France beneath, printed above the acrostic sonnet in the space covered by the portrait (Figure 4b).[5] Unlike Elizabeth, then, Henri does not introduce the maps of his kingdom in an exclusive and unified embodiment of the nation. Rather, on the verso of the second leaf, his figure and his name stand interchangeably with another figure, "GALLIAE REGNI POTENTISS. NOVA DESCRIPTIO." The icon of king-as-nation thus emerges mechanically from the manipulation of the half-page addition to the title page, a device that precludes viewing both images simultaneously. By contrast, the single icon of the queen-as-nation that introduces Saxton's atlas stands in place of any competing image or title for the collection of maps that follows.

I suggest that the Saxton title page functions so fully as an emblem for the whole atlas because the monarch it represents is female.[6] The land-based constructions of the nation that emerged and flourished in sixteenth-century England inevitably and centrally involved gender.[7] Their

SONNET ACROSTICHE
DE LA RENOMMEE.

AV ROY.

Heroique Monarque, Allexandre puiſſant,
E xercité en Mars: & ſecond Charle-Maigne
N oble en faits & en dits, le premier Henry-
    Maigne,
R ace de Sainct Loys par qui tu vas croiſſant.

Y ſſu du ſang Bourbon, tes ayeuls ſurpaſſant,
D iſcret, bening, vaillant ſur tout à la Campaigne,
E ntre les Martiaux, Vertu qui t'accompaigne
B urine en mon Autel ton Renom floriſſant.

O nc vn tel Pardonneur ne fut n'y ne peut eſtre
V ers les ſiens rebellez, auſquels il tend ſa dextre,
R enverſant l'Orgueilleux & honorant le bon.

B eny de l'Eternel, recouvriras Navarre
O bſtant ce vieil Maran, y planteras ton Phare,
N arrant par l'vnivers le nompareil BOVRBON.

               M. Bouguereau.

4a. Portrait of Henri IV in Maurice Bouguereau, *Le Théâtre François* (1594) (C.7.c.22), by permission of the British Library.

GALLIAE REGNI POTENTISS. NOVA DESCRIPTIO

SONNET ACROSTICHE
DE LA RENOMMEE.

AV ROY.

H eroique Monarque, Allexandre puiffant,
E xercité en Mars: & fecond Charle-Maigne
N oble en faits & en dits, le premier Henry-
    Maigne,
R ace de Sainct Loys par qui tu vas croiffant.

Y ffu du fang Bourbon, tes ayeuls furpaffant,
D iféret, bening, vaillant fur tout à la Campaigne,
E ntre les Martiaux, Vertu qui t'accompaigne
B urine en mon Autel ton Renom floriffant.

O nc vn tel Pardonneur ne fut n'y ne peut eftre
V ers les fiens rebellez, aufquels il tend fa dextre,
R enverfant l'Orgueilleux & honorant le bon.

B eny de l'Eter nel, recouvriras Navarre
O bftant ce vieil Maran, y planteras ton Phare,
N arrant par l'vnivers le nompareil BOVRBON.

M. Bouguereau.

4b. Map of France in Maurice Bouguereau, *Le Théâtre François* (1594)
(C.7.c.22), by permission of the British Library.

scholarly and aesthetic issues of gendered representation participated in a broader transformation of cultural and political representation. The mutually constitutive bodies of Elizabeth and the land produced a powerful feminine icon of the nation that was not easily supplanted in the succeeding reigns of James and Charles. The struggle to efface this feminine icon and replace it with a masculine image of the state lasted for almost fifty years after Elizabeth's death. Its early years coincided with the peak of topographical nationalism in the 1610s. Despite James's accession and insistently patriarchal style, the composite icon I call "Mater Terra" dominated the major nationalist projects of the first decade of his reign. In the following section, I demonstrate the persistence of this powerful feminine icon, and examine the Jacobean work of supplanting it that cleared the national stage for Hobbes's Artificial Man.

MATER TERRA AND THE PREVALENCE OF FEMININE ICONOGRAPHY

Michael Drayton's topographical epic *Poly-Olbion* is one of the most sustained examples of land-based nationalism produced in early modern England. Conceived at the end of the sixteenth century, the poem eventually surveyed all the counties of England and Wales, describing in its thirty songs the topography, local customs, historic events, and monuments of every corner of the realm. Drayton began work on the poem in the early 1590s, publishing the first eighteen songs in 1612 and the complete poem in 1622. The composition of *Poly-Olbion* thus stretches over almost thirty years, encompassing the last decade of Elizabeth's reign and virtually the whole of James's. Even so, Drayton was forced to abandon his original plan of including Scotland in order to terminate his vast project. The poem thus falls short of the promise inherent in its title of describing the whole island of Great Britain. Published and largely composed during James's reign, Drayton's poem does not leave the bounds of Elizabeth's realm.[8]

The title page of this Jacobean poem is also resolutely Elizabethan (Figure 5). The female personification of Great Britain appears in the same situation as Elizabeth on the Saxton title page. Both figures are enthroned with scepter and crown, Great Britain bearing a cornucopia in place of Elizabeth's orb. They are both framed by an arch with pillars, and flanked by allegorical figures. James's personified realm of Great Britain, draped in a map replete with Saxton's topographical symbols, her bare breast recalling the Amazon cult of Elizabeth's reign, is not so much a replacement of Elizabethan iconography as a perpetuation of the

5. Frontispiece to Michael Drayton's *Poly-Olbion* (1612), courtesy of Special Collections, Wellesley College Library.

symbolism wherein the queen's body and the land were mutually constitutive of the nation. Claire McEachern rightly warns against reading the complex and multiply divided *Poly-Olbion* through its frontispiece as an unproblematic tribute to wholeness (1996: 167–70). Yet the frontispiece itself does strongly recall the transcendant unity of Elizabethan national iconography,[9] and the insistent femininity of the personified Great Britain replays itself throughout the poem and its topographical engravings.

As the monarch who united the crowns of Great Britain, James is conspicuously absent from the poem's iconography. A profile engraving of Prince Henry, to whom the first part of the poem was dedicated, is one of the preliminaries, appearing two pages after the female personification of Great Britain and evoking none of its iconographical power. Neither the prince nor his royal father constitutes the land in his own body, as Elizabeth and the female personification of Great Britain do. And yet a gendered topography is everywhere present in *Poly-Olbion*, from the personification of Great Britain, her robe covered in topographical symbols and her pose suggesting the outline of the island, to the anthropomorphized deities of the landscape, both describing and representing its topographical features. To the extent that Drayton's epic can be said to have any action at all, it is a dramatization of gender and gender relations. Rivers marry each other or embrace islands and towns, daughter-rivers flow from their father Mount Helidon (1933: 23.37–44), the senex Clent Hill longs for the forest nymph Feckenham who has eyes only for the young River Salwarpe (14.9–60), and Thames prolongs his dalliance with the low-born River Mole, reversing his course by means of the tide and so deferring his arranged marriage to Medway (17.1–72).[10]

Drayton's emphasis on marriage as the chief means of uniting topographical features might lead one to expect a topography equally divided between male and female deities.[11] Yet topographical representation in *Poly-Olbion* is overwhelmingly feminine. Aside from hills, mountains, and ditches, which are consistently masculine, and the male partners in the river marriages, almost all the topographical features of the poem are feminine. The femininity of the landscape is even more pronounced in William Hole's engravings for the poem, from the Great Britain of the title page to the maps that illustrate the anthropomorphic topography of each county. The map of Warwickshire, dominated by female personifications of the Forest of Arden, the Vale of Redhorse and the three principal towns of Tamworth, Warwick, and Coventry, is a good example of his gendered topographies (Figure 6).[12] In addition to these large and detailed feminine personifications, each of the seventeen named rivers and streams on the map is represented as female, including the River Tame, here and elsewhere described as male in the text.

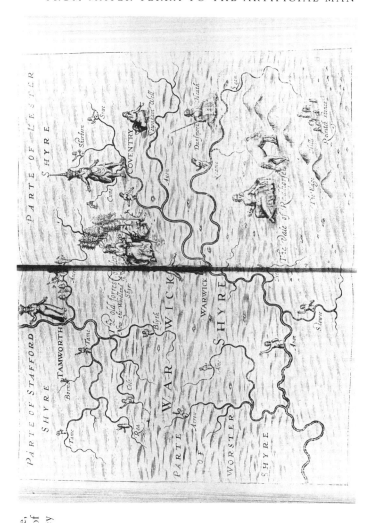

6. Engraved map of Warwickshire, *Poly-Olbion* (1612), courtesy of Special Collections, Wellesley College Library.

Celebrated as the "Hart of England" in Song 13, Hole's Warwickshire teems with topographical femininity.

Hole's engravings draw on the pictorial convention of topography as feminine, a long-standing set of assumptions that has been the subject of feminist work on European territorial expansion in the early modern period. This work emphasizes a relation of conquest and appropriation between the masculine colonizer and the feminized land, in which the masculine desire for sexual domination of the feminine and the imperial desire to dominate and control new territories come together.[13] The gendered model of colonial expansion had its analogues in national self-representation as well. Literary critics have noted the symbolic relation between Elizabeth's virginity and the impregnability of her island nation.[14] The persistent alignment of the female with nature and the male with culture in Jacobean and Caroline family portraits has also received attention, again emphasizing the connections between the female form and landscape (Goldberg 1986).[15] Peter Stallybrass approaches this gendered dichotomy of nature and culture in Bakhtinian terms, seeing the feminized landscape as both an emblem of masculine control and an embodiment of the constant threat to the patriarchal order of the grotesque natural world. Pointing to the idealization of Elizabeth I as an emblem of the perfect state, and the contemporaneous concern with unruly women at all social levels, Stallybrass argues that "within the dominant discourses of early modern England […] woman's body could be both symbolic map of the 'civilized' and the dangerous terrain that had to be colonized" (1986: 123–33).

Women's bodies did indeed figure prominently in resistance to patriarchal control over terrain in early modern England. Significant numbers of women participated in early modern enclosure riots, and men involved in these and other forms of local protest frequently adopted female dress (Davis 1975: 145–51). In enclosure riots and other defenses of common land rights, the identification of the land with women provided an emblem of resistance to patriarchal control. In his work on popular perceptions of the past in early modern England, Keith Thomas elaborates a set of legends that finds its most famous expression in Lady Godiva of Coventry, who rode naked through the City to prevent encroachment on the citizens' rights by her husband. She and other medieval noblewomen were cited in local protests against enclosures as having secured common lands by riding naked or walking barefoot over the disputed area (1983: 2–3). These myths suggest a connection between a woman's naked body and the land, indeed a sense of her body as a charter and guarantee of the originary relation of the people to the land. The threatened appropriation of the land figures as a masculine disruption of this originary relation, an attempt to subjugate both the land and the people under a new jurisdiction. This invocation of medieval noblewomen also suggests a historical dimension to the identification of the land with the feminine. It implies not only that the land is female, but that it is historically female, and that this historical femininity constitutes and guarantees the nature of communal relations.

This popular perception of an originary feminine charter for the local community finds an elite analogue in the antiquarian recovery of national origins and construction of national identity in this period. Scholars engaged in this project universally figured the ancient province of "Britannia" as female, both in their historiographical reconstructions of ancient Britain, and in the topographical representations of the nation that illustrated their works.[16] These scholars were educated, male recipients of political appointments and commissions, members or employees of that masculine elite that disrupts and appropriates the originary feminine charter in the Godiva legends. The antiquarians' relation to a feminine national iconography might indeed be read as a patriarchal desire to define and control national territory, history, and identity. Conceiving of their role in shaping national iconography in gendered terms, male historians, poets, artists, and cartographers could assume the dominant position *vis-à-vis* their feminized subject matter.

Stallybrass's insight that early modern representations of national territory as feminine embodied not only a patriarchal desire for control, but also patriarchal anxiety about the difficulties of such control, qualifies this reading. The feminine iconography of the nation, issuing from the mutually constitutive bodies of the queen and the land in late sixteenth-century England, did not go unchallenged in the early seventeenth century. In the same year Drayton published the first part of *Poly-Olbion*, John Speed completed his *Theatre of the Empire of Great Britain*, again invoking the ancient name of the island. The title page of this volume (Figure 7), the first full-scale revision of the county atlas genre, occupies a liminal place in the iconographical shift I explore. Its format – a central space framed by an arch with pillars and flanked by allegorical figures – is similar to both Saxton's atlas and *Poly-Olbion*.[17] In contrast to the other two examples, however, this space contains no figure. Rather, it bears the title of the work, a description of its contents, and the name of the author. With the exception of these written characters, the stage of Speed's *Theatre* is empty.[18]

This empty stage represents a turning point in the iconographical shift from Mater Terra to the Artificial Man. Standing about mid-way between the first county atlas and the *Leviathan*, the title page of Speed's *Theatre* offers neither male nor female images of the land. Indeed, it

7. Frontispiece to John Speed's *Theatre of the Empire of Great Britain* (1612), by permission of the Yale Center for British Art.

offers no image of the land at all. Yet it does retain marginal figures from earlier topographical works. Elizabeth was flanked by male personifications of Cosmography and Geography on the Saxton title page. On the *Poly-Olbion* title page, Great Britain is surrounded by what had become the conventional male representatives of the four peoples of British history: an ancient Briton, a Roman, a Saxon, and a Norman. In both cases, the surrounding male figures are subordinated to the central female personification, and in *Poly-Olbion*, they are on a much smaller scale. But Speed's title page treats these surrounding figures differently, both in terms of situation and emphasis. It replaces the figure of a Briton with a Dane, removing the Briton from one of the four corner positions occupied in the *Poly-Olbion* frontispiece to a central position surmounting the pillars that frame the title. The arch in which the Briton stands is equal in size to the frame occupied by the title, and the Briton himself is on a larger scale than the other four national representatives. He is also resolutely masculine, carrying a spear and buckler, and displaying a muscular chest and long mustache. The dominant place that the Artificial Man of Hobbes's *Leviathan* will occupy above the land is thus in preparation in Speed's *Theatre*, with its stage cleared of the conventional female embodiment, and its emerging masculine Briton above.

The masculine torso of the king on the title page of Hobbes's *Leviathan* is made up of the figures of individual men, clearly designated as male by their clothing (Figure 8).[19] This shift from the female embodiment of Elizabeth or Drayton's Great Britain to an all-male commonwealth is striking. In place of the landscape of *Poly-Olbion*, predominantly feminine in its parts and entirely so in its titulary personification, is the masculine figure of the Artificial Man whose torso, rising above the landscape, is formed by the bodies of individual men. Here indeed, Helgerson's "conceptual gap between the land and its ruler" has opened. No longer a figure of the land, the king emerges from behind it, only his torso and head visible, so that his upper body dominates the lower region of the earth. The verse from Job inscribed above his head, "*Non est potestas Super Terram quae Comparetur ei*," stresses both his separation from the earth and his mastery over it.[20] In the same year that Drayton published the first part of *Poly-Olbion*, with its feminine representations of the nation and its topography, Speed cleared the stage of his *Theatre* of these Elizabethan anachronisms. Shifting his enlarged male Briton to the superior position above the framed title, he moved national representation in a new direction, one that would eventually lead to the towering figure of Hobbes's Artificial Man. And yet, almost a decade into James's reign, Speed did not produce a central masculine personification of his "Empire of Great Britain." A radically different concept of the nation needed

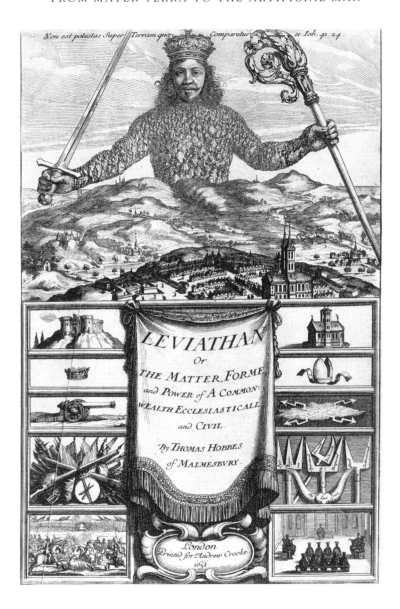

8. Frontispiece to Thomas Hobbes's *Leviathan* (1651), by permission of the Houghton Library, Harvard University.

to be developed before such an image would appear, a concept derived from the political representation of many men by one man, rather than from the symbolic representation of the nation in the mutually constitutive forms of the queen's body and the land.

THE ARTIFICIAL MAN AND THE FORGING OF
THE MASCULINIST STATE

Hobbes's theory of a commonwealth is heavily dependent on his metaphor of the One Person who represents the jointly yielded authority of every man:

> This is more than Consent, or Concord; it is a reall Unitie of them all, in one and the same Person, made by Covenant of every man with every man […] the Multitude so united in one Person, is called a COMMON-WEALTH, in latine CIVITAS. This is the Generation of that great LEVIATHAN.
>
> (1978: 2.17.227)

The great LEVIATHAN who rises above the landscape of Hobbes's title page transcends the Jacobean impasse of national iconography. Resolutely masculine in the parts and the whole of his multiply constructed "Person," Hobbes's Artificial Man supplants Elizabethan topographical allegories of the nation. At the same time, Hobbes's construct powerfully recalls Elizabeth's transcendent majesty in portraits like the "Ditchley" where she surmounts the globe, her feet planted on Saxton's England (Figure 2). Another Elizabethan portrait anticipates Hobbes's Artificial Man more precisely. Andrew Belsey and Catherine Belsey develop a reading of Elizabeth's portraits in terms of their stiff and rather heraldic formal qualities of English style in the last decades of her reign. Noting the complex composition of circles and semicircles in the queen's headdresses, collars, shoulders, and skirts, the Belseys comment on "the abstract geometry" of the later portraits, culminating in what they call the "pure geometry" of a series in the late 1580s. The most strikingly geometrical example of this trend is the frontispiece to John Case's *Sphaera Civitatis* (1588), where the arcs of the queen's shoulders, ruff and headdress surmount a circular diagram of the cosmos (Figure 9). The Belseys note Elizabeth's simultaneous embodiment of and detachment from the *civitas* figured in the diagram. Emphasizing her transcendent majesty over the cosmic figure, they suggest that Elizabeth usurps the position of God the Father as cosmic *primum mobile* and heavenly sovereign (Belsey and Belsey 1990: 11–35).

9. Frontispiece to John Case's *Sphaera Civitatis* (1588), by permission of the Houghton Library, Harvard University.

Hobbes's construction of the state as a geometrically determined "mortal god" seems less than original in the light of this Elizabethan frontispiece. But his image of the CIVITAS on the *Leviathan* title page does recast the geometry of the *Sphaera Civitatis*, replacing its circular schema with a series of rectangular frames ranging from the torso of the sovereign to the upper half of the title page in which he appears to the title itself and subdivided columns of the ecclesiastical and civil commonwealth in the lower half. All these frames contain images or text, and the images and text together represent the LEVIATHAN. Despite their mutual recourse to the theoretical order of Euclidean geometry, the Elizabethan *Sphaera Civitatis* and Hobbes's CIVITAS differ in their representational properties. Where Elizabeth's body (or similar female allegories) *figuratively* represented the nation, Hobbes's LEVIATHAN or Artificial Man constitutes the "reall Unitie" of the many men he represents *politically*. Just as, in Seyla Benhabib's formulation, the metaphor of the state of nature at times assumes the status of fact, so the metaphor of the Artificial Man represents a "reall Unitie" in Hobbes's articulation of the state. It is both an image of the union of all "men" under one sovereign, and the actual sovereign power that constitutes the state.

Representation is a political term in Hobbes's treatise, one that designates political authority and agency rather than figurative embodiment or analogy.[21] Yet Hobbes explicitly derives his use of this term from a theatrical concept of personation. Both his recourse to analogy to define the term, and the aesthetic context of his theatrical comparison, suggest how difficult Hobbes found it to isolate his new scientific language of politics from earlier figurative traditions.[22] Robert Stillman persuasively argues that Hobbes drew on the power of figurative language precisely to banish the "monsters of metaphor" from his scientific discourse. Nicely characterizing the *Leviathan* as "a peculiarly active and unsettling text" in this regard, Stillman suggests that "Given Hobbes's repeated strictures against the use of metaphor, any single figure of speech acquires an additional dimension of meaning (additional to its local affective or conceptual power) as an instance of unexplained contradiction" (1995: 806–7).[23]

In the following reading, I accord a high level of meaning to feminine figures of speech in the *Leviathan*. To Stillman's list of the binary oppositions informing the emergent scientific discourse of the *Leviathan* – "between the literal and the figural [, …] truth and falsehood, natural philosophy and poetry, philosophical discourse and rhetoric" (792) – I add the gender polarities of masculine and feminine. If, as Stillman argues, "Philosophy counters rhetoric, truth counters fiction, and logic counters metaphor in an ongoing effort to clear a rational domain for Hobbes's new discipline" (799), so masculine counters feminine in Hobbes's articulation of the state.

Indeed, Hobbes enjoyed a higher degree of success in the masculinization of his theory than in any of his other oppositional campaigns. For if he could not rid his monster text of constitutive metaphors, he achieved an almost complete effacement of feminine figuration.

Just as the bearded king's exclusively masculine torso supplants earlier feminine icons of the nation, so the text of the *Leviathan* resists and suppresses feminine figuration. Hobbes makes only the most sparing and conventional use of feminine personification in his treatise. His reticence in this regard marks a break with the conventional philosophical personification of abstractions as feminine, as well as with the national representational tradition of feminine iconography developed under Elizabeth and lasting well into the seventeenth century. Jean Bethke Elshtain warns against the danger of accepting the presumptive "neutrality" of Hobbesian mechanistic vocabulary in the *Leviathan*. Noting Hobbes's attempt to remove the language of his political science from its everyday contexts, she argues that the discourse of the *Leviathan* "erodes the meaning to human subjects of their own lives," sanctioning "the silencing of human speech by the all-powerful – those with the power to 'name names'" (1981: 114). In my consideration of Hobbes's figurative language, I argue for the gender-specific erosion of meaning to women as members of the polis, an effacement of the feminine in Hobbes's discourse of the state that is far from neutral. By articulating the state as a political construct, Hobbes transformed the nature of national representation from iconography dominated by feminine figuration to a political theory in which an artificial and masculine body constitutes the "reall Unitie" of the collective masculine political interest. And by emphasizing the political over the iconographical – the civil authority and agency of the Artificial Man over the symbolic power of Mater Terra – he paradoxically produced an exclusively masculine icon of the nation.[24]

The multiply masculine torso of the Artificial Man does not quite banish the earlier feminine iconography of Mater Terra. One of the rare feminine images in *Leviathan* invokes the female breasts that figured in earlier icons of the nation, from topographical allegories like Drayton's Great Britain to the recovered images of Britannia on Roman-British coins. In his chapter, "Of the Nutrition and Procreation of a Common-wealth," Hobbes uses maternal breasts as an image of plenty: "As for the Plenty of Matter, it is a thing limited by Nature, to those commodities, which from (the two breasts of our common Mother) Land, and Sea, God usually either freely giveth, or for labour selleth to man-kind" (2.24.295). The punning relation of "Matter" to "Mater" is particularly apparent in this analogy. Patricia Parker is right, however, in suggesting that in Hobbes's use of the term in this passage, the mastery of the female body as property and rhetorical display contains and defuses any power that the maternal breasts might once have exercised (1987: 149–51). The whole sentence emphasizes limitation and containment, from the immediate qualification of "Plenty of Matter" by its principal clause – "it is a thing limited by Nature" – to the actual bracketing of the reference to "(the two breasts of our common Mother)," and the final evocation of God as the owner and bestower of Matter to "man-kind." Thus bracketed and rendered incidental, the prior female body of national iconography is rhetorically subordinated in *Leviathan*'s text to the original of that "mortal god" whose masculine torso rises above the rolling landscape of its title page.

References to women in the *Leviathan* are similarly scarce and qualified. Only once does Hobbes imply their membership in the commonwealth, and this instance derives not so much from his own understanding as from a biblical precedent he invokes to guarantee the publishing of all civil laws to "every man that shall be obliged to obey them" (2.26.319).[25] Social historians studying the deterioration of the status of women in seventeenth-century England have emphasized that by the end of that century, women were no longer regarded as integral members of the state. In her pioneering work on women in seventeenth-century England, Alice Clark explained this exclusion as a shift from an understanding of the commonwealth as a union of families, including men, women and children, to a view of the state as made up of individuals, with the normative individual being male. She cited both Hobbes and Locke as the principal figures in developing this view of what she called the "mechanical State" (Clark 1982: 303–8).[26]

The political theorist Carole Pateman also identifies the seventeenth century as the crucial period of women's exclusion from the state. In her book *The Sexual Contract*, she reconsiders the development of contract theory, which assumes an originary social contract as the charter of all legitimate political authority. Contract theory depends on a conjectural history that presents civil authority as an agreement forged in the distant past by the original members of a commonwealth who consented to invest their individual rights in a representative body or person. It is this political fiction or "story" that opposes the patriarchalist concept of civil authority derived from natural law on the model of a father's natural authority over his children. Over the course of the seventeenth century, and particularly in Locke's polemic with Filmer, patriarchalism gave way to contract theory as the dominant model of English political thought. Yet Pateman argues that the movement from a patriarchal to a contractual model, while adequately explaining what changed in seventeenth-century political theory, does not address what remained constant, namely, its sexual politics.

In Pateman's revisionist history, the shift from patriarchalism to the social contract only represents half the story. Designating the original contract a "sexual-social pact," she excavates the repressed (and enduring) sexual politics of the transition from patriarchalism to the social contract:

> The story of the sexual contract is also about the genesis of political right, and explains why exercise of the right is legitimate – but this story is about political right as *patriarchal right* or sex-right, the power that men exercise over women. The missing half of the story tells how a specifically modern form of patriarchy is established. The new civil society created through the original contract is a patriarchal social order.
>
> (1988b: 1)

Central to Pateman's argument is a distinction between two current senses of the term "patriarchal" in the contemporary historiography of political theory. What Pateman calls the feminist meaning of the term (i.e., the dominance of men over women) is often obscured in accounts of the seventeenth-century shift from patriarchalism to contract theories of government. She argues that Locke's attack on patriarchalism does not imply any opposition to patriarchy in the feminist sense. For patriarchy in the latter sense suffered no interruption during the shift from patriarchalism to the social contract. To restore the repressed sexual contract in the historiography of political theory, Pateman rearticulates the seventeenth-century debate as a shift from "classic patriarchalism" to "fraternal patriarchalism," or the social contract.[27]

Pateman's revisionist history complements my argument about the masculinization of national iconography in early modern England. Examining the kinds of ascriptive, psychological bonds between men invoked by Locke (e.g., nationalism, patriotism, and fraternity), she notes how these "appeal directly to the masculine self's sense of identity" (1988a: 119). She goes on to address how this identity depends on an implied universalism of the masculine individual, a concept that itself depends on the abstraction from the body: "individuals have one of two bodies, masculine or feminine. But how can the feminine body become part of a (liberal or socialist) fraternal body politic?" (1988a: 120). Pateman's work looks forward to the full establishment of the modern state and its late twentieth-century challenges. Reading backwards from seventeenth-century contract theory to its immediate prehistory in English topographical and historiographical nationalism, I would rephrase Pateman's question about the feminine body and the body politic. The urgent question in the sexual politics of the seventeenth century was not so much how the feminine body could become part of a body politic, but rather, how such a representative body could be imagined as anything other than feminine.

The trajectory of national iconography I trace from Elizabethan land-based images or feminine personifications to the bearded king of Hobbes's frontispiece is determined by this struggle to reconceive the body politic without the (feminine) body. *Leviathan* is crucial in this process. In a text celebrated (and sometimes reviled) for its metaphorical language and argument, the virtual absence of feminine personifications and images, together with the insistent masculinity of all pronouns of political membership and agency, suggests not simply a default assumption of masculine universality, but rather an active exclusion or suppression of the feminine from the rhetoric of statehood. The seventeenth century was the watershed for the development of contract theory over patriarchalism, and Hobbes's *Leviathan* stands squarely in the middle of it. First published in 1651, it occupies a central place between Robert Filmer's *Patriarcha* (probably written in the late 1620s) and Locke's *Second Treatise of Government* (written at least in part as early as 1679–80).[28] Connected to both theoretical positions – like Filmer, an absolutist, and like Locke, a contract theorist – Hobbes articulates a masculinist model of the state in *Leviathan* that exceeds Filmer's patriarchalism while enabling the persistent patriarchy of the social contract.[29]

Yet Pateman gives little attention to Hobbes in her revisionist history of contract theory.[30] By jumping straight from Filmer to Locke, she misses the opportunity to examine *how* the feminine body was excluded from the emerging social contract. The recovery of the repressed sexual politics of the social contract cannot be fully accomplished without some attention to this immediate prehistory of the Lockean social–sexual contract. And that prehistory is the story of how a predominantly feminine national iconography was transformed and reconstituted as a masculine construct. My reading of Hobbes pursues these issues of gendered transformation in terms of the literary use of metaphor and personification. Over the course of this reading, I suggest that the primary sexual–political work of early modernism was the reconceiving of a previously feminine body politic in terms of a naturalized and exclusive masculinity. The patriarchal (in Pateman's feminist sense) resolution of this struggle emerges in the *Leviathan* by mid-century. Hobbes is the glue that holds paternal and fraternal patriarchalism together as against the excluded feminine body of earlier national iconography. At the same time, the seams show in the *Leviathan*; the strain of writing out the feminine is still evident, still not wholly naturalized, as Pateman argues it has become in Locke. In the following analysis of Hobbes's metaphors and rhetoric of statehood, I unpick some of the stitches in these patriarchal seams, demonstrating both the intensity and the success of Hobbes's will to articulate the state as masculine.

"THERE IS NOTHING I DISTRUST MORE THAN MY ELOCUTION": FIGURING THE LEVIATHAN

The *Leviathan* is notorious for the figurative language of its analogies and icons of statehood.[31] And yet Hobbes makes only the most sparing and conventional use of feminine personification in his treatise. In addition to the bracketed and subordinated maternal image for "Plenty of Matter," he refers in passing (and again in parentheses) to "need (the mother of all inventions)" (1.4.101), and develops a slightly longer treatment of Science as "the true Mother" of fortification and engineering (1.10.151).[32] With the exception of a single feminine pronoun in reference to Rome, these are the only gestures toward feminine personification in the *Leviathan* before the last two chapters. I discuss below the concentration in these last chapters of seven additional tropes of feminine personification and why they might appear near the end of the work. Like the earlier examples, they are formulaic and undeveloped (unless their comparative frequency in the closing chapters constitutes some form of development). As a group, they raise the total from five to thirteen instances of feminine personification over the whole of the *Leviathan*.

This paucity of feminine figuration in Hobbes's political language marks a break with the representational tradition of feminine iconography developed under Elizabeth and lasting into the seventeenth century. Just as the compoundedly masculine body of the Artificial Man in his frontispiece displaces feminine icons of the nation, so the language of his text resolutely excludes political and philosophical traditions of feminine figuration. Nature "itself" is neuter in Hobbes's lexicon, as are other formative and recurrent abstractions in his theory of a commonwealth.[33] The critical concept of Prudence, for instance, set off by typeface and capitalization at its introduction in Chapter 3, seems initially to invoke the convention of figuring philosophical concepts – from Fortuna to Lady Philosophy herself – as feminine: "Which kind of thoughts, is called *Foresight*, and *Prudence*, or *Providence*; and sometimes *Wisdome*" (1.3.97).[34] And yet these clustered abstractions, from which Prudence emerges as the dominant term, never achieve the full status of personification. Hobbes emphasizes instead the hypothetical "one man" who exercises prudence: "by how much *one man* has more experience of things past, than another; by so much also he is more Prudent" (1.3.97) [emphasis added]. And when Prudence becomes the subject of a later sentence, Hobbes uses neuter pronouns: "And though *it* be called Prudence, when the Event answereth our Expectation; yet in *its* own nature, *it* is but Presumption" (1.3.97) [emphasis added]. Finally, both Prudence and the hypothetical "one man" are subordinated to the greater "he" from whom all things proceed: "For the foresight of things to come, which is Providence, belongs *onely to him* by whose will they are to come. From *him onely*, and supernaturally, proceeds Prophecy" (1.3.97) [emphasis added]. Just as the maternal image for Plenty of Matter is quickly subordinated to God, so Hobbes shifts his rhetorical focus from the potentially feminine Prudence to its generically masculine possessor and ultimately to the exclusively masculine authority of "him onely" from whom prophecy supernaturally proceeds.[35]

If Hobbes concludes his initial discussion of Prudence by containing it within the masculine individual and subordinating it to an exclusive and masculine divinity, he also suppresses the feminine in preparing that discussion. In the paragraph immediately preceding his introduction of Prudence, he elaborates a definition of Remembrance in a threefold analogy:

> Sometimes a man knows a place determinate, within the compasse whereof he is to seek; and then his thoughts run over all the parts thereof, in the same manner, as one would sweep a room, to find a jewell; or as a Spaniel ranges the field, till he find a sent; or as a man should run over the Alphabet, to start a rime.
>
> (1.3.96–7)

Both the spaniel ranging the field and the man running over the alphabet are explicitly masculine. But the agent of the first part of the analogy is curiously gender-neutral: "as *one* would sweep a room, to find a jewell" [emphasis added]. This analogy implies a female agent, both in terms of social norms and literary precedent. Sweeping was a task generally delegated to women and girls, and its use to recover a valued object recalls one of Christ's analogies for repentance, in which a woman sweeps her house to find a silver coin.[36] And yet Hobbes refers to his sweeper as "one," withholding the gender of this actor in a way he does not for the spaniel ranging the field and the literate man running over the alphabet to start a rhyme.[37]

Hobbes concludes his discussion of Prudence with the articulation of an insistently masculine psychology:

> There is no other act of *mans* mind, that I can remember, naturally planted in *him*, so, as to need no other thing, to the exercise of it, but to be born a *man*, and live with the use of *his* five

Senses. Those other Faculties of which I shall speak by and by, and which seem proper to *man* onely, are acquired, and encreased by study and industry; and of most *men* learned by instruction, and discipline; and proceed all from the invention of Words, and Speech. For besides Sense, and Thoughts, and the Trayne of thoughts, the mind of *man* has no other motion; though by the help of Speech, and Method, the same Facultyes may be improved to such a height, as to distinguish *men* from all other living Creatures.

(1.3.98–9; emphasis added)

The words "man" or "men" and their correspondingly masculine pronouns are used a total of eight times in the paragraph's three sentences. Part 1 of the *Leviathan* is dedicated to the subject "Of Man," and I would argue that this term is not gender-neutral for Hobbes. His somewhat exaggerated insistence on the masculine near the end of Chapter 3 strikes me as a reaction to the suppression of feminine figuration in the analogies for Remembrance and the definition of Prudence. It is the mark of the strain of excluding femininity, even figuratively, from his articulation of the state. As Hobbes silently de-genders conventionally feminine figures in the opening chapters of the *Leviathan*, he volubly reiterates the masculinity of "Man," the subject of Part 1 and the representative member of his theoretical commonwealth.

The complement of this suppression of feminine figuration is the virtual absence of women from Hobbes's articulation of the state. This absence goes beyond the assumed and reiterated masculinity of the subject who possesses (or yields) power and rights in Hobbes's commonwealth. In the midst of a century in which women were claiming and exercising political agency on an unprecedented scale in England, Hobbes barely mentions them in the *Leviathan*. Almost all general references to women are in Part 1 and work to complement or elaborate Hobbes's account "Of Man." These references are brief and undeveloped and generally figure in lists elaborating the property, rights and powers of men, as in the description of how competition drives men to "use Violence, to make themselves Masters of other mens persons, wives, children, and cattell" (1.13.185).[38] References to women are even more scarce in Part 2, "Of Common-wealth." Only a quotation from Deuteronomy implies their membership in the commonwealth, and Hobbes invokes its authority merely to clarify the rights of men to know the law. Two other isolated references to women in Part 2 serve to elaborate the inheritance and property rights of men (2.19.250; 2.27.352). Nowhere do women figure as members of the body politic with rights or responsibilities.

Only in a section of the short chapter "Of Dominion Paternell and Despoticall" do the presence and roles of women in the commonwealth receive any extended treatment. Hobbes invokes the authority of mothers in this chapter to elaborate his distinction between paternal authority derived from nature, which he rejects, and that arising from the implied or explicit consent of the child, which he affirms as the contractual foundation of civil government:

> The right of Dominion by Generation, is that, which the Parent hath over his Children; and is called PATERNALL. And is not so derived from the Generation, as if therefore the Parent had Dominion over his Child because he begat him; but from the Childs Consent, either expresse, or by other sufficient arguments declared. For as to the Generation, God hath ordained to man a helper; and there be always two that are equally Parents: the Dominion therefore over the Child, should belong equally to both; and he be equally subject to both, which is impossible; for no man can obey two Masters. And whereas some have attributed the Dominion to the Man onely, as being of the more excellent Sex; they misreckon in it. For there is not always that difference of strength or prudence between the man and the woman, as that the right can be determined without War.
> (2.20.253)

This passage is remarkable not simply in its acknowledgment of parental equality, but in its very articulation of any female role or power.[39] It sets up Hobbes's assertion of dominion in the mother rather than the father in the state of nature, as well as his only theoretical reference to female sovereignty: "If the Mother be the Fathers subject, the Child, is in the Fathers power: and if the Father be the Mothers subject, (as when a Soveraign Queen marrieth one of her subjects,) the Child is subject to the Mother; because the Father also is her subject" (2.20.254). Hobbes also invokes in this section the (for him) historical example of the Amazons as an illustration of contractual government, again suggesting that female sovereignty is possible outside the state of nature.

The examples of matriarchal dominion and female sovereignty that emerge so startlingly in these paragraphs are subject to some of the same rhetorical qualifications that surround maternal figures of speech in the *Leviathan*. The reference to female sovereignty appears in parentheses – "(as when a Soveraign Queen marrieth one of her subjects)." The theoretical possibility under civil law of finding in favor of a mother's authority over a father's is mitigated by the assertion that "for the most part, (but not always) the sentence is in favour of the Father; because for the most part Common-wealths have been erected by the Fathers, not by the Mothers of families" (253). Here again, the exceptional theoretical possibility of maternal authority – "(but not always)" – is bracketed in a parenthetical aside. And despite the initial attention to matriarchal dominion in the state of nature and the possibility of female sovereignty in a commonwealth, the maternal term disappears later in the chapter when Hobbes describes a great family as itself "a little Monarchy; whether that Family consist of a man and his children; or of a man and his servants; or of a man, and his children, and servants together: wherein the Father or Master is the Soveraign" (257).

Yet I hesitate to explain away the striking theoretical invocation of maternal authority in Chapter 20, the more so because it stands in such marked contrast to the rare and brief references to women elsewhere in the Part 2.[40] Rather, I would argue that Hobbes here and exceptionally invokes matriarchal dominion as a way to discount earlier patriarchal theories of government. Hobbes's marginal note to the distinction between generation and consent as the basis of paternal authority invokes the term "contract": "Not by Generation, but by Contract" (2.20.253). Pointing forward to the fuller articulation of a social contract in Locke, Hobbes repeatedly rejects the patriarchalism epitomized in Robert Filmer's *Patriarcha*, where sovereign authority derives from natural law on the model of a father's natural authority as progenitor of his children.[41] Yet Hobbes's opposition to what Pateman calls classic patriarchalism should not be confused with feminist opposition to patriarchy. Indeed, his invocation of matriarchal dominion in Chapter 20 provides an excellent early example of Pateman's "sexual–social contract."

When Hobbes invokes matriarchal dominion in Chapter 20 of the *Leviathan*, he does so to demonstrate the fallacy of a patriarchalism that derives civil authority from a father's natural authority over his children. In the process, he reveals the suppressed gender construct that underwrites the "naturalness" of the father's authority:

> For as to the Generation, God hath ordained to man a helper; and there be alwayes two that are equally Parents: the Dominion therefore over the Child, should belong equally to both; [...] And whereas some have attributed the Dominion to the Man onely, as being of the more excellent Sex; they misreckon in it. For there is not always that difference of strength or prudence between the man and the woman, as that the right can be determined without War.
>
> (253)

What Hobbes reveals in this formulation is the consensual basis of pater-nal authority. Fathers are not by nature superior to mothers, or at least not invariably so. Once again invoking the adverbial qualification "not always," Hobbes acknowledges the possibility of the occasional natural superiority in strength or prudence of the woman over the man. The invariable subor-dination of maternal authority to patriarchal dominion in civil society must then derive from some form of consent rather than any natural imperative. And as with all forms of consensual authority in the *Leviathan*, this civil hierarchy exists to preclude the determination of right by war.

Hobbes invokes the possibility of matriarchal dominion in Chapter 20 to demonstrate that all civil authority, even the pre-eminent masculine authority of fathers over their children, has some form of contract at its origin, and owes something to civil law. But this deconstruction of pater-nal dominion as a natural phenomenon is not in the service of matriar-chy. Indeed, Hobbes identifies maternal dominion with the very state of nature he seeks to transcend through the contractual authority of the state. Only in "the state of meer Nature," where there are no laws but the Law of Nature and natural inclination, can there be said to be no contract. And where "there be no Contract, the Dominion is in the Mother" (253–4). Matriarchy for Hobbes is synonymous with that "state of meer Nature" where political right cannot always (if ever) be deter-mined without war. Only by establishing a sexual–social pact that denies maternal dominion can this primal chaos be resolved into the Artificial Man of civil government.

Hobbes's association of female sovereignty with a savage state of na-ture recalls early modern English fears about native origins. Uncivilized and tending to anarchy and civil war, the ancient Britons were also re-viled for having made no distinction of sex in government. Behind Hobbes's theoretical discussion of a generalized state of nature in the distant past lies this specifically English anxiety about the savagery of native origins. Pateman's concept of the sexual contract seems particularly appropriate here. At the same time that Hobbes invokes the matriarchal dominion that was one of the most disturbing elements of ancient British savagery, he also attacks the foundation of what Pateman calls "classic patriarchalism" in favor of the emerging "fraternal patriarchalism" of the social contract. Indeed, Hobbes's insistence on the masculine far exceeds Filmer's theory of patriarchal dominion, which allows for the exercise of female sover-eignty and makes explicit references to the roles and rights of women in the commonwealth.[42] In attacking this derivation of civil authority from the natural authority of fathers, Hobbes articulates a masculinist model of the state that exceeds Filmer's patriarchalism even as it enables the fraternal patriarchy of the social contract.

DE CLARIS MULIERIBUS: EXCEPTIONAL WOMEN IN THE LEVIATHAN

I have hitherto emphasized Hobbes's success in writing out or repressing both women and the feminine in the *Leviathan*. The example of Prudence suggests that the difficulty of avoiding feminine personification does leave some trace in the text, if only in the extraordinary suppression of all female references and conventions and the exaggerated insistence on normative masculinity in the paragraphs framing the discussion of that virtue. Yet there are places where feminine reference marks Hobbes's text by its presence as well as its absence. Few in number, they are the more remarkable in an otherwise rigorously masculine discourse. Two blocks of feminine figures and examples rise up in the last two parts of *Leviathan*, "Of a Christian Common-wealth" and "Of the Kingdome of Darknesse." Their exceptional presence reveals something of the struggle necessary to remove women and the feminine from political roles, rhetoric and iconography in mid seventeenth-century England.

There is only a handful of references to famous women in the *Leviathan*, and as in the case of feminine figuration, these examples are restricted to brief and unexplored invocations of conventional associations; e.g., Eve with marriage (3.38.479–81); or Miriam and the Sybil with visions and prophecy (3.36.457–8; 1.12.176). The brevity and conventionality of these references leaves little room for interpretation. And yet the predominance of biblical women associated with visionary powers or experiences suggests a connection between women and prophecy in a text famously hostile to the latter. More than half the women named in the *Leviathan* figure in Hobbes's treatment of the vexed question of prophecy, developed largely in Part 3, "Of a Christian Common-wealth." His brief references to these exemplary figures constitute the only discussion of women in that section of the work, a remarkable omission in a century when Christian social and political theory gave considerable attention to the place and roles of women.[43]

It is not surprising that prophecy should be the one subject where Hobbes acknowledges female models and agency in the *Leviathan*. Women prophets played prominent roles in the political, religious, and social debates of the English civil wars. Indeed, prophecy was the principal and often the only sanctioned means of engaging in political debate for women. Hobbes's references to women prophets consistently work to limit female agency and to discredit women's involvement in political debate. In Chapter 36, *Of the* WORD OF GOD, *and of* PROPHETS," he invokes Miriam to support his contention that praising God in church is the only form of prophecy open to women. From this narrowly defined example of laudable female prophecy, he moves quickly to the counterexample of the woman of Endor, whose false claims to prophecy contributed to the downfall of King Saul (3.36.457–8). Miriam later receives mention as Aaron's accomplice in the mutiny against Moses (3.40.504). Ultimately exceeding the narrow bounds of legitimate female prophecy, Miriam, like the woman of Endor, contributes to political rebellion against a sovereign male.[44] Hobbes's acknowledgment of biblical female prophets thus works to discredit the political agency of women in a Christian commonwealth.

The association of prophecy with rebellion was not based on scriptural evidence alone in seventeenth-century England. Women participated actively in the development of apocalyptic visions in the middle decades of the century, gaining entry into political debate and discourse through prophetic utterance. Phyllis Mack notes that in this period, prophecy offered women "virtually the only taste of public authority they would ever know" (1992: 4). Yet political prophets were not predominantly female, and those who were tended to be less radical in the claims of personal autonomy and independence from civil law that most disturbed Hobbes's absolutism.[45] His concern to restrict and discredit women's prophetic authority in the Christian commonwealth thus constitutes something of an overreaction to the unusual numbers of women prophets who rose up before and during the English civil wars. Partly provoked by this contemporary historical phenomenon, Hobbes's attention to female prophecy seems also to emerge from a theoretical opposition to women's presumed access to political discourse and agency through prophecy.

Indeed, the need to dismiss or discredit these female exemplars of prophecy owes something to Hobbes's own theoretical alignment of prophecy with government. "For he that pretends to teach men the way of so great felicity [i.e., one claiming prophetic powers], pretends to govern them," Hobbes warns. The only earthly prophetic authority, he counters, resides in the Civil Sovereign, "as when the Prophet is the Civill Soveraign, or by the Civil Soveraign Authorized" (466). To admit female prophets is thus to admit female political agency and, ultimately, female government. Yet to limit and discredit women's prophetic agency is nevertheless to mention women, something Hobbes does otherwise only in rare and brief instances. Chapter 36 thus paradoxically points to a contemporary instance of women's political engagement even as it attempts to disqualify it.

This paradox finds its rhetorical analogue in the chapter's visionary conclusion. Having carefully distinguished various forms of prophecy and limited its political use to the civil sovereign of a Christian commonwealth, Hobbes ends his chapter with a nihilistic vision worthy of a millenarian:

For when Christian men, take not their Christian Soveraign, for Gods Prophet; they must either take their owne Dreams, for the Prophecy they mean to bee governed by, and the tumour of their own hearts for the Spirit of God; or they must suffer themselves to bee lead by some strange Prince; or by some of their fellow subjects, that can bewitch them, by slander of the government, into rebellion […]; and by this means destroying all laws, both divine, and humane, reduce all Order, Government, and Society, to the first Chaos of Violence, and Civill warre.

(469)

This ironically apocalyptic conclusion to a chapter largely concerned with denouncing the political use of prophecy reads like a litany of everything Hobbes opposes in the *Leviathan*: sectarianism, foreign rule, rebellion, and the destruction of human and divine law. It represents the reversion of the commonwealth to the "state of meer Nature" with the inevitable outbreak of civil war. Indeed, it is one of the most developed descriptions of that state anywhere in *Leviathan*. Why does it emerge here, at the conclusion of a chapter addressing the Word of God and prophets in "Of a Christian Common-wealth"? I would suggest that the length and vehemence of this concluding "prophecy" are not unrelated to the unusual prominence of female examples in this chapter. The disruptive rhetorical force of these examples parallels the social and political disruptiveness of women during the English civil wars. Many works of early modern political, religious and social theory argue that a similar reduction of good government to anarchy follows directly from allowing women to exercise authority.[46] In most of the *Leviathan*, Hobbes ignores these contemporary gender debates by the simple expedient of ignoring women. Chapter 36 is one of the few exceptions to his silence on the subject. The threat that contemporary female prophets acting in the political arena posed to his theoretical commonwealth emerges in the apocalyptic conclusion to the chapter in which their biblical foremothers figure so exceptionally.[47]

Yet Hobbes does not address the specific case of female prophets in the ominous conclusion to his chapter on prophecy (although a passing reference to "the Witch of Endor" in the long final paragraph recalls the earlier discussion [468]). As in the exceptional discussion of maternal dominion in Chapter 20, the female examples drop out as Chapter 36 develops and concludes. But the prominent invocations of the state of nature in both chapters – explicitly in Chapter 20 and descriptively in the conclusion to Chapter 36 – suggest how much the exceptional consideration of female power could throw the *Leviathan* off its course. The civilizing project of Hobbes's treatise, its single-minded drive to establish a civil commonwealth with no connection to the state of nature or natural law, is also a project of masculinization. On the rare occasions when Hobbes admits female references – either to distinguish his project from earlier patriarchalist theories or to respond to a contemporary political phenomenon – he also admits the state of nature and its inevitable consequence of civil war. Both the difficulty of determining the right between mother and father in Chapter 20 and the danger of yielding to prophetic authority in Chapter 36 raise the specter of civil war. Part of Hobbes's response to this terrible possibility is to suppress the female examples that raise it in both chapters. These two chapters contain the only instances of anything approaching a sustained treatment of women's roles and authority in the *Leviathan*. And in both cases, the admission of a female presence in the commonwealth is bound up with the state of nature and the real possibility of degeneration into that "first Chaos of Violence, and Civill warre."

The exceptional presence of women in Chapters 20 and 36, and their subsequent disappearance, suggest both the difficulty and the ultimate success of Hobbes's masculinization of the commonwealth. These chapters reveal the strain of writing women out of the secular and Christian commonwealths even as they articulate the political consequences of female power. In Part 4, "Of the Kingdome of Darknesse," Hobbes reaches a similar breaking point in his rhetorical avoidance of feminine figuration. In the last two chapters before the Review that concludes the *Leviathan*, he invokes four feminine personifications and refers several times to "old wives tales." As in earlier chapters, these references are conventional and undeveloped, yet their relative frequency (more than in the rest of the *Leviathan* combined) makes them remarkable. His feminine personifications are largely positive, developed in a section of Chapter 46 to illustrate his history "Of the Beginnings and Progresse of Philosophy" (683). Invoking the conventional Renaissance derivation of learning and the arts from leisure, Hobbes develops his own construct of the commonwealth's priority in a two-generational maternal analogy: "*Leasure* is the mother of *Philosophy*; and *Common-wealth*, the mother of *Peace, and Leasure*" (683). Brief and conventional though it is, this analogy contains the only female image of the commonwealth in the *Leviathan*. It is followed in Hobbes's history of the development of philosophy by references to "Geometry, which is the Mother of all Naturall Science" (686) and to the restricted study of philosophy itself, which (to Hobbes's scorn) "hath no otherwise place, then as a handmaid to the Romane Religion" (688).

These dead metaphors would not seem to merit discussion, so embedded are they in the conventions of philosophical discourse. And yet they occur in the final chapters of a long and highly metaphorical treatise that virtually excludes the convention they model. Why do they appear here, after forty-five chapters containing only four other comparable figures and a single feminine pronoun in reference to Rome? Does Hobbes let down his rhetorical guard to admit the feminine as he moves toward the conclusion of his vast treatise? Does he tolerate feminine figures in the kingdom of darkness as he did not in the first three parts of the *Leviathan*? Are these figures perhaps appropriate to the articulation of the "anticommonwealth" in Part 4? Or do they represent the return of the repressed near the end of the treatise, the flickering of a tradition of feminine figuration all but extinguished in Hobbes's theory of a commonwealth?

Chapters 46 and 47 round out Part 4 of the *Leviathan*, in which Hobbes anatomizes spiritual darkness and the papacy as its primary author and beneficiary. In the final pages of his last chapter, he invokes "the old Wives" three times as he develops his comparison of the Kingdom of the Fairies and the Papacy.[48] In these multiple references to old wives' tales, Hobbes builds a set of connections between the feminine, the literary, and spiritual darkness, a nexus he maps out explicitly in his second-last paragraph:

> as the *Fairies* have no existence, but in the Fancies of ignorant people, rising from the Traditions of old Wives, or old Poets: so the Spirituall Power of the *Pope* (without bounds of his own Civill Dominion) consisteth onely in the Fear that Seduced people stand in, of their Excommunication [...].
>
> (714)

Rhetorically interchangeable with "old Wives" as creators and perpetuators of a belief in fairies, the "old Poets" stand for a concept of literature as fabulous, feminine, and spiritually aligned with darkness. As he approaches the end of his treatise, Hobbes returns again and again to this set of associations between the feminine, the literary, and the kingdom of darkness that threatens to overwhelm his theoretical commonwealth. And just before concluding his extended and highly metaphorical treatise, he attempts to disown the literary entirely.

"There is nothing I distrust more than my Elocution," Hobbes writes in the final pages of his "Review and Conclusion" (726). Assuming a posture of principled neglect, Hobbes presents himself as the virtuous champion of reason over the formal temptation to empty ornamentation: "That I have neglected the Ornament of quoting ancient Poets, Orators, and Philosophers [...] proceedeth from my judgment"

(726–7). This willful exclusion of ancient literary, rhetorical and philosophical precedents seems less a matter of neglect than of active rejection. Stillman reads the anti-rhetorical stance of Hobbes's conclusion as
a strategy that empowers the sovereign at the expense of the traditional
humanist celebration of the orator (803).[49] I understand Hobbes's attitude to feminine figuration in similar terms. Hobbes's "neglect" of the
feminine in the *Leviathan* is programmatic. It extends from a disregard
for questions of women's place in the commonwealth – questions that
were of urgent contemporary interest – to a suppression of conventional
feminine personifications in his theoretical discourse. And the beneficiary of Hobbes's willful neglect of the feminine is the absolute and exclusive masculinity of the Artificial Man.

Hobbes was not alone in his desire to restrict and control the political
and spiritual agency of women in the commonwealth. What distinguishes
him from most other theorists of the period is that he so thoroughly
suppresses even the discussion of women in the *Leviathan*. Only in reference to theoretical patriarchalism in Chapter 20 and to women prophets
in Chapter 36 does something of the urgency of seventeenth-century
gender debates break through. The pressure of these contemporary phenomena – theoretical and political – leaves its mark on Hobbes's treatise. At the same time, the female examples in these chapters mark the
virtual absence of women elsewhere in the *Leviathan*. Women are not
merely silent and subordinate in Hobbes's commonwealth. With brief
and rare exceptions, they are not there at all.

From the notorious title page to the "Review, and Conclusion" of the
Leviathan, Hobbes excludes women and conventions of feminine figuration from his articulation of the state. *Leviathan* bears almost no sign of
the prior tradition of the nation as female. Even the Jacobean struggles
to supplant that female body leave little trace on the figure of the Artificial Man, whose sovereignty is virtually unchallenged. Hobbes's radical
exclusion of feminine figuration is the rhetorical complement to his political argument for absolute sovereignty. From the de-gendering of conventional feminine personifications to the insistent masculinity of his
metaphors and rhetoric of statehood, Hobbes's argument in the *Leviathan* is as much figural as it is rational. Paradoxically, the very rhetorical
practice that creates the absolute sovereignty of the Artificial Man also
provides the vehicle for rare instances of feminine resistance to a totalizing
masculinity. In the closing chapters of his vast treatise, as he anatomizes
his "anticommonwealth" or "Kingdome of Darknesse," the banished figures of feminine personification return to haunt Hobbes's conclusions.
Recalling other moments when the strain of effacing the feminine leaves
its mark on the *Leviathan*, these clustering figures reveal that the author

who conceived the Artificial Man did not quite exercise the absolute dominion over his literary practice that he ascribed to the sovereign in his political theory.

POST-RESTORATION FEMALE SOVEREIGNTY: ELIZABETH AND THE EMPRESS OF THE BLAZING WORLD

One woman does figure in the final chapter of the *Leviathan*, that most exceptional woman in early modern England: Elizabeth I. Citing her authority twice against the assembled powers of old Wives, old Poets, and spiritual darkness, Hobbes presents the old Queen as his principal champion against the papacy. In the first citation, he invokes the glorious sovereign of the Elizabethan Church Settlement and the post-Armada years: "First, the Power of the Popes was dissolved totally by Queen Elizabeth; and the Bishops, who before exercised their Functions in Right of the Pope, did afterwards exercise the same in Right of the Queen and her Successours" (4.47.711). Hobbes's phrasing of these achievements invests Elizabeth with a high degree of agency and power. He magnifies her independent authority by presenting the dissolution of papal authority in England as her absolute and exclusive achievement. And in the upper-case emphasis on the "Right of the Queen," he highlights her female sovereignty and power. His second and final reference to Elizabeth is more qualified. In the last paragraph of "The Kingdome of Darknesse," she shares the honor of expelling the papacy with her father: "It was not therefore a very difficult matter, for Henry 8. by his Exorcisme; nor for Qu. Elizabeth by hers, to cast them out" (714). Following her father's example, her very title of "Queen" abbreviated, Elizabeth's female sovereignty is limited and derivative, amounting to no more than the repetition of her father's not very difficult exorcism. Yet she stands with him at the head of the last paragraph in the body of the *Leviathan*. The paucity of female examples throughout the rest of the treatise makes her presiding role at the end of its final chapter all the more remarkable.

The old Queen is in fact the last person named in the work. Exceptional as a female reference, Elizabeth is unique among the historical figures named in the *Leviathan* in having been a contemporary of Hobbes, who was her subject for the first fifteen years of his life. Her presence near the end of the *Leviathan* thus represents a double departure from Hobbes's rhetorical practice elsewhere in the work. Not only does she figure in the return of the rhetorically repressed feminine; she also represents the pressure of contemporary history, also carefully excluded from

the *Leviathan's* theoretical argument.[50] Does recent history, both political and iconographical, irrupt into the conclusion of the *Leviathan*, even
as the feminine figuration suppressed in its theoretical discourse makes a
qualified return in the final chapters? Having labored throughout the
Leviathan in word and image to develop an exclusively masculine construct of the state, Hobbes seems at his conclusion to revert to the greatest feminine icon of the nation in early modern England.

Yet I do not think the invocation of Elizabeth at the end of the *Leviathan* signals the continuity of the Elizabethan afterlife that flourished in
Jacobean icons of the nation. Rather, it seems to me that the detailed
and programmatic masculinization of the state in Hobbes's *Leviathan*
marks a definitive break with the earlier feminine, land-based images of
the nation. By the time Hobbes's political hopes were realized with the
restoration of the monarchy, the feminine no longer played a constitutive role in shaping or resisting national iconography. Elizabeth is curiously absent from the popular historical literature of the Restoration,
which focused rather on English kings in general and her father in particular.[51] When the Stuarts were restored to the throne, queenly images
of the land conformed to the domestic model of wifely subordination
(Fabricant 1979). This iconographical shift away from powerful female
embodiments of the nation participated in the general movement to
contain and appropriate female power in this period, both symbolically
and politically. The ultimate success of this movement is as evident in
Hobbes's ability to articulate an artificial and exclusively masculine model
of the state as it is in the ultimate containment of women within the
privatized domestic sphere by the end of the seventeenth century.

Let me temper this rather grim conclusion with a brief account of its
most notorious counterexample. Margaret Cavendish, Duchess of Newcastle, began publishing her own political reflections in 1655 while in
exile with her royalist husband in Antwerp. In 1666, she published *The
Description of a New World, Called The Blazing World* as the companion
piece to her *Observations Upon Experimental Philosophy*, an elaborate treatise
of natural philosophy in which she took issue with Robert Hooke's
Micrographia (1655).[52] Like Hobbes, she was a political absolutist who
believed in the scientific articulation of political theory. Her *Blazing World*
is a utopian fiction developed from Hobbesian principles of unity of law
and authority, and the derivation of government from an originary contract. In this fiction, Cavendish broadens Hobbes's theoretical focus on
the nation, imagining whole worlds operating on his principles of political science. The theoretical perfection of her Blazing World rests on its
absolute unity of government, having "but one sovereign, one religion,
one law, and one language, so that all the world might be but as one

united family without divisions" (1992: 201).[53] And the originary contract of national government in Hobbes receives universal application in
Cavendish: "Although there be numerous, nay, infinite worlds," her sages
assert, "yet none is without government" (184–5).

Hobbes was a frequent guest in the Cavendish household while he
was composing the *Leviathan* in the late 1640s in Paris. Although Cavendish
herself later claimed not to have exchanged more than twenty words
with him, she was present at the intellectual soirées hosted by her husband, and privy to his long-standing philosophical correspondence with
Hobbes. Both Cavendishes supported Hobbes's political views and maintained their philosophical allegiance to him after the Restoration.[54] Yet
Margaret Cavendish's intellectual allegiance to Hobbes in *The Blazing
World* stops short of his totalizing masculinity. She devotes her authorial
power to the creation of an idealized female sovereign, replacing the
Leviathan as "mortal god" with her own Empress as "uncreated goddess." Through the emblematic character of her Empress, Cavendish
undoes the masculinizing work of Hobbes's *Leviathan*, reconceiving its
divine majesty as insistently feminine. In one of her most splendid appa-
ritions, Cavendish's Empress leads her own scientifically sophisticated
navy against the assembled ships of an entire world:

> the Empress appeared upon the face of the water in her imperial
> robes; in some part of her hair she had placed some of the star-
> stone, near her face, which added such a lustre and glory to it,
> that it caused a great admiration in all that were present, who
> believed her to be some celestial creature, or rather an uncreated
> goddess, and they all had a desire to worship her; for surely, said
> they, no mortal creature can have such a splendid and tran-
> scendent beauty, nor can any have so great a power as she has,
> to walk upon the waters, and to destroy whatever she pleases,
> not only whole nations, but a whole world.
>
> (215)

Recalling Hobbes's scriptural claim for his central metaphor, inscribed at
the top of his title page – "*Non est potestas Super Terram quae Comparetur
ei*" – Cavendish endows her Empress with unequaled dominion over the
waters and vast destructive powers. Indeed, the Empress's appearance
"upon the face of the water" implies a power exceeding that of Leviathan, whose destructive, created majesty merely inhabits that realm.
Envoking the movement of the holy spirit "upon the face of the waters"
in the opening verses of Genesis, Cavendish equates the imperial majesty
of her Empress with the divine power to create, as well as destroy, whole

worlds.[55] Less explicit than Hobbes's title-page quotation from *Job*, Cavendish's envocation of Genesis nevertheless suggests several claims to precedence over her mentor's brainchild. Through the allusion, she places her Empress at the very moment of creation, before the world or any of its creatures existed. And if Leviathan is later described as preeminent among creatures in *The Book of Job*, the Spirit of God in Genesis is the creative power itself. Taken with her explicit reference to the Empress's destructive potential, Cavendish's allusion to Genesis frames this iconographical description of the Empress with claims for unlimited powers of creation and destruction.[56]

The creative powers of the holy spirit in Genesis also have persistently feminine associations in western exegesis.[57] Cavendish's "uncreated goddess," her lustrous and transcendent beauty inspiring the desire to worship her, does indeed feminize Hobbes's "mortal god." And yet her feminine splendor is not so much a reconceiving of Hobbes's masculine sovereign as it is a return to earlier feminine icons of the nation. A frontispiece used indiscriminately in several of Cavendish's publications seems modeled on these earlier feminine topographical allegories. It displays the female author standing in a niche framed by figures of Athena and Apollo, her classical drapery revealing bare feet and round breasts (Figure 10).[58] Recalling Drayton's Great Britain and other feminine personifications, this image of Cavendish as author draws on the feminine authority of topographical allegory. Indeed, much of the Elizabethan iconography banished from the *Leviathan* finds new life in Cavendish's descriptions of the Empress of the Blazing World. The detail of the "star-stone" in the Empress's hair, adding its luster to her face, recalls the "moon-jewel" headdresses of Elizabethan portraiture. The cult of Elizabeth as Cynthia, or the moon, also implied her sovereignty over the ocean, and Roy Strong suggests that its ascription to the queen of "cosmological powers" prepared the way for later portraits like the "Ditchley" and the "Rainbow" (1987: 125–9). Frances A. Yates quotes a 1584 description of Elizabeth in terms that strikingly anticipate the imperial dominion of Cavendish's Empress:

> If her earthly territory were a true reflection of the width and grandeur of her spirit, this great Amphitrite would bring far horizons within her girdle and enlarge the circumference of her dominion to include not only Britain and Ireland but some new world, as vast as the universal frame, where her all-powerful hand should have full scope to raise a united monarchy.[59]

In her 1666 description of her Empress's dominion over the waters, Cavendish imaginatively realizes the incorporation of "some new world"

Here on this Figure Cast a Glance,
But so as if it were by Chance,
Your eyes not fixt, they must not stay,
Since this like Shadowes to the Day
It only represent's; for Still,
Her Beuty's found beyond the Skill
Of the best Paynter, to Imbrace,
Those lovely Lines within her face,
View her Soul's Picture, Judgment, witt,
Then read those Lines which Shee hath writt,
By Fancy's Pencill drawne alone
Which Peice but Shee, Can justly owne.

10. Frontispiece portrait to the Duchess of Newcastle's *Plays* (1668) (HEW 7.10.19), by permission of the Harry Elkins Widener Collection, Houghton Library, Harvard University.

into the feminine dominion of Elizabeth's girdle. And by imagining her Empress as the sovereign of a whole world, she transcends the island nationalism of Elizabethan iconography to an extent that exceeds even Hobbes's theoretical articulation of a commonwealth in the *Leviathan*.

Elizabethan iconography nevertheless plays a formative role in visions of the Empress of the Blazing World. Cavendish's loving descriptions of her bejewelled Empress throughout her fiction recall portraits of Elizabeth more strongly than they do the fashions of the Restoration court. Her first account of the new Empress's "accoutrement" combines attributes of several branches of Elizabethan iconography:

> on her head she wore a cap of pearl, and a half-moon of diamonds just before it; on the top of her crown came spreading over a broad carbuncle, cut in the form of the sun; her coat was of pearl, mixed with blue diamonds, and fringed with red ones; her buskins and sandals were of green diamonds: in her left hand she held a buckler, to signify the defence of her dominions; which buckler was made of that sort of diamond as has several different colours; and being cut and made in the form of an arch, showed like a rainbow; in her right hand she carried a spear made of a white diamond, cut like the tail of a blazing star, which signified that she was ready to assault those that proved her enemies.
>
> (133)

Attributes like the half-moon of diamonds or the rainbow recall iconographical associations of Elizabeth I with Diana and Astraea. Even more strongly, they point to specific portraits of Elizabeth, especially the "Rainbow" portrait, where the queen holds a rainbow and wears a crown surmounted by a jewelled crescent moon (Figure 11).[60] The Empress's buckler and spear, signifying her readiness "to assault those that proved her enemies," recall the tradition of an armored Elizabeth addressing her troops at Tilbury,[61] as well as the iconographical figures of ancient Britons, Saxons, Romans, and Danes on Elizabethan and Jacobean frontispieces. Altogether, the armored and bejewelled Empress revives earlier feminine icons of the nation, from similarly splendid visions of Elizabeth in the Armada, Rainbow, and Ditchley portraits to the framing figures of topographical allegories.[62]

One might argue from the Empress's absolute sovereignty over the Blazing World and her iconographical resemblance to Elizabeth I that Hobbes's masculinization of the state in *Leviathan* left no impression on Cavendish's political imagination. And yet *The Blazing World* is marked

NON SINE SOLE
IRIS.

11. "Rainbow" portrait of Elizabeth I, attr. Marcus Gheeraerts the Younger (1603?), courtesy of the Marquess of Salisbury.

throughout by the difficulty of conceiving and exercising female sovereignty. Early in her reign, the Empress learns and accepts the Hobbesian catechism of unified government.[63] Later, she laments that there is nothing for her to change in the government of the Blazing World, "by reason it was so well ordered that it could not be mended" (189). The Empress's regret points, I think, to a similar desire in Cavendish to revise the political apparatus she received from Hobbes. Cavendish introduces herself as a character in the middle of her work, summoned from her own world ("our world") to be the intellectual companion and scribe to the Empress. The purported function of this character ("the Duchess of New-castle"), is to record the "Jewish Cabbala," which the Empress's spirit advisors will not entrust to any of a host of male philosophers named by the Empress. These philosophers range from ancients like Aristotle and Plato to contemporaries like Hobbes. The spirit advisors reject the an-cients on the grounds that they are "so wedded to their own opinions, that they would never have had the patience to be scribes," and the moderns, whom they acknowledge to be "fine ingenious writers," be-cause they are "yet so self-conceited that they would scorn to be scribes to a woman" (181).

The Empress's need for a scribe in this regard is one of the more ob-scure points in Cavendish's fiction. The real point of this episode seems to be to reject the western pantheon of male philosophers and to sum-mon a female intellectual companion for the Empress, namely, her au-thor. Once "the Duchess" arrives, she and the Empress soon abandon the Jewish Cabbala in favor of creating intellectual worlds of their own. The Duchess embarks on her imaginary world with the intention of com-bining the best in all philosophical systems, from Pythagorus to Hobbes. This attempt sins against the first Hobbesian principle of unity, the vari-ous parts of the nascent world pressing and driving each other like wolves and sheep or dogs and hares (188). Her imaginative encounter with this intellectual version of the state of nature determines the Duchess to make a world entirely of her own invention. Before she can do so, how-ever, she suffers the nearly incapacitating mental effects of her initial experiment:

> her mind was so squeezed together, that her thoughts could nei-ther move forward nor backward, which caused such an horri-ble pain in her head, that although she had dissolved that world, yet she could not, without much difficulty, settle her mind, and free it from that pain which those pressures and reactions had caused in it.
>
> (188)

The Duchess's attempt to remake the imaginary worlds of male philoso-phers is nearly fatal. Even the dissolution of her intellectual monster can-not, "without much difficulty," free her mind to make a world of her own invention. When she finally succeeds in this endeavor, the Duchess cre-ates a world "so curious and full of variety, so well ordered and wisely governed, that it cannot possibly be expressed by words, nor the delight and pleasure which the Duchess took in making this world of her own" (188). Little more than an abstract principle of "sensitive and rational self-moving matter" is given in description of this world. Its chief importance seems to be not so much its nature as the delight its female author takes in creating "this world of her own."

The Empress's regret at having nothing to improve in the perfect Hobbesian government of the Blazing World is separated by one short paragraph from the Duchess's delight in making a world of her own invention.[64] This juxtaposition emphasizes both the Empress's frustration at having no scope for political creativity, and the Duchess's nearly fatal attempt to create within a masculine philosophical tradition stretching from Pythagorus to Hobbes. These two reactions suggest something of an authorial impasse for Cavendish, caught between the pre-existent "perfection" of Hobbesian political theory and the crush of a masculine tradition that despite its diversity leaves no space for independent feminine authority. Despite the Duchess's eventual delight in making a world of her own, her authorial original seems unable to describe in detail an independently conceived and governed feminine polis. And yet, if the full elaboration of an original political philosophy along the lines of the *Leviathan* is beyond Cavendish's authorial powers in *The Blazing World*, she does find some scope for revision. And the recurrent focus of these revisions is gender.

For all the Empress's expressions of regret, she has in fact improved the government of the Blazing World. Not long after learning her Hobbesian catechism of unified government, she observes to her priests and statesmen, "I thought you had been either Jews, or Turks, because I never perceived any women in your congregations" (135). The involved response of these male advisors ranges from the unfitness of allowing men and women to be "promiscuously together in time of religious worship" to the prohibition on marriage for the priests and statesmen of the Blazing World, who are all eunuchs. The guiding principle of their response is that "women and children most commonly make disturbance both in church and state," causing as much or more mischief secretly by prevailing with husbands and parents "than if they had the management of public affairs" (135).

The Empress's only demur to the location of all civil discord in women and children is to observe that "women and children have no employment in church or state" (135). Later, however, having decided to convert the people of the Blazing World to her own (unidentified) religion, the Empress establishes what is essentially a female church:

> she resolved to build churches, and make also up a congregation of women, whereof she intended to be the head herself, and to instruct them in several points of her religion. This she

had no sooner begun, but the women, which generally had quick wits, subtle conceptions, clear understandings, and solid judgements, became, in a short time, very devout and zealous sisters; for the Empress had an excellent gift of preaching, and instructing them in the articles of faith; and by that means, she converted them not only soon, but gained an extraordinary love of all her subjects throughout that world.

(162–3)

The female domination of this institution, from the Empress as head to the congregation of women who convert all her subjects, stands in direct opposition to the all-male political world described by the priests and statesmen. The detailed praise of the women's intellectual capacities for public service also counters the earlier masculine accusations of secret mischief to the state arising from the inappropriate domestic influence of women. In putting these charges into the mouths of her imaginary priests and statesmen, Cavendish exposes the implicit misogyny of Hobbes's radical exclusion of women from church and state in the *Leviathan*. Her Empress's "excellent gift of preaching, and instructing them in the articles of faith" responds to the one place where Hobbes's exclusion of women is explicit, in his attack on prophets and prophecy in Chapter 36. Where Hobbes discredits and dismisses women prophets, Cavendish imagines a congregation of women convoked and inspired by the prophetic gifts of its female sovereign.

The Empress's female sovereignty over the church plays havoc with the exclusive masculinity of unified government in Hobbes. Observing contentedly "that both church and state was now in a well-ordered and settled condition" (164–5), the Empress exemplifies the Hobbesian ideal of unified sovereignty over church and state. Located in the sovereign, her prophetic gifts of preaching and instruction are also perfectly consistent with Hobbesian theory, where "the Prophet is the Civill Soveraign, or by the Civil Soveraign Authorized" (3.36.466). But the civil sovereign of the Blazing World is female, and the massive prophetic campaign she authorizes to effect the union of church and state is accomplished through the spiritual and political agency of women.

If Cavendish's Empress learns her catechism of Hobbesian absolutism, her author does not allow its exclusive masculinity to go unchallenged. The Empress's early observations that women do not appear in congregations and that "women and children have no employment in church or state" apply as much to Hobbesian political theory in the *Leviathan* as to its application in the Blazing World. Far from leaving intact the theoretical "perfection" articulated in the *Leviathan* and exemplified in the government of the Blazing World, Cavendish both identifies and remedies its radical exclusion of women and the feminine. In doing so, she articulates an alternative commonwealth, shaped and conceived by the art and ingenuity of a female sovereign:

> the Empress, by art, and her own ingenuity, did not only convert the Blazing World to her own religion, but kept them in a constant belief, without enforcement or blood-shed; for she knew well, that belief was a thing not to be forced or pressed upon the people, but to be instilled into their minds by gentle persuasions; and after this manner she encouraged them also in all other duties and employments, for fear, though it makes people obey, yet does it not last so long, nor is it so sure a means to keep them to their duties, as love.
>
> (164)

United under one sovereign who heads both church and state, the Blazing World is indeed in a state of Hobbesian perfection. And yet Cavendish's closing description of how the Empress and her female converts realize this absolute and peaceful monarchy of church and state directly contradicts the premise of all government in Hobbes. Throughout the *Leviathan*, Hobbes reiterates his conviction that all forms of government are created in response to fear. Only out of fear of chaos and civil war do "men" enter into contract with one another, yielding their individual sovereignty to one representative man or body.[65] The "art" and "ingenuity" of Cavendish's Empress represent a radical critique of Hobbes's first premise. For Cavendish's Empress relies on love rather than fear to guarantee her sovereignty, drawing on the "gentle persuasions" of her women's congregation to effect the unity of church and state advocated in Hobbesian absolutism.

Despite her character's regret at having nothing to change in the Hobbesian perfection of the Blazing World's government, Cavendish does effect a radical revision of Hobbes's theory in two respects: (1) she argues for the love and persuasion of her female sovereign over the fear and force of the Artificial Man as the means of establishing and maintaining a stable government; and (2) she accords full political membership to women at all levels of government, from the multiple agents of religious conversion to the single and unchallenged absolute sovereign of the Blazing World. In short, Cavendish writes women and the symbolic power of the feminine back into Hobbes's masculinist theory of the state. At the same time, I think it would be an overstatement to claim that Cavendish's imaginary world stemmed the masculinist tide of late seventeenth-century political theory. Although she published her *De-*

scription of a New World, Called The Blazing World as the companion piece to a scientific treatise where she takes issue with another male philosopher, she conceived it nevertheless as a fiction. Hobbes's scientific articulation of political philosophy in the *Leviathan* breaks down in Cavendish's double publication of *The Blazing World* with her *Observations Upon Experimental Philosophy*. The sequestering of her political revisions to the fictional half of that double volume suggests how difficult it had become by 1666 to articulate the state as feminine. Although Cavendish drew on earlier feminine icons of the nation to imagine and enhance the power of her female sovereign, that female sovereignty and its iconography had lost their political agency by the time she wrote her fiction. Their symbolic power had not altogether expired, but even Margaret Cavendish could only imagine them in the setting of another world.

2

KING LEAR AND THE TRAGEDY OF NATIVE ORIGINS

> We are younger than ever, we Europeans, since a certain Europe
> does not yet exist. Has it ever existed? And yet we are like these
> young people who get up, at dawn, already old and tired. We are
> already exhausted.
>
> Jacques Derrida, "The Other Heading"

With his characteristic flair for refreshing constitutive tropes in the western
tradition, Jacques Derrida offers this as the "first axiom" of "the very old
subject [*cap*] of European identity" (1992: 5) in his essay, "The Other Heading
[*L'autre cap*]." Replete with French wordplay on *cap* as head(ing), shore,
direction, capital, subject, Derrida's reflections on European identity emerge
self-consciously from the perspective of one himself born on the "other
shore" of the Mediterranean. The self-alienating perspective and language
of these late twentieth-century reflections are also strikingly evocative of
early modern English attempts to articulate national identity in relation to
the "other shore" of continental Europe. In Derrida's suggestion that his
subject – "the very old subject of European identity" – may still retain "a
virgin body" (5), the paradoxical flourishing of Elizabeth's virgin iconography in her last decades blooms once again for all Europe. And in his insistence on the language of spatial orientation and perspective, the topographical
obsessions of *Lear* – from the map of the kingdom to the storm on the heath
to the illusion of Dover cliff (*cap*?) – finally achieve that playful turn into
romance so relentlessly denied them in Shakespeare's tragedy.[1]

In this and the following chapter, I develop complementary readings of
the two plays Shakespeare set in ancient Britain, juxtaposing what I call
the "tragedy of native origins" in *King Lear* with the "romance of Roman
Britain" in *Cymbeline*. Adapted from Elizabethan chronicle sources, both
plays also include icons of topographical nationalism from the previous
reign, ranging from the map of the kingdom and Edgar's description of
Dover cliff in *Lear* to the Queen's celebration of Britain as "Neptune's

park" and the Tudor dynastic associations with Milford Haven in *Cymbeline*. The anxieties inherent in Elizabethan projects of national description and recovery also persist in both plays, from the prominence of savage British queens to the difficult negotiation of Rome's role in national history. Responding to these persistent tensions in the first decade of James's reign, Shakespeare adapted the materials of Elizabethan nationalism quite differently in the tragedy of *Lear* and the romance of *Cymbeline*. In *Lear*, he exploded them, sending the king out to wander at the mercy of the elements after his disastrous use of the map, poising Gloucester within a foot of the verge of an illusory Dover cliff, and killing the one British queen whose female sovereignty received unmitigated praise in early modern accounts. In *Cymbeline*, he redeemed these anxieties about national identity and gender, developing the Welsh idyll of Belarius and the princes, remaking Imogen as the Roman page "Fidele," and substituting *pax romana*-with-honor for the bellicose nationalism of the "wicked Queen."

The generic distinctions between *Lear* and *Cymbeline* are very much effects of their different approaches to the problem of native origins. Similarly, the formal properties of the two genres enhance the relative sense of Britain's cultural isolationism in these plays. The unredeemed tragedy of *Lear* is set in a fiercely insular Britain bent on self-destruction at the personal, familial, and national levels. Its tragic intensity is bound up with the relentless cultural insularity of its setting in British prehistory. By contrast, the mixed genre of romance allows for the development of a Roman–British hybrid in *Cymbeline*. Facilitating the replacement of the Queen's isolationist nationalism with what I call "the masculine embrace of Roman Britain," it defuses problems of gender, sexuality, and national identity in the complex set of personal and national connections that unfolds in the play's long concluding recognition scene. Put in the simplest terms, *Cymbeline* is a "romance" because it incorporates "Romans."

Lear, on the other hand, is a tragedy because it is inescapably locked in the *huis clos* of pre-Roman Britain. No one really leaves or enters the island in *Lear*. Gloucester's desperate attempt to throw himself off Dover cliff dramatizes the boundedness of *Lear*'s Britain, where a blinded old man is deceived that he stands within a foot of its verge, and where no one reaches Dover. The ephemeral suitors France and Burgundy leave no impression on the benighted earth of Britain, and although Cordelia seems to make an early (if painful) escape, she returns to die as *Lear*'s daughter rather than the Queen of France, her foreign identity and power nullified once she rejoins her father. And yet *Lear* incorporates many of the romance conventions Shakespeare exploits in *Cymbeline*, from children and counselors misjudged, lost, and restored to pastoral retreat, forgiveness, and the promise of national renewal. The romance redemption of *Cymbeline* takes place at Milford Haven, the overdetermined site in Wales that brings the play's Romans and Britons together in anticipation of the landing there some fifteen hundred years later of Henry Tudor. In contrast, the action of *Lear* staggers toward a Dover it will never reach, smelling its way to the sea whose other shore is the distant and yet-to-be-encountered civility of Europe. It is in this sense that I invoke *Lear*'s relentless denial of romance in my heuristic juxtaposition of Derrida's reflections with Shakespeare's tragedy. In *Lear*, every gesture toward Romans, romance, and a historical afterlife falls a foot short of the verge of Dover.

Lear's tragic inversion of pastoral romance has long been recognized, and more recently cultural-materialist work has brought a new critical emphasis to this question of genre. Associating the play's romance elements with Jacobean reconstructions of national and political origins, these readings emphasize the interrelation of national myths of origin and early modern attempts to stabilize the social and political orders. My own consideration of *Lear* as a tragedy of native origins, while more focused on the intellectual context of topographical and historically based nationalism, shares a number of topoi with these materialist interpretations, particularly regarding the intersection of issues of social disintegration, national history, and dramatic genre. My contribution to this discussion will be to emphasize that what John Turner calls "powerful familiar tales of national origins" (1988: 87) did not come ready-made as romances in this period. Shakespeare's composition of a British tragedy some time before his Roman–British romance itself adheres to the pattern of romance, exemplifying the necessary passage of time before recuperating the tragic inevitability of ancient British savagery. In this chapter, I consider how Shakespeare exploded the elements of topographical and historically based nationalism in his tragedy of British prehistory. In the subsequent chapter on *Cymbeline*, I suggest how he remade them in the masculine image of Rome.

GYNARCHY AND PATRIARCHA

In his reading of *Lear* as a "tragic romance," John Turner links the play's disappointment of generic expectations with its subversion of "the mythical charter of its own country." Arguing that *Lear* "tells not of a civilization won for the present with heroic difficulty in the past, but of a civilization lost with anguish for all time," Turner locates this loss in a timeless breakdown of social reciprocity (98). Responding in part to Turner's essay in his own exploration of *Lear*'s politics and genre, Richard

Halpern notes the tensions between the play's romance associations and its politically coherent examination of the problem of kingship in Jacobean England.[2] Observing that Lear's "*hysterica passio*" was in fact "*historica passio*" in all editions before the 1685 folio, Halpern puts the problem of history at the heart of the drama. Grappling with the question of how drama can represent historical processes, he renders *historica passio* as "the bearing or enduring or manifestation of historical force through one's person and one's body" (1991: 215, 218), thus locating historical suffering or loss in individual characters (especially Lear). Both these readings emphasize *Lear*'s composition at a time of political, social, and economic disruption in England, and both argue that the play's inversions of romance conventions betray contemporary desires to ground the modern nation on a morally stable vision of the national past.

Both readings also assume, however, a consistent romance quality to stories of native origins. Rightly locating Lear's reign in "the earliest and most violent days of British history" (91), Turner nevertheless characterizes the pervasive injustice of Shakespeare's *Lear* as an inversion of "the heroic past out of which Tudor and Stuart moralists drew their mythic charter" (111). Halpern similarly asserts that "the mythic tales of early chronicle history" implicitly supported Jacobean theories of absolute monarchy (224). Both critics develop persuasive and finely nuanced connections between *Lear*'s tragic aesthetic and the material contexts of perceived and real social disintegration in early modern England. Yet despite their sophisticated accounts of the historical significance of dramatizing one of the earliest British reigns, neither writer appreciates the inherently tragic implications of the ancient British chronicles for modern national identity. Although (as I discuss later) the barbaric divisiveness of the early royal lines does intersect unexpectedly with Robert Filmer's political theory of patriarchal monarchy, the savagery of Britain's prehistory in *Lear* was not Shakespeare's invention. The premise of my own reading of Shakespeare's tragedy is that, far from enacting the irreparable loss of civilization, *Lear* dramatizes a period *before* civilization. *Lear* is not so much a chronicle of historical loss as it is the tragic representation of originary barrenness. *Lear*'s tragic intensity as a dramatization of native origins derives from this failure to incorporate any civil foundation for the modern nation.

Jonathan Dollimore's reading of *Lear* as representative of the humanist failure to redeem the natural world is revealing in this regard. Contending that " 'nature' as ideological concept [was] fast losing its power to police disruptive elements" in early modern England, he quotes Albany's lines: "That nature which contemns its origin / Cannot be bordered certain in itself" (4.2.32–3). Dollimore suggests that social disintegration emerges in this image as an ideological problem in which origin, identity, and action can no longer maintain a natural unity (1984: 200). Albany's definition of nature in terms of origins and borders also evokes the construction of national identity in early modern England, with its emphases on historical recovery and topographical iconography. Based as it was on a perceived relation between native origins and contemporary identity and destiny, early modern English nationalism depended precisely on a belief in the natural unity of origin, identity and action. And yet the chronicle reigns of Lear and other ancient kings hardly provided a civilized ground for the modern nation. Set in the most remote period of native origins and relentlessly dramatizing its primitive savagery, Shakespeare's *Lear* reveals the tragic double-bind of savage origins in early modern England, betraying both the historiographical project of recovering native antiquity, and the intellectual principle on which it was based, namely, the natural unity of origin and identity.

The tragic form that Shakespeare gave to the Leir story famously exceeds the brutality of his source material. In his much-maligned decision to kill Cordelia before her father, Shakespeare departed from the comic or romance versions of Leir's reign in contemporary chronicles and drama. Samuel Johnson's celebrated denunciation of the death of Cordelia suggests some of the moral, aesthetic, and cultural issues involved in Shakespeare's choice: "Shakespeare has suffered the virtue of Cordelia to perish in a just cause, contrary to the natural ideas of justice, to the hope of the reader, and, what is yet more strange, to the faith of chronicles (1968: 704). Johnson invokes an odd mixture of universal and particular criteria in rendering this verdict. Articulating his moral judgment in terms of the three aesthetic categories of the sublime ("natural ideas of justice"), the beautiful (the more familiar and humane "hope of the reader"), and the strange ("the faith of chronicles"), Jonson shifts from an Olympian perspective of moral judgment to the reader's private disappointment to the strange breach of faith with the English chronicles. In a specific sense, the "chronicles" that close Johnson's survey are those of Holinshed, Spenser, *The Mirror for Magistrates*, and the old *Leir* play. Shakespeare's betrayal of "the *faith* of chronicles," however, suggests a more serious breach than the mere (and characteristic) departure from source material. In using the term "faith" in this context, Johnson recalls the debates and anxieties about national historiography that had raged almost two hundred years earlier when the Elizabethan chronicles were first compiled, and when both dramatizations of the Leir material were written. The historicity of the chronicles of ancient Britain had not been at issue for some time when Johnson published his commentary on *Lear* in 1765. Shakespeare's decision to kill Cordelia in the face of an otherwise universal tradition of her survival is certainly worth comment (and has certainly received it), but why does Johnson turn it into a question of the faith of chronicles he himself surely regarded as fabulous?

I submit that when Johnson invoked the strangeness of Shakespeare's having broken with "the faith of chronicles," he was trying to articulate some way in which the bard had betrayed national history as well as universal ideas of justice and the private (if shared) hope of the reader. Thus revealed as contrary to universal, private, and national expectations, the death of Cordelia could have no justification. This tripartite distinction of universal, personal, and national realms parallels Johnson's simultaneous deployment of the three aesthetic categories of the sublime. Johnson's Lear-like insistence on tripartite division is also implicit in his use of the terms "justice," "hope," and "faith" in his series. Elaborating Shakespeare's indifference to the virtue of Cordelia, Johnson himself subjects her virtue to a tripartite division, refracting it through the prism of his own insistent parallelism into a merciless version of the three Christian virtues, where "ideas of *justice*" replace charity alongside "the *hope* of the reader" and "the *faith* of chronicles." The religious implications of "faith" in this last phrase are thus bolstered by Johnson's insistent rhetorical and ideological trinities. Aesthetically, morally, and theologically reprehensible, Shakespeare's decision to suffer the death of Cordelia invests the "faith of chronicles" by contrast with all the virtues of artistic, cultural, and religious truth.

At the same time that Johnson invokes the faith of chronicles alongside universal moral and aesthetic ideals, however, he qualifies his own moral universalism with reference to the play's historical sources and the primitive period of its setting. Countering criticism that Lear's conduct in dividing the kingdom is improbable, he asserts that the king "is represented according to histories at that time vulgarly received as true." Expanding on this historical relativism, Johnson reminds his readers of "the barbarity and ignorance of the age to which this story is referred," suggesting that they might still find such behavior credible "if told of a petty prince of Guinea or Madagascar" (703). Thus eliding the native barbarity of ancient Britain with eighteenth-century English perceptions of Africa, Johnson estranges his modern readership from the primitive period of *Lear*'s ancient British setting. And in his allowance for Shakespeare's reliance on "histories at that time vulgarly received as true," he (erroneously) ascribes a historiographical primitivism to the period in which *Lear* was composed. Johnson's defense of *Lear*'s dramatic credibility emphasizes the play's historical distance from eighteenth-century England – doubly removed in time by its ancient dramatic setting and its primitive early modern historiography – as well as implying its geographical distance in the African analogy. Invoking these comparisons, Johnson responds to Shakespeare's tragedy as though it were both the representation and the product of a foreign culture.[3]

The early modern need to transform or project the savagery of native origins resurfaces in Johnson as a desire to distinguish the more fully modern English nation from the primitivism of *Lear*'s setting *and* from the earlier period of its historiographical recovery. And yet Johnson's assumption of the vulgar reception of histories like Lear's notwithstanding, the "faith of chronicles" in this earlier period was itself somewhat weak with regard to the first reigns of British antiquity. Early modern chroniclers continued to recount the legendary reigns of pre-Roman Britain even as they dismissed their historicity, arguing that there was nothing else to put in their place. Holinshed's introduction to these primitive beginnings is typical of this early modern historiographical ambivalence:

> But sith the original in manner of all nations is doubtful, and even the same for the more part fabulous (that always excepted which we find in the holy scriptures) I wish not any man to lean to that which shall be here set down as to an infallible truth, sith I do but only show other men's conjectures, grounded nevertheless upon likely reasons, concerning that matter whereof there is now left but little other certainty, or rather none at all.
>
> (1587: 1)

Relatively few early modern dramas were drawn from this fabulous period of British prehistory, playwrights preferring to base their historical formulations of national identity on the less distant Norman reigns, despite the invention of the native history play with *Gorboduc*.[4] The social and Christian orthodoxy of the old *Leir* play, however, indicates that the material of this reign need not present the nation's earliest history as irredeemable. Indeed it was precisely Shakespeare's revision of the older play and the chronicle histories that created the tragedy of native origins in *Lear*.

In the revision of his literary and historical sources, Shakespeare effected a tragic conclusion beyond any hope of personal or national redemption. In contrast to her demise before the end of her father's reign in Shakespeare, Holinshed's Cordeilla both succeeds in rescuing her father and the nation, and lives to succeed Lear as the first reigning queen of Britain. One of the more striking historiographical results of Shakespeare's revision of Holinshed, then, was the elimination of the first female reign in the history of Britain. The short paragraph describing the reign of Cordeilla is introduced in the 1587 edition of Holinshed with the heading "The gunarchie of queene Cordeilla," and her reign is singled out as the only one to merit that title throughout the line of Brute:[5]

> Cordeilla the youngest daughter of Leir was admitted queen and supreme governess of Britain in the year of the world 3155, before the building of Rome 54, Ukia then reigning in Juda, and Jeroboam over Israel. This Cordeilla after her father's decease ruled the land of Britain right worthily during the space of five years, in which meantime her husband died, and then about the end of those five years, her two nephews Margan and Cunedag, sons to her aforesaid sisters, disdaining to be under the government of a woman, levied war against her, and destroyed a great part of the land, and finally took her prisoner, and laid her fast in ward, wherewith she took such grief, being a woman of a manly courage, and despairing to recover liberty, there she slew herself, when she had reigned (as is before mentioned) the term of five years.
>
> (1587: 13)

Not only did Cordeilla rule in her own right, and for at least some period without the benefit of a husband's counsel, but she also ruled "right worthily" and met her fate stoically as "a woman of a manly courage." A woodcut in the 1577 Holinshed emphasizes these qualities, depicting a resolute (if not scowling) monarch with muscular forearms, a crown, and scepter (Figure 12) (Holinshed 1577: 20). If Cordeilla's conduct as queen was admirable, however, her reign nevertheless suffered from the familial divisiveness that cursed the Brutan line. The single sentence in which Holinshed praises her reign and then charts her ruin and the destruction of "a great part of the land" by her nephews emphasizes the constant degeneration associated with this period of ancient British history, where the establishment of a new monarch was generally the first stage in the next cycle of war and division. Indeed, Book II of *The History of England* ends shortly after Cordeilla's deposition with the collapse of the line of Brute into Hobbesian civil war and eventual extinction.

Throughout Holinshed's history of this ancient line, the Brutan monarchs are characterized by what J. P. Brockbank has called "the arbitrary spleen and malevolence that Geoffrey [of Monmouth] often found antecedent to the rule of law" (1958: 44). The rule of law begins in the Third Book of *The History of England* with the reign of Mulmucius, who set the laws of ancient Britain. The period from which Shakespeare drew his material for *King Lear* was thus the most savage and chaotic of ancient British history, antecedent not only to the civilizing

12. Woodcut of Cordeilla in Raphael Holinshed, *Chronicles* (1577), by permission of the Houghton Library, Harvard University.

presence of the Romans, but even to such laws as the British them-selves had devised. The reigns of the Brutan line also precede the ro-mance material of Arthurian legend, as Lear's Fool suggests with his line, "This prophecy Merlin shall make, for I live before his time" (3.2.95–6). Antecedent to both the rule of law and the civility of romance, the reigns of Cordeilla and her father are paradoxically exempted from the general savagery of this period in Holinshed. Cordeilla rules "right worthily" for five years and Leir is characterized as "a prince of right noble demeanor, governing his land and subjects in great wealth" (12). Singled out as examples of royal integrity and national prosperity, the chronicle reigns of Leir and Cordeilla are exceptional in their promise of a romance-like recuperation of the civility of the Trojan founding, that moment of national and dynastic civility dissipated in Brute's division of Britain between his sons and the cyclical recurrence of division in his royal line (Leir was the tenth monarch in that line). By suffering Cordelia to predecease her father, Shakespeare collapsed the romance potential of his source material, subjecting it to the tragic compression of a single reign in which a father unnaturally survives his children, leaving no heir in the royal line.[6]

In Shakespeare's tragedy, the compressed histories of Leir and Cordeilla become a prime representation of the spleen and malevolence to which they seemed to offer the only potential exception in Holinshed's chronicle of the Brutan kings. And yet, in eliminating both the only "gynarchy" and the sole gesture toward order and prosperity in this earliest period of native history, Shakespeare did not, I think, break faith with the early modern chronicles. Rather, in his tragic adaptation of the Leir material, Shakespeare removed what ran contrary to the faith of chronicles, compressing Lear's reign into his terrible old age, nullifying Cordelia's familial and national powers of renewal, and eliminating in the process the nation's founding gynarchy and its only early example of idealized female sovereignty. Shakespeare thus brought the reigns of Leir and Cordeilla into line with early modern anxieties about native origins, developing two memorable examples of savage (would-be) queens, and allowing native barbarism to run its inevitable course of national ruin in the familial inversions and strife of the first British line of kings.

This national history of internecine strife was one of the primary counterexamples used in early modern English political theory. I discussed in Chapter 1 how Hobbes's metaphor of the state of nature recalled these earlier historiographical accounts of ancient Britain in its emphasis on the self-destructive savagery that pre-exists the rule of law. Hobbes's contemporary and (classic) patriarchalist adversary also drew on this period of British history to ground his own theory of the state. Robert Filmer probably composed his *Patriarcha*, the period's most elaborate derivation of civil authority from paternal dominion, in the years 1628–31 when Charles I and his advisors were beginning to consolidate his personal rule under Thorough. Intellectually as well as politically conservative, Filmer was well versed in Elizabethan and Jacobean reconstructions of native origins, drawing extensively on these earlier projects of national recovery to provide the historical evidence for his derivation of civil authority from paternal dominion.[7]

Filmer invokes nationalist stories of origin early in the *Patriarcha*, using the example of the sons of Noah to support the assertion of his first chapter, "That the first kings were fathers of families":

> Most of the civillest nations in the world labour to fetch their original from some one of the sons or nephews of Noah, which were scattered abroad after the confusion of Babel. In this

dispersion we must certainly find the establishment of regal power throughout the kingdoms of the world.

(1991: 7)

Thus deriving regal power from Noah's paternal dominion over his sons, Filmer associates his political theory with the historiographical project of establishing national civility. The confusion of Babel and the subsequent "dispersion," however, are oddly implicated in Filmer's account of the founding of civil nations. Indeed, if Hobbes regarded divided government as the downfall of the state, Filmer takes it as the foundation of civil authority and the proof of its derivation from paternal dominion. His seeming affinity for nationalist reconstructions of civil origins thus gives way before his theoretical need to derive patriarchal sovereignty from the atomistic government of individual fathers at the origins of "the civillest nations."

Filmer also invoked the divided government of his own nation's origins to support his more general derivation of patriarchalism from paternal dominion:

Caesar found more kings in France than there be now provinces there, and at his sailing over into this island he found four kings in our county of Kent. These heaps of kings in each nation are an argument that their territories were but small, and strongly confirm our assertion that erection of kingdoms came at first only by distinction of families.

(1991: 9)

The petty barbarism of British antiquity that threatened the foundation of the modern nation in the histories of Holinshed and Camden becomes in Filmer's theoretical model the historical evidence for patriarchal authority.[8] Filmer's dependence on the historicity of divided government in British antiquity has important implications for the political absolutism of *Lear*. Where Hobbes associated the state of nature with maternal dominion, Filmer conceives of originary political atomism as the founding moment and historical proof of patriarchalism. Lear's very insistence on dividing the kingdom, his laying aside of the sovereignty that constituted the "reall Unitie" of his symbolic office, thus returned Britain to the originary political moment when patriarchal authority was coterminous with paternal dominion.

Understood in Filmerian terms, Lear's division of the kingdom is not the tragic error that destroys the possibility of sovereignty, but rather the paradoxical assertion and affirmation of the monarch's natural patriar-

chal authority. John Turner addresses this paradox of political absolutism in terms of the grotesque, arguing that *Lear*'s "grotesqueness is its
mode of re-creating the political fragmentation of Lear's Britain, and
thus of establishing the living connexion between the present and its
imagined prehistory." Turner goes on to observe that in Lear's virtual
identity with Britain when he calls for the map in the opening scene, "his
absoluteness only serves to draw out the contradictions within the ruling
classes of his kingdom" (1988: 112–13). Consistent with Turner's general thesis of a social ideal (feudalism) succumbing to its own internal
contradictions (87), the Filmerian reading I am proposing of the division
of the kingdom also exposes the internal contradictions of a political
absolutism that depended on the historical fragmentation of its origins.
Here indeed, "That nature which contemns its origin / Cannot be bordered certain in itself."

In *King Lear*, Shakespeare dramatized a primitive absolutism that reveals the internal contradictions of early modern patriarchalism. Simultaneously staging patriarchal sovereignty and the divided nation that
was its historical charter, he effected a tragic compression of Filmer's
political theory very like the compression he imposed on the chronicle
histories of Leir and Cordeilla. The tragedy of native origins is a function
of both these historical compressions. Insisting on the savagery of the
early Brutan line, Shakespeare was in fact true to the faith of chronicles
when he fused the reigns of Leir and Cordeilla, eliminating the only
ancient examples of native civility and laudable gynarchy after Brute's
initial division of Britain. Resisting the turn to romance in other contemporary versions of this material, he realized the tragic potential of the
historiography of native origins. His similar compression of early modern
patriarchalism with its supposed historical origins precluded any recuperation of native antiquity in terms of primitive patriarchal absolutism.

CARTOGRAPHICA PASSIO

I shift my interpretive focus in this section from the historiographical issues
of Shakespeare's tragic revisionism to the representational problems of the
play's topographical icons. Ranging from the map of the divided kingdom
to the imagery of Renaissance cartography to Edgar's virtuosic description
of Dover cliff, these icons confirm the historiographical associations between national representation and tragedy in *Lear*. Elaborating my sense of
the play's primitive absolutism in terms of *Lear*'s cartographical obsessions,
I explore Shakespeare's engagement with the anxieties provoked by
early modern cartography and topographical description and their roles in

defining the nation. My exploration of problems of cartographical representation in *Lear* intersects with readings that engage the play's technical issues of perspective, particularly with regard to theatrical representation. Although I do not elaborate an argument about the conditions of representation in the early modern theater, I do note the coincidence of certain crises of theatrical representation with similarly complicated moments of cartographical representation.

My subtitle invokes Richard Halpern's profound meditation on the *historica/hysterica* crux in *Lear*. Adapting his definition of *historica passio* to the play's striking evocations of place rather than time, I propose a reading of the effects of "*cartographica passio*" in *Lear*. Both Lear and Gloucester submit to "the bearing or enduring or manifestation" in their persons and bodies of cartographical forces. These forces range from the technical imperatives of Ptolemaic mapping and the necessary distortions of mathematical projection, to the inescapable confusions of history and topography at overdetermined national sites like Dover. The humanist dream of taming the natural world through rational explanation and precise description collapses under the pressure of *cartographica passio* in *Lear*, subject to the same tragic compression that reveals the internal contradictions of native historiography and patriarchalist political theory. To demonstrate the peculiar intensity of *cartographica passio* in Shakespeare's tragedy of native origins, let me begin with a counterexample from a comic history set in the more recent national past.

In Act 3 of *1 Henry IV*, Hotspur, Mortimer, and Owen Glendower meet in Wales to plot their uprising against the king. The farcical note of the gathering is set within the first five lines by Hotspur's observation that they have forgotten the map. It is further developed by Owen Glendower's exaggerated claims about the heavenly portents that heralded his birth, and Hotspur's mocking dismissal of Glendower's pretensions to supernatural power.[9] Yet when they finally return to the subject of their meeting and locate the map, the conspirators discuss the division of the kingdom in ways that strikingly anticipate the opening of *King Lear*. Mortimer describes the map, which like Lear's has already been divided into three portions:

> The Archdeacon hath divided it
> Into three limits very equally.
> England, from Trent and Severn hitherto,
> By south and east is to my part assigned;
> All westward, Wales beyond the Severn shore,
> And all the fertile land within that bound,

To Owen Glendower; and, dear coz, to you
The remnant northward lying off from Trent.
(3.1.71–8)

The tripartite division, the references to rivers and bounds, and the fertile land all look forward to the similar description of Goneril's portion in Act 1 of *Lear*. Similarly, the division into Southeast, Southwest and North suggests the rough division of Lear's kingdom into the southeastern region of Dover and Kent's duchy, which may have been initially intended for Cordelia, and the southwestern and northern regions of Cornwall and Albany. The scene anticipates *Lear* more generally in its setting in Wales, the early modern remnant of ancient Britain, and in the Welsh Glendower's exaggerated description of the elements. Glendower's cosmological pretensions also evoke the primitive absolutism that might have belonged to a king in the period of Britain's legendary origins, but that in the context of a historical Norman reign provoke only Hotspur's amused scorn.[10]

The scene's final measure of difference from the high seriousness of *Lear*'s opening is the preposterous dispute over whether to change the course of the river Trent. This discussion is entirely governed by the conventions of the map, from Hotspur's initial complaint that "this river comes me cranking in / And cuts me from the best of all my land / A huge half-moon, a monstrous cantle out" (3.1.97–9) to Glendower's exclamation, "Not wind? It shall, it must! You see it doth" (105) to Worcester's assurance that "but a little charge will trench him here […] And then he runs straight and even" (110, 112). The conventions of Ptolemaic cartography, in which the map bears an empirical rather than a schematic relation to the land it represents, are mocked here in the conspirators' assumption that a river's course may be shifted as simply as a line may be redrawn on a map. The topographical nationalism of late sixteenth-century England was indeed concerned with such shifts, from the correction of misidentified place names to the attempted reconstruction of ancient rivers that were discovered to have dried up or changed course over time. The conspirators' meeting thus mocks Elizabethan projects of national representation as well as the magical and legendary associations of Wales with ancient Britain (associations that Shakespeare treats with greater seriousness in *Cymbeline*).

The farcical nature of this scene is appropriate to the comic plot of *1 Henry IV*, helping to maintain the play's buoyancy by undercutting the seriousness of the threat posed by the conspirators. This lightness plays no part in the corresponding scene in *Lear*, where the ancient king's real cartographical power results in the actual division of the kingdom in civil war. Like the map in *1 Henry IV*, Lear's map has already been divided before the scene opens, and Gloucester and Kent begin the play by discussing its implications. Unlike the disputed division in *1 Henry IV*, however, the lines on Lear's map have been drawn so that "equalities are so weighed that curiosity in neither can make choice of either's moiety" (1.1.5–7). This preternaturally perfect division emerges as a similarly utopian plenitude in Lear's description of Goneril's portion:

> Of all these bounds, even from this line to this,
> With shadowy forests, and with champains riched,
> With plenteous rivers, and wide-skirted meads,
> We make thee lady.
>
> (1.1.65–8)

Regan's portion, identical in "space, validity, and pleasure" (1.1.83), confirms the idealized proliferation of topographical bounty. Lear has included every pleasing form of topography in England, from shadowy forests for game and the hunt to rich champains for crops, plenteous rivers for irrigation and travel, and wide-skirted meads for grazing. What would be unprofitable, dangerous, or unpleasant – from marshy ground to the barren mountainous regions that had yet to receive the aesthetic cachet of the sublime – is eliminated from this Edenic vision of the kingdom. The introduction of the map in *Lear*, then, from Gloucester's opening evocation of its perfect division to Lear's own catalogue of the bounties it represents, suggests an idealized and iconographical representation of the kingdom that testifies both to its bounty and to the absolute sovereignty of Lear.

There is no external evidence as to the kind of map used on stage for this scene, or even if any image was visible at all to the audience. Shakespeare seems to have relied primarily on the few lines describing Goneril's portion to suggest the image of the map for his audience. This description emphasizes topographical detail in a way that would only be possible in a survey of a small region or in a composite national map based on such individual surveys. Saxton's 1579 county atlas of England and Wales answers to this description in both the composite map of the realm and the individual maps of the counties. These county maps would have been the most familiar cartographical image in England by the time of *Lear*'s composition.[11] And like Lear's map of the kingdom, they were also founded on the principle of division. When Lear refers to Goneril's portion as extending "even from this line to this," he suggests the defining feature of Saxton's maps, namely, their indication of the kingdom's internal division into counties.[12] Saxton's maps defined the nation in terms of its internal divisions, just as Lear's map presents his kingdom as already divided between his daughters.

As the first known complete survey of a country by its constituent parts, Saxton's atlas represented the one major English contribution to the expanding art of cartography in the sixteenth century. Lear's map is thus not simply a pictorial representation of his kingdom, but also an icon of late sixteenth-century English nationalism, evoking the county atlas that was England's unique cartographical triumph and constituting the realm as a land-based nation. *Lear* opens, then, with an idealized vision of topographical plenitude that is both an icon and an instrument of royal control. By the end of this opening scene, however, Lear has lost all control of the carefully orchestrated display of royal power. His youngest daughter has defied his attempts to force a more than axiomatic expression of her love and reverence for him, and his careful provision for the succession has been thrown over in favor of a rash division of the kingdom between those who least honor it. What began as an administrative division on the map ends as a literal division of the kingdom, torn apart by the familial conflict and civil war that follows. The very sign of Lear's sovereignty, his absolute power to make real the lines he draws on the map, becomes the source of his destruction.[13]

Lear's absolute power to divide the kingdom also points to the sixteenth-century cartographical claim to present an empirical replica of the world rather than the schematic diagram of medieval world maps. With the recovery of Ptolemaic geography in the early fifteenth century, western cartographers began to conceive of maps as a set of geometrically determined coordinates representing the actual shapes and spatial relations of land masses. A line drawn on a map was meant to bear some real relation to the feature it represented, as opposed to the lines on medieval world maps, which indicated purely schematic divisions.[14] The literalization of Lear's division of the kingdom is thus itself a literalization of the Ptolemaic convention of cartographic realism. Catherine Belsey has speculated on the relation of these two different modes of cartographic representation to the staging of tragedy in early modern England (1985: 13–54).[15] She begins with an analysis of the *mappamundi*-like stage plan that survives for the early fifteenth-century morality play *The Castle of Perseverance*. This plan sketches a dramatic situation where the subject is surrounded by the audience, which lines the circular plan where the battle for the subject's soul takes place. The audience is thus part of the cosmic drama, neither inhabiting a separate sphere from the action nor developing any detached perspective on it. Similarly, the subject of the drama has no separate or transcendent identity, simply suffering the various trials inflicted upon it by the dramatic situation. In Belsey's argument, the subject of tragedy does not develop a unified and transcendent identity until the establishment of classic realist theater in the late seventeenth century, with its isolation of the world of the fiction from the world of the audience. This separate identity is created by the fixed perspective of the audience, which now reads, maps, and masters the scene from its isolated position apart from the stage. The isolated stage of realism thus presents an empirical replica of the world rather than an emblematic representation, following the conventions of a Ptolemaic map rather than a *mappamundi*. Between the theater-in-the-round of *The Castle of Perseverance* and the classic realism of the Restoration, Belsey defines a transitional period that runs from the opening of Burbage's Theater in 1576 to the closing of the theaters in 1642. In her reading, this period witnessed the collision of the emblematic medieval geography of the stage with the emergent illusionism of the isolated empirical replica.

The period of collision defined by Belsey also represents the great age of English nationalist drama, in which the dramatic subject was frequently the nation as much as it was as any individual character.[16] Indeed, I believe that the collision she describes is central to the representation of the nation in *Lear*. *Lear* begins by exploiting the new Ptolemaic perspective in the map and the control of the kingdom it offers. Edgar's description of Dover Cliff is another such moment of fixed and isolated perspective, foregrounding the illusionism Belsey defines as the identifying characteristic of the emerging empirical theater. Stephen Orgel and Jonathan Goldberg have approached Edgar's verbal illusion in terms of the contemporary introduction of illusionistic scenery in court theatricals. Contemporary accounts of this new scenery indicate the degree to which it baffled its audiences, who had yet to be educated in this new convention of staging. It was nevertheless the new convention that eventually prevailed over the older emblematic representation deriving from the *mappamundi*/morality play tradition.[17] Marshall McLuhan also considered Edgar's speech in terms of the relation between medieval and Renaissance conventions of representing the world. In *The Gutenberg Galaxy*, he defined the Renaissance map as the "key to the new vision of peripheries of power and wealth" and argued that the map in the opening scene of *Lear* brings forward the play's principal theme of the isolation of the visual sense as a kind of blindness. McLuhan found Edgar's speech in 4.6 to be emblematic of this paradox, its isolation of sight from the other senses conferring the illusion of a third dimension – the only instance, in McLuhan's view, of verbal three-dimensional description in all literature. McLuhan nevertheless ended his consideration of *Lear* by situating the play in the older tradition of emblematic representation, calling it "a kind of medieval sermon-exemplum or inductive reasoning to display the madness and misery of the new Renaissance life of action" (1962: 11–17).

There is indeed much in the staging of *Lear*'s world that derives from the *mappamundi*/morality play tradition. The storming stage directions and cosmic invocations of the heath scenes suggest the all-encompassing world scene of *The Castle of Perseverance*, even as Lear's helpless sufferings there recall the hapless protagonists of the morality plays. The nation in *Lear* is subject to the same collision of representational modes. More than just the tragedy of an individual, *Lear* represents the tragedy of the whole nation, whose collapse is as absolute as Lear's own demise. National topography assumes its own subjectivity in the play, from the use of territorial names for many of the characters to the almost human agency assumed by the map of the kingdom.[18] This national subject is caught in precisely that collision of representational modes described by Belsey. If the map in the opening scene promised a detached and empirical perspective from which to control national representation, the scenes on the heath annihilate this comfortable distance, both for Lear and for his audience. Yet the return to empirical perspective in Edgar's description of Dover Cliff fails to restore representational unity. Self-consciously presented as a healing illusion, Edgar's description is as inadequate to the play's representational crises as it is to its moral questions. While he succeeds in making his father believe in his illusion, Edgar fails both to restore the right order of familial relations in the play and to avert its tragic conclusion. Indeed, the collision of the emblematic and the empirical in *Lear* serves ultimately to destroy the redemptive potential of either mode of representing the nation. The right relation of all parts to the whole that characterizes the *mappamundi* is revealed merely as imprisonment in an intolerable world in *Lear*. Similarly, the promise of transcendence and a separate identity based on the fixed perspective of classic realism degenerates into isolation and fragmentation. Possessing neither an integrated place in a larger cosmos, nor a separate and transcendent identity of its own, Lear's Britain is a nightmare of internal division from which there is no escape.[19]

The sixteenth-century advances in cartography also implicated national representation in technical problems of perspective. Although the role of mapping in the development of national subjectivity is well-established, the particular effects of Ptolemaic principles also merit examination. In the following pages, I compare a didactic English interlude on the subject of cosmography, which was written and performed in London in the early sixteenth century, with the scenes Shakespeare wrote nearly a century later to dramatize Lear's rage against the winds and hurricanoes of the storm on the heath. I consider both cosmic dramas in terms of the technical problems of Ptolemaic mapping, particularly with regard to the production of world maps. This early interlude and *Lear* frame the century in which the great Renaissance world maps were produced according to Ptolemaic principles. Full of promise for human mastery over the natural world, these maps exploited the developing technologies of printing and mathematical projection even as they enabled and recorded advances in navigation. The same humanist confidence animates the English cosmographical interlude, which was written when Ptolemaic maps were only beginning to be introduced into England. Almost uncannily, the humanist language of this interlude resurfaces in Lear's raging speeches on the heath. Drawing on the linguistic coincidence of Lear's madness and the interlude's rational explanation, I explore the connections between his despair on the heath and the earlier, hopeful invocation of cosmographical enquiry.

In 1517 or 1518 the London bookseller, lawyer, merchant, and civil servant John Rastell wrote and produced an interlude entitled *The Nature of the Four Elements*. Closely tied to the morality play tradition, Rastell's interlude was nevertheless more concerned with the humanist process of education than with the cosmic drama of salvation. In particular, Rastell (a brother-in-law to Thomas More) was eager to introduce into England the principles of humanist scholarship and the new fields of knowledge that were already being developed on the continent. Rastell's interlude has been cited as the first work on modern geography by an English author, characterized as "a versified cosmography for the stage" (E. G. R. Taylor 1930: 8–9). In this cosmography, Ptolemaic geography emerges as the key to the new world of humanist learning. Presenting geographical information about the shape and dimensions of the earth and its continents in the dialogue, Rastell also caused a world map or globe to be brought on stage as a prop to illustrate Ptolemaic principles of empirical representation (1979: 704–876).[20]

Rastell has his geographical figure brought on stage by the character "Nature," thus suggesting the derivation of its depiction of the world according to empirical principles, or "from nature." This suggestion is further developed by the character "Experience," who is able to verify the figure's accuracy, having traveled throughout the world (695). Rastell's emphasis on nature and experience as the purveyors of the figure indicates his attempt to dislodge the more emblematic world view of the *mappamundi* in favor of the empirical representation of Ptolemaic geography. Yet *The Nature of the Four Elements* is not utterly divorced from its origins in the inclusive cosmos of the morality play. The first task of "Experience" is to indicate England on the figure, pointing also to Scotland and Ireland, and describing the situation of both islands as surrounded by water (708–14). He moves quickly to identify the other countries on the map, beginning with Europe and its colonial holdings in the Americas, and eventually including the East, Africa, and a final discussion of the two hemispheres (715–46, 829–76). "Experience" thus presents England as part of a greater whole, beginning with its immediate position in the British Isles, and elaborating its place in its relation to the other countries of Europe, the three Ptolemaic continents and the Americas, and finally the two hemispheres of the globe. The internal division of England, constitutive of both map and national identity in *Lear*, appears nowhere in *The Nature of the Four Elements*. Indeed, despite its insistence on Ptolemaic principles, Rastell's interlude incorporates both emblematic and empirical modes of representation without any sense of indecorum. The collision that represented the tragic situation of the nation in *King Lear* passes unnoticed in this earlier dramatic presentation of England's geographical situation.

The reasons for this distinction between the two dramas lie in the near century that separated their composition. Between the writing of *The Four Elements* in 1517 and *King Lear* in 1605, the whole drama of English topographical nationalism was enacted. In contrast to the ability of Shakespeare's audience to derive a mental image of the map of the kingdom from hearing the brief description of Goneril's portion, Rastell's dialogue indicates that even his large and clearly visible figure had to be explained in detail before his audience would know what to make of it. This contrast is the more striking when one considers that Rastell's audience was almost certainly a learned one, given the technical nature of much of his dialogue, whereas Shakespeare composed *Lear* for the general audience of the Globe. Rastell's work dates from the very earliest stage of the introduction of humanist knowledge into England. Indeed, he begins the drama with a lament on the sad state of English scholarship and publishing, and calls for the translation of "cunning Latin books" so that the "subtle science" of the continent might become more widely available to English readers (15–35). Rastell's gloomy assessment of the contemporary state of national learning gives way to a corresponding optimism for the nation's future once England begins to participate in the humanist revolution of the continent. This optimism is most evident in Rastell's cheerful confidence that the workings of the elements can be both understood and mastered through the new science of cosmography. The section of the interlude in which

"Experience" explains the science of the elements is lost. Its argument survives, however, and in the list of topics lies a curious anticipation of Lear's dramatic encounter with the elements almost a century later.

The section of Rastell's argument devoted to the working of the elements reads as follows:

> Of the cause of the ebb and flood of the sea.
> Of the cause of rain, snow and hail.
> Of the cause of the winds and thunder.
> Of the cause of the lightning of blazing stars and flames flying in the air.
>
> (Argument, 28–31)

Given the general catechetical technique of Rastell's dialogue, these topics were probably presented in question form. The young student of the drama may well have approached the workings of thunder with the question, "What is the cause of thunder?" "Experience" no doubt drew on the large chart of the elements that was another prop of the interlude to develop his cosmographical explanation of this phenomenon. Thunder, like the other natural phenomena listed, would lose its mysterious power in the face of this rational enquiry and tamely take its place on the chart. The dramatic situation in which Lear poses his question nearly a century later offers no such comfort. In contrast to the sheltered environment of Rastell's interlude with its ordered chart, the stage directions of Shakespeare's *Lear* repeatedly call for the illusion of the elements themselves to be brought into the theater and visited on the head of the king who seeks to understand their workings. As Lear turns to the poor, bare, forked animal on the heath and asks "What is the cause of thunder?" the stage directions continue to indicate, as they have regularly throughout the heath scenes, "Storm still" (3.4.158).[21]

Lear's approach to that question nevertheless points back to the humanist assumptions of *The Four Elements* and similar scholarly works of scientific explanation, for he begins by saying "First let me talk with this philosopher" (3.4.157). In the course of the next thirty lines, as Kent and Gloucester desperately try to bring him to shelter, Lear addresses Poor Tom four more times with scholarly epithets: "I'll talk a word with this same learned Theban. What is your study?" (160–1); "Noble Philosopher, your company" (175); "I will keep still with my philosopher" (178); and "Come, good Athenian" (183). Learned Theban, noble philosopher, good Athenian – this is the language of Renaissance humanism, with its desire to return to classical principles of order, to recover Greek science and philosophy, and to submit the natural world to rational investigation and explanation. Their use in this context suggests not only the collapse of the classical ideal of stoic suffering in *Lear*,[22] but also the failure of Renaissance projects of topographical and cosmographical mastery. If Rastell could introduce these disciplines to England with full confidence that they would provide not only understanding but mastery of the natural world, Shakespeare responds a century later with the words of the naked madman addressed so grandiloquently by his mad king. "Tom's a-cold," says Edgar, and "Child Rowland to the dark tower came; / His word was still, 'Fie, foh, and fum, / I smell the blood of a British man" (3.4.176, 185–7).

Shakespeare's juxtaposition of humanist tags with Poor Tom's mad patter invokes not only the inescapable human vulnerability to cold but also the persistence of medieval romance and folklore after a century of rigorous humanist investigation of the national past. Lear's personal anguish and bafflement also give expression to this corporate failure, as though he were beholding the utter ineffectuality of the nationalist projects that sought to master both native topography and national identity through empirical research and representation. Turning away from this prospect, Lear returns to the cartographical iconography with which the play began. Having unleashed the disintegration of the kingdom through his own literalized act of division, the mad king now calls for the destruction of the whole Ptolemaic world:

> Blow, winds, and crack your cheeks. Rage, blow!
> You cataracts and hurricanoes, spout
> Till you have drenched our steeples, drowned the cocks.
> You sulph'rous and thought-executing fires,
> Vaunt-couriers of oak-cleaving thunderbolts,
> Singe my white head. And thou, all-shaking thunder,
> Strike flat the thick rotundity o'th'world,
> Crack Nature's molds, all germains spill at once,
> That makes ingrateful man.
>
> (3.2.1–9)

The imagery of these lines, although inspired by Lear's experience of the natural world, points in fact to the cartographical world of its empirical representation. Invoking the round-cheeked wind gods and the water spouts banished to the edges of the great Renaissance world maps, Lear calls on them to reclaim the center of that ordered world and return it to chaos. Yet Lear does not merely describe the images found on Renaissance maps; he also invokes the technical procedure that allowed for their empirical accuracy. When he calls on the all-shaking thunder to

"Strike flat the thick rotundity o'th'world," he invokes the destructive power of that natural force in terms of the mathematical projection of the round world onto flat paper.

Lear's image evokes the technical problem of mapping a sphere onto a plane, possibly the greatest challenge and eventual triumph of Renaissance cartography. The thick rotundity of the earth was mapped onto the flat page by a variety of projections in the sixteenth century. (A projection is any regular system of parallels and meridians on which a map can be drawn.) Because no flat representation of the globe can present both area and angles accurately, any map projection is at best a compromise of their respective distortions. Mercator's Projection, developed for his world map of 1569, solved the problem of representing the shape and relation of land masses accurately at the price of grossly distorting their relative area. Its reasonably accurate replication of shape and direction made Mercator's 1569 world map especially useful for navigation, and his projection quickly became the standard for world maps.[23] J. B. Harley notes, however, that this improvement in the technical production of maps produced as its corollary a growing concern about their accuracy and reliability, particularly in terms of surveys and projections (1983: 27). Even as mathematical projection allowed for the first relatively accurate depiction of the round earth on flat paper, it also raised both expectations for and anxiety about cartographical accuracy.

When Shakespeare had Lear call on the all-shaking thunder to "Strike flat the thick rotundity o' th' world," he also invoked these issues of distortion and error inherent in mathematical projection. His image of the world-flattening thunder suggests that cartography is inevitably a process of distortion and destruction, annihilating the plenitude of the natural world and flattening it into the two dimensions of the page. In this evocation of cartography as destruction, Shakespeare also articulated the implications of Lear's own rash act of cartographical division. Just as Lear's call to the world-destroying thunder invoked the cartographical principle of projection, so his earlier division of the map of the kingdom literalized the Ptolemaic principle outlined by Rastell in *The Four Elements*, where lines on the map represent real divisions in the world. What for Rastell was a triumph of empirical replication becomes in Shakespeare's *Lear* a nightmare of literal representation, where the fragmenting and distorting properties of cosmography invest the real world rather than its replica. Raging on the heath at the all-shaking thunder even as he incites it to global destruction, Lear becomes the subject of "*cartographica passio*," bearing, enduring, and manifesting the internal division and distortion of his own cartographical act.

(DOVER)

When Edgar makes his perspectival description of Dover Cliff in 4.6, he does not re-establish the safe empirical distance that Lear loses on the heath. Rather, he reveals that distance as an illusion that both isolates and deceives the viewer. Despite Edgar's claim that he perpetrates it in order to "cure" his father, there is nothing saving in this deception. What I examine in the last section of this chapter is the curious way in which the word "Dover" stands for the saving, redemptive possibility that Shakespeare excised from his tragic revision of the Lear story. In Gloucester's belief that it will provide his deliverance, as well as Kent's intelligence of Cordelia's projected landing there, Dover assumes something like the saving function of Jerusalem on a *mappamundi*. Jerusalem stands at the center of schematic medieval world maps, indicating the centrality of the Crucifixion and Resurrection in the Christian drama of salvation. Just as Jerusalem marks the centrality of death and resurrection in medieval Christian theology, so Dover becomes the ultimate destination of those seeking death and redemption in *Lear*.[24] And yet no one reaches Dover in Shakespeare's tragedy, and no one finds redemption. I put parentheses around (Dover) in my subheading as one might circle a point representing an unreached limit on a graph, or indicate an open set in mathematical notation. I use this device to denote the status of (Dover) as the unreachable and indefinable point toward which the action of the last acts of *Lear* is directed.[25]

The symbolic quality of (Dover) in *Lear*'s action suggests more than one parallel with the central informing presence of Jerusalem on the medieval *mappamundi*. As Jerusalem was for Henry IV, Dover is a place of penitential pilgrimage in *Lear*. And just as Henry was famously cheated of his prophetic death in the Holy Land, so Gloucester is duped into making his false leap from the illusory cliff. Dover's status more broadly in English cartography also suggests a shared function of definition with Jerusalem. But where Jerusalem marked the center of the *mappamundi* and its schematic vision of the drama of salvation, Dover represented the easternmost edge of England. On one of Matthew Paris's medieval maps of England, Dover is placed at the bottom of the island as the base of a line of towns that runs up the center as far as Newcastle. No attention is given to the east–west axis in this itinerary of the major towns between Dover and Newcastle. Paris noted "South" or "Auster" directly below Dover, which was indeed the port of entry and departure for lands south of England, despite its position on the east coast of the island (Harvey 1980: 140–2). The placing of Dover at the center of the bottom of the map also recalls the emblematic position of the Pillars of Hercules at the bottom of medieval *mappaemundi*, which were oriented to the east. The Pillars of Hercules, marking the westernmost edge of the Mediterranean, were synonymous with the end of the world. Dover exercises this function in the more limited context of Paris's map, where it marks the end of England. The emblematic function of the white cliffs of Dover as the traveller's first and last view of native topography already figured on sixteenth-century maps of England. The first modern map of the British Isles, published in Rome in 1546, shows a profile view of the cliffs of Dover surmounted by Dover Castle on the easternmost point of the island (Lynam 1934).

That Dover should mark the eastern edge of the island is significant in historiographical terms also. Just as the tragedy of *Lear* strains toward the unreachable point of Dover, so the last two acts of *Cymbeline* are governed by a similarly pervasive need to reach Milford Haven on the west coast. This westward drive brings the action into Wales and the legendary world of pre-Roman Britain at the same time that it evokes the recent history of the Welsh Tudor dynasty, founded after Henry Tudor's landing at Milford Haven and subsequent usurpation of the English crown (Jones 1961). In *Lear*, the drive is in the other direction, back toward the classical civilizations of the continent whose records provided the only contemporary descriptions of ancient Britain. As the first part of the island seen and later described by Julius Caesar in his *Gallic War* (1986: 4.23), Dover represented the founding place of recorded national history. A certain amount of confusion had reigned in medieval histories of Caesar's landing, stemming from the difficulty of identifying Roman place names and Geoffrey of Monmouth's faulty but influential rendering of a line describing the first battle in Caesar. As early as Wace's *Brut* of 1155, however, the site of "Douvres" was given for Caesar's landing. Wace was also the first medieval historiographer since Gildas to adopt a *felix culpa* view of the Roman invasion, offering a strongly pro-Roman interpretation of events despite his heavy use of Geoffrey's pro-British *Historia Regum Britanniae* (Nearing 1949a). By the early sixteenth century, English antiquarians resolved the problem of identifying the location of the first Roman–British encounter by designating Dover as the site of Caesar's first vision of Britain and its native defenders, and nearby Deal as his first true place of landing after being repulsed at Dover. The long-standing legendary association of Caesar with the building of Dover Castle nevertheless persisted throughout the sixteenth century, demonstrating widespread popular belief in his landing at Dover, and functioning even in scholarly accounts as oral evidence for some historical association of Caesar with the site (Nearing 1949b).[26]

The historiographical confusion about the site of the momentous first encounter between Rome and Britain suggests something of the difficult emblematic role of Dover in *Lear*. By dividing the originary moment of Roman Britain into the two stages of Caesar's initial vision at Dover followed by his eventual landing at Deal, early modern historiographers acknowledged their inability to fix a unified point of origin for the nation's written history. Just as it remains always beyond the verge of longing in Shakespeare's tragic recasting of the Lear story, so (Dover) eluded the grasp of nationalist historiography. It represented the vanishing point of national history, that threshold between the unrecorded and the recorded past beyond which the more distant point of native origins receded.

The inevitably disrupting effects of this overdetermined site register in the topographical survey of the *Britannia*. Like Caesar, the *Britannia* also made two approaches to the first Roman–British encounter, initially in its introductory narrative of Roman Britain and subsequently in the county-by-county description of England that made up the body of the work. In the introductory narrative, the *Britannia*'s English translator simply provided a translation of Caesar's own account in the *Gallic War* (1610: 34–7). Restricted to Caesar's own historical eye-witness, this initial account does not name the site of arrival (35). In the description of Dover in its proper topographical setting, however, the voice of Camden dominates, asking leave self-consciously "to disgress a while out of my course" when he reaches Deal and launching on a long and scholarly account of legends about Deal and Dover and the invasion (342–4). This account does not recapitulate the exposition in the introductory history of Roman Britain. Rather, it surveys the native historiography of the invasion, citing poetry as well as prose histories and evaluating their relative merits in contributing to the understanding of the historic events. At the end of his excursus, Camden outlines his own historiographical position, namely, that Caesar's own account (already translated as part of the earlier historical narrative) is the only reliable document about the invasion. In reference to the many other legends that had grown up independently of the *Gallic War*, Camden drily observes that "neither as yet have I met with that old father a Briton […] who avowed that he was present at the battle in which they assayed to keep Caesar from landing when he came to war upon them." This dismissal of oral history leads directly into a disavowal of the whole historical digression just concluded: "neither is it any part of my meaning now to write an History, but a Topography" (343). Camden's disavowal suggests that he felt himself to be on firm ground (as it were) in elaborating his "Topography," whose empirical evidence was before his eyes, than when evaluating local legends about Caesar's landing, whose proverbial eye-witness was lost in time. That he should be moved to such a historiographical digression at this point in his topographical survey indicates the inescapable associations of Dover not only with national history, but also with methodological questions of national historiography. Just as (Dover) produces a collision of representational modes in *Lear*, so in Camden it becomes a place of historiographical confusion, both in the competing identifications of the site of Caesar's arrival, and in the competing poetic and scholarly genres of historically based nationalism.

This fusion of history and topography was the hallmark of early modern English nationalism. Within that vision of the nation, (Dover) emerged as a place of topographical and historiographical crisis, a verge or beginning to both the island and its history that could neither be reached nor defined as a unified locus of origin. In Shakespeare's tragic vision of native origins and topography, the consciousness that bears the ultimate "*historica-cartographica passio*" is Gloucester's. His terrible journey toward Dover so that he might throw himself from its verge dramatizes the conflicted early modern longings both to reach that point of historical origins and to escape the confines of national history and topography that it represented. A pro-Roman nationalist like Camden might locate the tragedy of *Lear* in its failure to reach Dover, the place where written history begins. That place both ushered in the first historically verifiable period of national history and conferred on it the empirical certainty of topography as opposed to oral history. And yet Camden's own troubled survey of national historiography, poetry, and legend at the site of Dover testifies to the impossibility of maintaining a stable place of origin, either as a topographically unified point of arrival, or as a historiographically pure narrative of the founding of Roman Britain. An anxiety about the nature of his project that remains otherwise unacknowledged in Camden's masterful survey of national history and topography emerges at Dover. From the perspective of this scholarly anxiety, Gloucester's terrible need to cast himself from Dover cliff might be construed as a desire to escape the empirical world of topographical description and historiographical reliance on eye-witness accounts – precisely the kind of witness that Gloucester himself could no longer provide. Understood in these terms, Gloucester's pilgrimage of despair dramatizes the tragic inadequacy of empirical or emblematic visions of national history and topography. In Shakespeare's decision to direct the last acts of his most ancient British tragedy toward Dover, he rejected both the Christian redemption of the old *Leir* play and the civic humanism of early modern English nationalism, which sought its salvation in the historical record of Roman Britain. Neither the empirical humanist world of accurate historical record and topographical description, nor the emblematic Christian world of the *mappamundi* and morality play could deliver Shakespeare's tragedy of native origins from its internal dynamic of division and self-destruction.

3

CYMBELINE AND THE MASCULINE ROMANCE OF ROMAN BRITAIN

> Nationalism had a special affinity for male society, and together
> with the concept of respectability legitimized the dominance of
> men over women.
>
> George L. Mosse, *Nationalism and Sexuality*

Recent work on the mutually informing constructs of nationalism and sexuality defines nationalism as a virile fraternity guaranteed by its rejection of overt male homosexuality and its relegation of women to a position of marginalized respectability. George L. Mosse, from whose *Nationalism and Sexuality* I take the epigraph to this chapter, was the first to elaborate the interdependence of these two phenomena of modernism, associating both terms with the contemporaneous development of bourgeois respectability in European culture (1985: 67). Sexuality is also implicit in much of Anderson's *Imagined Communities*, emerging explicitly in the closing pages, where he posits two versions of eroticized nationalism that also suggest how attitudes to race and miscegenation figure in this complex (1992: 199–203). Although both Mosse and Anderson identify the eighteenth century as the period when these interrelated phenomena emerged, local studies inspired by their broader theoretical arguments suggest that similar constructs were already beginning to operate in Anglo-American culture in the early seventeenth century, and in Anglo-Irish colonialism, as early as the sixteenth century.[1]

In my reading of *Cymbeline* as masculine romance, I argue that the gendering and sexualizing of the nation elaborated or implied in the work of Mosse and Anderson was current by the early seventeenth century in England. English anxiety about the female savagery of native origins indicates how sexual concerns were already shaping nationalism in this period. Sexual tropes were particularly useful in the difficult articulation of the Roman role in national historiography. Jacobean dramas set in Roman Britain often conclude with a masculine embrace, staged literally or invoked rhetorically as a figure for the new relation between Rome and Britain. These concluding masculine embraces depend on the prior death of the central female character who has advocated or led the British resistance to Rome. Shakespeare's romance recuperation of the tragedy of native origins, I argue, is largely a function of his successful deployment of this civilizing masculine embrace in *Cymbeline*.

The exorcism of savage female resistance grounds the stable hybrid that crowns these plays with a promise of peace for Britain and wider membership in the Roman world of civilization. And yet it is precisely the savage females banished from the conclusions of these dramas – ancient queens such as Fletcher's Bonduca or the wicked Queen of Shakespeare's *Cymbeline* – who articulate British nationalism and patriotism. In my exploration of Shakespeare's romance of Roman Britain, I take up this paradox of savage female patriotism, exploring the play's complex national issues in terms of gender and sexuality. Pursuing the interrelation of nationalism and sexuality in the recovery of native origins, I also consider the connections between two important traditions of *Cymbeline* criticism: the historicist and the psychoanalytic. One of the projects of this (historicist) chapter is to demonstrate that these two interpretive lines need not be mutually exclusive.

NEPTUNE'S PARK

The Queen's great patriotic speech in 3.1 has long been a stumbling block in interpretations of *Cymbeline*. Combining appeals to native topography, history, and legendary origins, it recalls the highest moments of Elizabethan nationalism:[2]

> Remember, sir, my liege,
> The kings your ancestors, together with
> The natural bravery of your isle, which stands
> As Neptune's park, ribb'd and pal'd in
> With rocks unscaleable and roaring waters,
> With sands that will not bear your enemies' boats,
> But suck them up to th' topmast. A kind of conquest
> Caesar made here, but made not here his brag
> Of "Came, and saw, and overcame:" with shame
> (The first that ever touch'd him) he was carried
> From off our coast, twice beaten: and his shipping
> (Poor ignorant baubles!) on our terrible seas,
> Like egg-shells mov'd upon their surges, crack'd

As easily 'gainst our rocks. For joy whereof
The fam'd Cassibelan, who was once at point
(O giglot fortune!) to master Caesar's sword,
Made Lud's town with rejoicing-fires bright,
And Britons strut with courage.

(3.1.17–34)

The Queen's opening command to remember invokes the restitutive drive
of early modern English nationalism. The nation's glorious past – its
resistance to the great Julius Caesar, its ancient line of kings, and the
antiquity of its capital – depends paratactically on this command, emerging in the incantatory power of names like "Lud's town" and Cassibelan
and the powerful icon of native topography.[3] Moved by this nationalist
appeal, Cymbeline refuses to pay the tribute demanded by the Roman
emissaries, thus setting Britain and Rome at war.

As the last of the play's many reversals, however, Cymbeline agrees
to pay the tribute and announces his submission to the Roman emperor. In place of the bonfires of victory remembered by his queen, he
commands that "A Roman and a British ensign wave / Friendly
together" as both armies march through Lud's town (5.5.480–4). This
volte-face is the more remarkable in that the Britons have just defeated the Romans in battle. Honor, not force, dictates Cymbeline's
decision, as he invokes the promise made by his uncle Cassibelan to
Julius Caesar, from which he recalls, "We were dissuaded by our wicked
queen" (5.5.459). Despite everything else she does to earn this epithet,
Cymbeline accords it here in the context of her opposition to the
Roman tribute. Her intervention in this matter, her disruption of the
masculine network of kinship, promises, and honor that binds Cymbeline
to Rome, is what constitutes her wickedness.[4] In this final assessment
of the political plot, the king's full censure falls on the radical nationalism articulated by "our wicked queen."

Critics who wish to read *Cymbeline* as a straightforward celebration
of national identity dismiss the Queen's motivation as mere self-
interest (failing to interrogate the corporate self-interest that animates
nationalism).[5] They further marginalize the Queen by focusing on the
oafish Cloten as the main proponent of an objectionable patriotism,
thus avoiding the problem of how to interpret her delivery of one of the
great nationalist speeches in Shakespeare. Even those who do acknowledge
the interpretive difficulties of this scene find ultimately that the nationalist voices of the Queen and Cloten must be rejected to effect the
play's romance conclusion.[6] G. Wilson Knight's masterful account of
Shakespeare's interests in Roman and British historiography remains

the most instructive. He casts Cymbeline's refusal to pay the tribute, the main national interest in the play, as a "question of Britain's islanded integrity." Noting Posthumus's introduction of this sentiment in his reference to Julius Caesar's respect for British courage (2.4.20–6), Knight nevertheless recognizes that the Queen expresses it much more satisfyingly in 3.1. He argues, however, that the Queen and Cloten are types Britain must ultimately reject in order to recognize freely her Roman obligation and inheritance. Writing shortly after the Second World War, Knight comments that the national situation in *Cymbeline* serves "as often in real life, to render violent instincts respectable" (1947: 136).[7]

Mosse's argument about nationalism and sexuality, which culminates in an analysis of Nazi Germany, also rests on this term "respectable." Indeed, in Mosse's analysis, an alliance between nationalism and respectability is crucial to the formulation and dissemination of both. He traces naturalized concepts of respectability to the eighteenth century, when modern nationalism was emerging, and finds both to be informed by ideals of manliness and the place of women. Men were to engage actively with one another in a spirit of brotherhood, while women were to remain passively within the domestic sphere, exercising a biological maternal function that in no way challenged the spiritual bonding of adult males. "Woman as a national symbol was the guardian of the continuity and immutability of the nation, the embodiment of its respectability," Mosse writes, noting that the more respectable nationalist movements become, the more respectable their feminine icons look (18). When Knight commented in 1947 on how the national situation serves "to render violent instincts respectable," he intuited the naturalized alliance between nationalism and respectability that Mosse was to theorize forty years later. Knight's insight that something like this alliance might be at issue in *Cymbeline* bears further consideration.

Cymbeline's Queen is hardly a figure of national respectability. Even her maternal devotion to Cloten does not escape censure,[8] and the rest of her career as evil stepmother, would-be poisoner, and, finally, suicide fully earns Cymbeline's concluding approbation of the "heavens [who] in justice, both on her and hers, / Have laid most heavy hand" (5.5.460–1). Yet Cymbeline's insistence on her political intervention as the mark of her wickedness suggests a critique of the nationalism she articulates *per se*. This convergence of national and personal wickedness indicates the difficulty of forging national identity before the eighteenth-century alliance of nationalism and respectability. Indeed, the complex and somewhat clumsily resolved romance of *Cymbeline* dramatizes the immediate prehistory of that alliance and its constitutive elements.

Early modern England certainly had an ideal of respectable womanhood, one that (as in the eighteenth century) rested on the chastity and subordination of women within the patriarchal household. Susan Amussen has demonstrated, however, that the terms of this ideal were neither so clear nor so universally accepted in the seventeenth century. Definitions of wifely obedience in particular were contested by seventeenth-century Englishwomen, despite their general acquiescence to the principle of feminine subordination. Only by the late seventeenth and early eighteenth centuries do these challenges disappear, suggesting that the naturalized ideal of feminine respectability Mosse invokes as an element of nationalism had been fully internalized by women (Amussen 1988: 118–23). The difficulties of constructing and ensuring this sexual ideal in the seventeenth century reveal themselves in the complex formation of a national ideal in *Cymbeline*.

If respectable nationalism depends in part on respectable womanhood, someone other than the wicked Queen must embody it. Imogen, so beloved of the Victorians for her wifely devotion and forbearance, might figure as the wicked Queen's respectable double, and she does indeed come to represent an alternative nationalism.[9] Yet her progress through a series of disguised identities and alliances, not all of them British, indicates the amount of work needed to construct a national icon of feminine respectability, just as the messages from and about the Queen in the final scene assert the impossibility of resolving the drama without invoking her feminine wickedness. This feminine duality of respectability and wickedness reveals how deeply early modern English nationalism was fraught with fears of the unrespectable, or to use the language of the period, the uncivil or barbaric. It also indicates how important gender was as a category for working out these anxieties. Indeed, work that applies Mosse's analysis of nationalism and sexuality to the early modern period emphasizes the identification of the feminine with the barbaric in nationalist discourse. Jonathan Goldberg's reading of *Plimoth Plantation* as the inaugural text of a national American literature notes its persistent alignment of Anglo women and Indians. Although not precisely identical, he argues, they must both "be effaced in order for history to move forward as the exclusive preserve of white men" (1992: 63–4).[10]

The collapse of women and "savages" also informs *Cymbeline*. Nationally inflected gender anxiety haunts the drama, emerging particularly in contests over Roman–British relations. If it is most apparent in the caricature of feminine wickedness represented by the Queen who tries to come between Britain and Rome, it also informs masculine characters in all-male settings. After the Queen's intervention in 3.1, British articulation and enactment of male bonding becomes increasingly important, from Belarius's reconstitution of an all-male family in the Welsh cave, to the princes' further bonding with Posthumus on the battlefield and the ultimate reconciliation of Rome and Britain at the play's conclusion. Although Imogen appears in all these settings, she does so only in boy's dress, a costume she retains even after the revelation of her womanly identity. I shall discuss the implications of her disguise further in the last section of this chapter, but point out here that it shifts not only her gender, but also her status and age from married adult to single youth.[11] These shifts make more apparent the exclusion of adult women, particularly mothers, from the scenes of male bonding in *Cymbeline*.[12] Something like the historiographical concern over originary females seems to be enacted here in familial terms. The construction of the wicked Queen as a figure of savage excess, even (and perhaps especially) in her maternity, recalls Goldberg's formulation of the necessary effacement of women and savages "in order for history to move forward as the exclusive preserve of white men." One might alter his last words to read "civilized" or perhaps "Romanized men" in the context of *Cymbeline*. All roads of male bonding lead to Rome in this play, and correspondingly to a place in the exclusive preserve of Roman history.[13]

Critics reading *Cymbeline* from the perspective of early modern historiography are divided on the question of Rome's role. Those who identify the play's romance resolution with the Romans cite the importance of Rome in British chronicle history, and Jacobean enthusiasm for Augustan analogies.[14] Others argue that in *Cymbeline*, Shakespeare exorcises his fascination with Roman history in favor of a more humane British national ethic.[15] Early modern responses were not so one-sided. In their attempts to reconcile ancient British patriotism and a civilized union with Rome, English historians acknowledged and developed the doubleness of nationalist response to the Roman Conquest. Violently patriotic queens played an important role in negotiating this doubleness. Indeed, the hierarchical binarism of gender, fundamental to the construction of early modern society, also governed that period's construction of the ancient British relation to Rome. In the section that follows, I shall examine this phenomenon through the early modern historiography of two ancient Britons, Boadicea and Caractacus. Although separated historically by almost twenty years, these two figures of ancient British patriotism converge in early modern accounts of Roman Britain. Their dramatic juxtaposition reveals much about the gendering and sexualizing of national origins and identity in early modern England.

A FRIEND'S PART

Cymbeline's Queen has no direct source in Holinshed's reign of Kymbeline. She bears a striking resemblance, however, to Voadicia, or Boadicea, who appears roughly sixty years later in Holinshed's narrative of Roman Britain.[16] Like Cymbeline's Queen, Boadicea opposed the Roman conquerors but ultimately failed to free Britain of the Roman yoke, taking her own life (or dying of "a natural infirmity") after the last battle. Also like the wicked Queen, she was famous for her nationalist stance, especially in her great speech on British freedom and resistance to Roman tyranny, when she opposed the payment of tribute to Rome and invoked the same topoi of the island's natural strengths and the glorious history of her people and kings. And ultimately, Boadicea too suffered condemnation as a "wicked queen" for her ruthless defense of this position. In contrast, Caractacus won unqualified historiographical praise, both for his initial resistance and his eventual submission to Rome. In AD 43, he led the western tribe of the Silurians in revolt against Rome. Although he too was defeated, he did not end his life, but was taken to Rome to appear in a triumph of the Emperor Claudius. There, he so distinguished himself by the dignity of his speech and bearing that he won freedom and commendation of his manly courage from Claudius himself.

Caractacus's "manliness," his Roman *virtus*, is the focus of early modern accounts of his uprising. The patriotic oration Caractacus delivered before Claudius never suffered condemnation. Rather, the 1587 Holinshed cites it as both laudable and successful, calling it the "manly speech to the Emperor Claudius, whereby he and his obtain mercy and pardon" (30), in contrast to the earlier condemnation of Boadicea's revolt as an example of feminine government. This distinction between Caractacus's manly *romanitas* and Boadicea's feminine savagery became a standard feature of early modern accounts of Roman Britain. Camden begins his collection of "Grave Speeches and Witty Apothegms of Worthy Personages of this Realm in Former Times" with a twelve-line citation of the "manly speech" of Caractacus before Claudius. He follows this quotation with a mere three lines from Boadicea, and a reference to her letting a hare out of her lap as a token of the Romans' fearfulness. Wryly noting how this superstitious piece of barbarism met with the fate it deserved, Camden remarked that "the success of the battle proved otherwise" (1984: 205–6). As late as Milton's *History of Britain*, this distinction was maintained. Milton cites in full Caractacus's manly speech, and offers him as a classic exemplum of masculine virtue. When he comes to Boadicea's rebellion, however, he refuses to include her oration, saying that he does not believe in set speeches in a history, and had only quoted Caractacus because his words demonstrated "magnanimity, soberness, and martial skill" (1971: 70–2). Indeed, Milton accuses his classical sources of having put words into Boadicea's mouth "out of a vanity, hoping to embellish and set out their history with the strangeness of our manners, not caring in the mean to brand us with the rankest note of barbarism, as if in Britain women were men, and men women" (79–80).[17] In this standard pairing of the masculine and feminine British rebels against Rome, then, Boadicea represented "the rankest note of barbarism," that state in which gender distinctions collapsed, "as if in Britain men were women, and women men." But Caractacus was a figure of exemplary manliness, invoked to counterbalance the overwhelming female savagery of Boadicea, and to re-establish British masculinity.[18]

Fletcher seems to have followed this example in composing his drama *Bonduca*. Although he derived most of his historical information from classical sources and Holinshed's "History of England," he also included a character named Caratach, Bonduca's cousin and general of the Britons.[19] Caratach consistently conducts the war by Roman rules, for which he expresses great admiration. He chastises Bonduca for her extravagant speeches against the Romans, thus anticipating Milton's rejection of her female oratory. Bonduca is made to bear full responsibility for the Britons' eventual defeat, having meddled in men's affairs against Caratach's frequent orders that she return to her spinning. Despite her eponymous role as subject of the drama, she dies in Act 4, leaving the "Romophile" Caratach to represent Britain in the last act. During that act, he earns the further admiration of the Roman soldiers, who publicly honor him and praise him for his Roman virtues. The play ends with his embrace by the Roman commander Swetonius, and the latter's words "Ye shew a friends soul. / March on, and through the Camp in every tongue,/The Vertues of great *Caratach* be sung" (1966: 5.3.201–3).

Other plays of the period dealing with British rebellion against Rome end with the same masculine embrace. In *The Valiant Welshman*, a dramatization of Caractacus's rebellion, he is betrayed into Roman hands by the duplicitous British Queen Cartamanda, and brought before the Emperor Claudius. Claudius then recalls the Briton's valor in battle, lifts him up from his kneeling posture, and celebrates his valiant name ("R. A." 1902: 5.5.39–58). In William Rowley's *A Shoemaker a Gentleman*, a disguised British prince twice saves the life of the Emperor Dioclesian [*sic*] and the Roman Eagle from the Vandals and Goths in succession (1910: 3.4). On resigning his trophies to Dioclesian in the next scene with the words, "Now to the Royal hand of Caesar I resigne / The high Imperiall Ensigne of great Rome," the prince is bidden by the emperor to "Kneele downe, / And rise a Brittaine Knight" (3.5.17–49). The defeated Vandal Prince

Roderick kneels in turn at the end of this scene, promising to confine his people to Germany, to which Dioclesian responds, "And that obedience Roderick weele imbrace" (3.5.64). *Cymbeline*'s combination of British victory with submission to the embrace of empire is thus refracted through a third nation in this probably contemporaneous drama of Roman Britain.[20] Despite an unusual emphasis on Roman atrocities (invoked throughout in the context of Christian persecution), Rowley's play too presents a Roman emperor praising the valor of a British prince in the final scene, with Dioclesian's words: "It is a man, whose Fate / Vpheld the glory of the Roman State" (5.2.22–3).

Fuimus Troes, or the True Trojans, a play about Julius Caesar's Conquest, ends on a metaphorical embrace of empire, with the words "The world's fourth empire Britain doth embrace" (Fisher 1825: 5.7). With the exception of Rowley's *Shoemaker*, these plays work toward a reconciliation between Rome and Britain that is exclusively masculine.[21] Any women who might have figured in the action (and they usually do so in invented love plots) have been killed off, leaving the stage free for the men to conclude the matters of true historic import. With their exclusion from the action, the stage of Roman Britain becomes the exclusive preserve of men, both British and Roman. This triumph of exclusion is figured in the masculine embrace that becomes the dominant trope of these final scenes, invoked as a metaphor of empire, and embodied in the staged embraces of male Britons by Roman commanders and the symbolic merging of their national emblems.[22]

If the masculine romance of Roman Britain delivers Britain from the self-destructive violence of the wicked queen, however, it also defines the province of Britannia as the passive object of Roman desire.[23] Mosse emphasizes the fear of male homosexuality that haunts the fraternal bonding of nationalism (23–47). Goldberg expands on this in his analysis of *Plimoth Plantation*, citing Bradford's need to separate the pervasive homosociality of his founding American fantasy of all-male relations "by drawing the line – lethally – between its own sexual energies and those it calls sodomitical." Commenting on Bradford's reluctant inclusion of "a case of buggery" because "the truth of the history requires it," Goldberg sets the unrealizable desire to distinguish originary male bonding from sodomy at the heart of Bradford's history: "The truth of the history, as I am reading it, is the entanglement of the 'ancient members' with and the desire to separate from the figure of the sodomite who represents at once the negation of the ideal and its literalization" (1992: 67–68). Fear of homosexuality is neither so clear nor so lethal in early modern constructions of Roman Britain, where female savagery is the primary object of revulsion. When Fletcher and Shakespeare attempt the literalization of this masculine ideal in terms of a purely British nationalism, however, they produce scenes of male bonding characterized by feminine and domestic behavior.[24]

The assumption of women's work, speech, and familial roles characterizes male bonding among Britons in *Bonduca* and *Cymbeline*. Wales, the last preserve and final retreat of pure Britishness, provides the setting in both cases.[25] In *Bonduca*, this nationalist male bonding dominates the last act, where Caratach, hiding from the Romans, cares for his nephew Hengo, the last of the royal Iceni line after the deaths of Bonduca and her daughters. In doing so, Caratach takes on the maternal role that Bonduca, in her unnatural lust for battle, refused to accept. His whole concern in this last act is the nursing and feeding of the boy Hengo, who is dying of sickness and hunger after the British defeat. Caratach's language to the boy is tender and protective; he tries to shield him from the knowledge of their loss, and soothes him with such endearments as "sweet chicken" and "fair flower." Hengo's name (Fletcher's invention) points to Hengist, the first Saxon ruler in Britain, who was often used as the representative of England's Saxon heritage in early modern iconography.[26] The moving spectacle of the old warrior nursing the last sprig of British manhood thus suggests an imaginative attempt to construct a native, masculine genealogy proceeding directly from ancient Britain to the Saxon heptarchy, and excluding both women and Rome from the national past.[27] The death of Hengo signals the failure of this fantasy. Only after the collapse of this last hope for the continuation of the British line does Caratach allow himself to be won over by the brave courtesies of the Romans, who promise the boy honorable burial (Fletcher 1966: 5.3.185–8). Caratach's embrace by Claudius follows the failure of this domestic interlude in Wales, in which he has tried to keep alive the generative fantasy of a purely masculine Britain.[28]

The experiment in an all-male British world is more developed in *Cymbeline*. In the middle of Act 3, after ties with Rome have been broken, Shakespeare introduces the Welsh retreat of Belarius, Guiderius, and Arviragus. This idyll represents as full a retreat to pure Britishness as the wicked Queen's opposition to the payment of tribute. Just as her opposition to Rome fails, ending in her own death and that of her son, so too does the primitive fantasy of the Welsh cave fail to avert the ultimate embrace with Rome. In the latter case, it is not the death of the British heirs that ends this hope, but rather their anticipated lack of a historical afterlife. When Belarius praises the purity of their Welsh retreat, as against the tales he has told the boys "Of courts, of princes; of the tricks in war" (3.3.15), the elder son responds: "Out of your proof you speak: we poor unfledg'd, / Have never wing'd from view o'th'nest; nor know not / What air's from home" (3.3.27–9). He concedes that the quiet life of their retreat may be sweeter to Belarius than the court, but asserts that "unto us it is / A cell of ignorance" (3.3.32–3). His younger brother then adds:

> What should we speak of
> When we are old as you? When we shall hear
> The rain and wind beat dark December? How
> In this our pinching cave shall we discourse
> The freezing hours away? We have seen nothing:
> We are beastly.
>
> (3.3.35–40)

What the brothers protest is their exclusion from history. They have seen nothing; they are beastly. Confined to their pinching cave in Wales, they have, quite literally, no history to speak of. This conflict between the princes and their presumed father comes to a head when they want to enter the battle against the Romans. Belarius takes their zeal as an irrepressible sign of their royal blood, which longs to "fly out and show them princes born" (4.4.53–4). It is equally, however, a sign of their desire to enter the world of history. Belarius's own sense of having been shaped, however painfully, by a wider experience only fuels this desire. "O boys, this story / The world may read in me: my body's mark'd / With Roman swords" he claims (3.3.55–7), as though his body were a literalization of the Roman writing of ancient British history. Without fighting the Romans, the princes will have no such marks to read by the winter fire when they are old. The masculine rite of passage this represents for them personally is a version of Britain's entry into history by means of the Roman invasion. Like the princes, Britain too would have remained outside history without entering into battle with the Romans.[29]

This convergence of the personal and the national in the forging of masculine identity offers the possibility of reconciling two of the most important interpretive traditions of *Cymbeline*: the psychoanalytic and the historicist. Where historicists find the battle and its aftermath puzzling and inconclusive in terms of the play's treatment of Roman–British relations, psychoanalytic critics focus on the battle as the play's central masculine rite of passage, interpreting it in archetypal terms that sometimes ignore its historiographical complexity.[30] In her historicist reading of *Cymbeline*, Leah Marcus highlights the battle as an essentially mysterious and unassimilable episode, recapitulated four times in forms that exemplify the insoluble nature of the play's many riddles of interpretation (1988: 139–40). Most psychoanalytic critics interpret the Welsh cave as a form of maternal protection from which the princes must emerge into battle with the Romans, an experience that restores them to their father and their patrilineal identity. Caesar functions in these readings as the ultimate father, with whom Britain works out its relationship through the Roman conflict and its resolution (Schwartz, Skura, Landry). In contrast Janet Adelman regards the Welsh retreat as an exclusively male preserve where Belarius can raise Cymbeline's sons free from the tainted maternity that haunts masculine imagination in the play (1992: 203–4). David Bergeron, while not discussing the battle, notes that the Welsh retreat affords the princes no opportunity for sexual experience, arguing that their seclusion is another version of the play's sterile or incomplete sexuality (1983: 167).

The battle is not so unreadable historiographically as has been claimed, however; nor is the princes' assumption of masculine sexual identity so successfully divorced from historiographical complexity. Indeed, the approach I have been advocating, developed from Mosse's insight about the interrelatedness of nationalism and sexuality, historicizes the development of sexual and national identities as it demonstrates their interdependence. Adelman, recognizing the historiographical complexity of Cymbeline's submission to Rome, interprets it in psychoanalytic terms as "the conflicted desire for merger even at the root of the desire for autonomy" (207).[31] Applying her psychoanalytic insight to my own historiographical concerns, I would argue that an originary engagement with Rome was necessary for the formation of an autonomous national identity in early modern England. Roman Britain came to play a foundational role in the recovery of native origins because it provided the male bonding that characterizes modern nationalism, as well as exorcising the feminine savagery that challenged both its autonomy and its respectability.

Engagement with Rome also brought Britain into the masculine preserve of Roman historiography. It is battle with the Romans that affords Cymbeline's sons, the male Britons of the next generation, that historical identity they found lacking in their pastoral retreat. In the dramatization of this episode, they achieve it instantly, not because they rewrite Roman history or win a lasting victory, but rather because that victory is immediately described and preserved in historiographical forms. As soon as the princes' stand with Belarius has been presented dramatically, Posthumus recapitulates it as a historical battle narrative, complete with citations of brave speeches and descriptions of the terrain and deployment of troops (5.3.1–51). His interlocutor responds by producing an aphorism to commemorate their action: "A narrow lane, an old man, and two boys" (5.3.52), which Posthumus improves into a rhymed proverb: "Two boys, an old man twice a boy, a lane, / Preserv'd the Britons, was the Romans' bane" (5.3.57–8). The transformation of the dramatic stand in 5.2 into the narrative, aphorism and proverb in 5.3 shows a process of instant historicization. This making of history issues directly from engagement with the Romans, which incidentally leads to the princes' restoration as Cymbeline's male heirs. Both the continuance of the masculine British line and the entrance of its youngest branches into written history require the abandonment of the purely British romance of the cave in Wales.[32]

FIDELE

Imogen alone remains as a possible icon of pure Britishness in the complex of gender, sexuality, and nationalism I have been describing. Surely in her we have Mosse's icon of respectable womanhood to bless the virile bonding of nationalism.[33] She, more than her father or brothers, presents and experiences Britain, wandering through it, calling up its place names, and describing its natural situation. Her very name, invented by Shakespeare for the heroine he adds to his historical material, is derived from that of Brute's wife, Innogen, mother of the British race.[34] And like other ancient queens, Imogen too voices a lyrical celebration of the island:

> I' th' world's volume
> Our Britain seems as of it, but not in't:
> In a great pool, a swan's nest.
>   (3.4.139–41)

The image of the swan's nest is as evocative of national identity as that of Neptune's park in the Queen's speech, suggesting among other things Leland's great chorographic song of the Thames, *Cygnea Cantio*.[35] The context of the speech, however, is quite different from that of the Queen's national celebration in 3.1. In contrast to the Queen's radical "Britocentrism," Imogen asserts in 3.4 that Britain is only a small part of a larger world, a world from which it is in fact separate. Her line "Our Britain seems as of it, but not in't" raises the historiographical concern about Britain's isolation from the civilized world. It has been suggested that the line is a version of the Vergilian verse, "*Et penitus toto diuisos orbe Britannos*," cited in Holinshed's "History of Scotland" (Brockbank 1958: 48; Holinshed 1587: 2).[36] Whether the image is derived from a Roman source or not, it perpetuates the imperial view of Britain's separation from the world of civilization. Rather than lauding this separation, as would Boadicea or the wicked Queen, Imogen suggests that there is a world outside Britain where she may fare better than at the hands of the Queen and her son.

As in early modern accounts of ancient Britain, this flight from native isolation leads inevitably to Rome, for Pisanio answers Imogen's speech with the words:

> I am most glad
> You think of other place: th' ambassador,
> Lucius the Roman, comes to Milford-Haven
> To-morrow.
>
> (3.4.142–5)

Lucius the Roman and Milford Haven will shape Imogen's identity between them for the rest of the play. Their joint role in doing so indicates the way British national identity is formed from the interaction of the Roman invaders with the native land. If there is a magic of place in *Cymbeline*, it is in Milford Haven. The place name takes on an almost incantatory power as Imogen and the other characters make their way to the haven of final recognition and reconciliation.[37] Critics since Emrys Jones have emphasized the importance of Milford Haven in Tudor mythography as the place where Henry Tudor landed before marching to defeat Richard III at the Battle of Bosworth Field.[38] They have built on this historiographical reading to develop a sense of Milford Haven as a sacred or enchanted place that saps the strength of those who invade it and grounds the resistance of those who defend it. This understanding of Milford is very satisfying in terms of Tudor–Stuart mythography, with its claims of Arthurian and British precedence, but it does not explain why Lucius the Roman, rather than Cymbeline, lands there in anticipation of the future Henry VII of England.

The first Britons Lucius encounters on landing are the disguised Imogen and the headless corpse of Cloten in Posthumus's clothes. His attempt to reconstruct the story of the sleeping or dead page on the "trunk […] / Without his top" issues in a series of questions that demand a recapitulation of the play's action no single character could provide (4.2.353–67), one that will indeed occupy much of the lengthy recognition scene at the play's conclusion. The unreadability of this headless tableau of masterlessness emphasizes the confusion of British national identity by Act 4, with Cymbeline under the domination of his wicked Queen, Cloten dead in Posthumus's dress, the princes in hiding and unaware of their royal identity, Imogen disguised and believing Posthumus to be dead, and Posthumus himself at large and still deceived as to her fidelity.[39] Imogen voices this confusion in response to Lucius's final, blunt question, "What art thou?:"

I am nothing; or if not,
Nothing to be were better. This was my master,
A very valiant Briton, and a good,
That here by mountaineers lies slain. Alas!
There is no more such masters: I may wander
From east to occident, cry out for service,
Try many, all good: serve truly: never
Find such another master.

(4.2.367–74)

Recalling medieval laments over the dead body of the feudal lord, Imogen invents an account of a youth who has lost all identity of status or place after the death of the "very valiant Briton" "he" calls master. In this invented identity, she gives voice to the inner despair of her presumed widowhood – her sense of being nothing or worse at the seeming death of her husband – in terms of a nationless wandering from east to west. As in the princes' entry into battle, the personal and the national intersect in Imogen's crisis in Wales.

And yet the upward turn of Imogen's fortunes, and those of her nation, is not far to seek. If there is any straightforwardly respectable character in *Cymbeline*, it is the Roman commander and emissary Lucius. He conducts himself with honor in the council scenes of 3.1 and 5.5, and succors the disguised Imogen with grace and generosity in 4.2. He is also resolutely masculine, deriving his identity from military and political functions, and appearing in the masculine situations of the council chamber, the march, and the battlefield. Here indeed is a virile antetype for Henry Tudor at Milford, and an ancient predecessor on which to found a stable, masculine identity for the nation.[40] When he questions the disguised British princess about the identity of her dead "master," she gives the latter's name as "Richard du Champ" (4.2.377), suggesting an analogy between his body and the ground. Without putting undue pressure on this analogy, I would suggest that Lucius, in raising Imogen from the ground, also releases her from her quest to reach Milford Haven, from her ritualized laying out by the princes and Belarius, and from her second "death" on the body of "du Champ." In taking her from this multiply constructed British ground, he gives her a new identity in his Roman entourage.

The nature of this new identity remains unclear. In her fictional relationship to "du Champ," Imogen says she served a master, but such a one as shall never be found again. Lucius tells her, "I will not say / Thou shalt be so well master'd, but be sure / No less belov'd" (4.2.382–4). Imogen promises to follow him, if he pleases to entertain her, and he answers,

"And rather father thee than master thee" (4.2.395). Complicated issues of the nature of obedience and subordination are played out in
these two exchanges, issues of significance for both political and gender
relations in the play. Imogen believes she replaces a husband with the
Roman commander, and something of the difficulties of defining wifely
subordination between the poles of love and mastery emerges in this first
exchange with Lucius.[41] The paternal model Lucius invokes in the second
exchange also implicates Imogen's political allegiance, as replacing her
father also means replacing her king. Lucius's inability to articulate the
new mastery he offers Imogen, his shifting and uneasy invocations of
husbandly and paternal love, reveals how thoroughly nationalism and
sexuality are entangled in the play's two plots, and how difficult it is to
resolve the issues of identity they raise. In this Roman–British encounter
scene, Imogen negotiates the terms of the new relationship that replaces
both her marriage to Posthumus and her filial allegiance to father and
nation. Yet what Imogen is to Lucius cannot quite be defined. The Roman male is not in a position of absolute mastery, although the British
female, disguised as a boy, has agreed to follow him.

One term remains constant in Imogen's shift of identity in this scene,
and that is her assumed name, Fidele. It is her proper epithet, and yet, for
a personification of unwavering marital fidelity, Imogen changes allegiance
a remarkable number of times. Her initial defection from her father precedes but informs the play's action, and one might even read in her decision to reject the death planned by Posthumus, or her mistaken abandonment
of her marriage while her husband yet lives, a kind of defection from absolute fidelity to him also.[42] Certainly, she moves from one allegiance to
another in the middle acts of the play, where she gives up the princes and
Belarius, the seeming corpse of Posthumus, and ultimately Lucius himself
when she refuses to plead for his life before Cymbeline (5.5.104–5).[43] Both
in this series of shifts between British and Roman identifications and in
the wager plot, the question of Imogen's fidelity is of central importance.
Posthumus reviles Imogen and all women for faithlessness when he believes she has betrayed him (2.5.20–35), and Lucius makes a similar generalization about those who place their trust in girls and boys when she
abandons him to his fate (5.5.105–7).[44] By the conclusion of the play,
however, Imogen reconciles all her conflicting fidelities. Cymbeline is again
her father, Posthumus, her husband, and the princes, her brothers. Last of
all these bonds, she restores her relation to Lucius, to whom she says, "My
good master, / I will yet do you service" (5.5.404–5).

This last restoration immediately precedes the final reversal of the
play, in which Cymbeline restores Britain's tributary relationship to Rome,
and puts the blame for disrupting it on the nationalism of his "wicked

queen." Imogen's final act of fidelity, like her father's, is an acknowledgment of Rome as master, even in defeat.[45] The Latin name Fidele that she assumes as a badge of her wifely constancy suggests the general importance of Rome in the construction of British faithfulness. Imogen's personal quest to prove her marital fidelity becomes involved in the complex question of national fidelity when she decides to follow Lucius. It is Lucius who raises her from ritualized death and failure in 4.2, and he who gives her the context in which to reconstruct her identity as Fidele when she acknowledges herself reduced to nothing by the apparent death of Posthumus. Even when she seems to deny Lucius, Imogen reaffirms the Roman bond, telling Cymbeline, "He is a Roman, no more kin to me / Than I to your highness" (5.5.112–13). Throughout the period of her disguise, she is constituted as her Latin name Fidele, as though her disgrace could only be lifted, her fidelity reconstructed, in Roman terms.[46]

The role of Fidele involves a shift not only in national identity, but also in gender, Lucius's generalization about those who put their trust in girls and boys being truer than he knows. Imogen's new relationship with Lucius is a version of the bonds between male Britons and Roman commanders in other Roman–British dramas. Like Caractacus, she is lifted from the ground by a Roman leader who celebrates her virtue, and in Lucius's redefinitions of their hierarchical relationship, she becomes increasingly the object of his love, not his mastery. The masculine embrace of Roman Britain is thus figured in the relationship of the disguised Imogen and the Roman Lucius even before the Roman and British ensigns "wave friendly together" at the play's conclusion. The complexity of what Imogen represents in this embrace, in terms of both gender and sexuality, illustrates the complicated nature of British national identity in the play. Neither her imagined female body nor the boy's disguise that makes visible the cross-dressing of the theater offers a stable, masculine identity for Britain. Indeed, the instability of the gender, status, and national identities represented in this figure of disguise and much-questioned fidelity troubles the construction of any stable identity, personal or national.[47]

The resolution of the play's many riddles of identity depends on the *deus ex machina* of the oracle Posthumus wakes to find on his bosom after dreaming of his family and lineage in 5.4. As in the princes' entry into battle, this restoration of personal identity has its national analogue. The Roman Soothsayer who explicates the oracle of Posthumus's identity is the same who prophesied the merger of Cymbeline's emblem of the radiant sun with the Roman eagle, as he recalls in the penultimate speech of the play (5.5.468–77). When he reads Imogen into the oracle, he identifies her as "The piece of tender air […] / Which we call *mollis aer*; and *mollis aer* / We term it *mulier*: which *mulier* I divine / Is this most constant wife" (5.5.447–50). This display of pseudo-etymology recalls the involved and equally fanciful antiquarian derivations of the name Britain. (Indeed, but for its context, it would stand as a parody of such pedantry, in the style of a Don Armado or a Fluellen.) Camden begins the *Britannia* with a survey of such theories, including Humfrey Lhuyd's derivation from the Welsh "Prid-Cain," meaning a "pure white form," a phrase that resonates with the Soothsayer's "piece of tender air" in its attempt to articulate an ethereal purity (Camden 1610: 5–6). As in the Soothsayer's derivation of *mulier* from *mollis aer*, it also works to disembody and desexualize the loaded term "Britannia." Even so, by presenting Imogen as a piece of tender air, the Soothsayer completes the separation from the earth begun by Lucius when he lifted her from the ground of Wales and the body of "du Champ." This fancy antiquarian footwork restores Imogen to her husband by reconstituting "woman," strongly identified with the land in both Imogen and the wicked Queen, as air so that she might take her place in the prophetic new order of Roman Britain.[48]

Imogen never regains the visual trappings of her femininity. If she represents a version of ancient British respectability, it is one riddled with the problems of gender and sexuality that characterize the British relation to Rome. To the extent that she re-emerges as a respectable ideal at the end of the play, it is in a series of alliances with the male characters, both British and Roman, from whom she derives her identity. Cymbeline's daughter, Posthumus's wife, the princes' sister, and still in some sense the servant of Lucius, she does not raise the specter of feminine autonomy and leadership suggested by the wicked Queen's machinations and the model of Boadicea behind her. The anxieties provoked by these ancient British queens are ultimately defused in the series of bonds established by Imogen at the end of the play. These bonds emphasize the necessary subordination of the feminine within the patriarchal structures of marriage and empire. The fact that Imogen achieves these bonds while still in her boy's disguise indicates the degree of anxiety about the feminine power to destroy them. Like *Bonduca*, *The Valiant Welshman* and *The True Trojans*, *Cymbeline* concludes with the image of an exclusively male community.

I would like to conclude with a word about the relative roles of homophobia and misogyny in early modern constructions of national origins. In Mosse's formulation, the greatest threat to the male bonding of nationalism is overt male homosexuality, a perception that Goldberg demonstrates as early as the 1630s in *Plimoth Plantation*. Both theorists emphasize the interrelatedness of homophobia and misogyny in the formation of masculine national identity. In the masculine romance of

Roman Britain, fears of effeminacy and of women are also intertwined. It strikes me, however, that the latter are much more explicit than the former, which indeed might be understood as an extension of misogyny. A fear of originary feminine savagery was what consistently drove early modern historians and dramatists of ancient Britain to take refuge in the Roman embrace. The complexities of Britain's position in this embrace certainly raise issues of sexuality, but these seem to me to be subordinated to an overriding concern about the gender of native origins. British origins in all these works emerge as unavoidably feminine, either in the savagery of a wicked queen, or in the feminized domesticity and submission to the Roman embrace of the British male. I take the violence with which dramatists and historians rejected the figure of the ancient British queen as an indication of how thoroughly their failure to transform the femininity of native origins disturbed them. Their attempts to avoid this originary femininity led them ultimately to embrace subordinate status in the Roman empire. Although this new status also consigned Britain to a feminized role, it avoided the savagery of the purely British nationalism articulated by ancient queens. It also allowed for a historical afterlife for Britain. In contrast to the ancient queen's savage refusal of empire, the masculine embrace of Roman Britain became the truly generative interaction, producing a civil, masculine foundation for early modern English nationalism.

PACKING SLIP:

Amazon.co.uk Marketplace Item: **The Legacy of Boadicea:**

Gender and Nation in Early Modern England

[Paperback...

Listing Id: 0323H363988

Purchased on: 16.01.2008

Dispatched by: <u>stewart@bridge12345.freeserve.co.uk</u>   Thank you for

your order

Francesca Vassallo

f It has only a little cytoplasm so that it can have a thin, streamlined shape.

2 a On the diagrams below label where the **adaptations** in question 1 are found. Just use the letters for the labels. _____

4

THE DOMESTICATION OF
THE SAVAGE QUEEN

I earnestly recommend it to every Father to have his Child nursed
under his own Eye.

William Cadogan, *Essay on Nursing*

Throughout the preceding chapters, I have emphasized connections between early modern concerns about contemporary gender relations –
particularly the perceived threat to social stability from unruly women –
and the projection of female savagery onto native origins. In my introduction, I suggested that Holinshed resolved the complicated national
issues of Boadicea's uprising by imposing a masculinist gender hierarchy
on the British and Roman armies. Thus recasting the national contest in
terms of early modern gender conflict, he transformed the potentially
tragic history of a native queen into a comic narrative of the reimposition
of masculine authority. In my discussion of the *Leviathan* in Chapter 1, I
noted the persistence of these earlier projections of female savagery onto
native origins in Hobbes's formulation of the state of nature, particularly
with regard to his discussion of dominion paternal and maternal. I also
suggested that the exceptional presence of female examples in his denun-
ciations of prophecy might be understood as a response to the numbers of
women engaging in religious and political prophecy in mid-seventeenth-
century England. The perceived danger to the state from publicly insubordinate and outspoken women also played a large part in my readings of
the complementary dramas of *Lear* and *Cymbeline*, from the erasure of
Britain's first "gynarchy" in Shakespeare's revision of the Leir story to the
nationalist oratory of Cymbeline's wicked Queen.

In my final chapter, I would like to elaborate these claims by situating
historiographical and literary representations of Boadicea in a more fully
developed social and cultural history of early modern English gender relations. Drawing on accounts of a crisis in gender relations in this period – a
phenomenon documented over the last two decades by historians and
literary and cultural critics of early modern Europe – I examine the early
modern reception of Boadicea's uprising as an example of contemporary

anxiety about gender reversal. Received in the socio-cultural context of early modern England, classical accounts of barbaric savagery and defeat were shaped into a cautionary tale about the dangers of unrestricted female agency and rule. For the elite male authors of early modern histories and literary representations of the ancient queen, Boadicea's cruel excess and eventual self-destruction were straightforward effects of her gender. Undisciplined by nature, she inevitably sank into savagery without the direction and control of a masculinist gender hierarchy.

And yet the early modern reception of Boadicea is not quite so straightforward. Some writers – most notably Edmund Spenser – drew more complex pictures of the ancient queen. Representing a native patriotism they could not entirely dismiss, Boadicea was invoked by other Elizabethan poets as a type of their own queen – the most powerful female sovereign of early modern Europe. In her classic study of "Women on Top" in sixteenth-century Europe, Natalie Zemon Davis examined the strain imposed on the period's masculinist social structures and theories by the historical phenomenon of female sovereigns and regents (1975: 124–51). Boadicea's female patriotism, particularly in conjunction with the early modern iconography of Elizabeth, posed similar problems in the articulation of a masculine and historically based national identity in early modern England. Typologically linked to Elizabeth, Boadicea was the "woman at the bottom" of national identity, threatening the establishment of a masculine foundation for the early modern nation even as she anticipated the female sovereignty of Gloriana.

The violent rejection of Boadicea in most early modern accounts may reflect anxieties about Elizabeth's female rule as well. Two sides of the same coin of female sovereignty, Boadicea and Elizabeth occupied the extreme positions of vilification and glorification that structured other misogynist definitions of femininity in the period, from the madonna and whore to the chaste wife and sexually voracious virago. Early modern representations of Boadicea and Elizabeth are rich in potential comparisons. Both were native queens who led their people in government and war, and both vigorously opposed the incorporation of Britain into an expanding continental empire. Both were also famous for their exceptional use of the masculine art of oratory, especially with regard to inspiring nationalist sentiment and inciting their people against foreign invaders. Boadicea's oration in Holinshed contains a long passage of topographical celebration similar to that associated with visual representations of Elizabeth (1587: 43–4). Just as images of Elizabeth – juxtaposed with maps or perpetuated in topographical personifications – embodied the nation in early modern iconography, so Boadicea invoked native topography in early modern texts. Her outspoken celebration of British topography suggests not simply her championship of the island, but her virtual identity with it. In her state of natural savagery and insistent isolationism, Boadicea personified the untamed island in its pristine state, inherently separate, as in Imogen's paraphrase of the Virgilian *divisa orbe*: "I' th' world's volume / Our Britain seems as of it, but not in't" (3.4.139–40). Representing the polar opposite of Elizabeth's virgin body, whose inviolate purity symbolically guaranteed the island's impregnability to foreign invasion, Boadicea's female excess was directed toward the same isolationist result, threatening to cut ancient Britain off from any form of (masculine) civilization.

Yet despite this rich field of potential comparisons, Boadicea was only rarely invoked in Elizabethan iconography, and the ancient queen did not emerge as a national heroine until well over a century after Elizabeth's death. The history of Boadicea's reception provides an excellent example of changing English attitudes to women in power. From her violent rejection in the nationalist historiography of the early modern period, to her incorporation into national and imperial iconography in the eighteenth and nineteenth centuries, her early-twentieth-century invocation by British suffragettes, and her 1980s return to the national stage in misogynist caricatures of Margaret Thatcher, the figure of Boadicea registers masculinist concern about female authority.[1] The modern transformation of the ancient queen into a figure of British patriotism follows the same trajectory of gendered exclusion I traced in my readings of national iconography and Hobbesian political theory in Chapter 1. Far from indicating a greater tolerance for female authority, the eighteenth-century adoption of Boadicea as a national heroine marked the eclipse of female rebelliousness as a subject of public concern.

As women's public authority and agency diminished, eventually restricted to a newly privatized household, so the threat posed by Boadicea's female rebellion lost its contemporary analogues. By the Restoration, comic revisions of earlier tragedies like *Bonduca* had begun presenting the queen in a gentler light, excising much of her martial valor and emphasizing her proper maternal solicitude for her daughters. This is the process I refer to as the "domestication of the savage queen." Following the arc of a broader socio-political domestication of women in the latter seventeenth century, this process was particularly dependent on the patriarchal subordination of what Hobbes called "Dominion in the Mother," or the primal authority of mothers over their children. Maternal authority was under sustained attack in the period, from sermons and tracts shifting the familial emphasis from motherhood to subordinate wifehood, to popular accounts of murderous mothers, to elite masculine appropriations of powerful maternal attributes of fruitfulness and nurture. Over the course of the seventeenth century, as English mothers were increasingly confined to a household that was itself losing its public status, the powerful cultural role of the mother lost its earlier authority, both symbolically and in practice. As maternity lost its connotations of independent female authority, so the savage queens of national historiography became less disturbing.

Scholars and artists engaged in the recovery of native origins participated in the cultural campaign to subordinate and defuse maternal power. Negotiating the particular difficulties of historically based English nationalism, with its disturbing examples of savage maternity, these early modern writers contributed to the broader cultural work of subordinating, vilifying and masculinizing icons of maternal dominion. In this chapter, I locate their struggles with Boadicea's savage nationalism within the context of early modern anxiety about maternal agency and authority. Reviewing the terms of the nature/culture debate of the 1970s and 1980s, I examine how the gendered polarities of recent cultural theory illuminate early modern attitudes to native origins even as they throw into relief the resistances and alternatives to these cultural binarisms that were still available in the seventeenth century. Within this theoretical context, I return to the Boadicean atrocity story I discussed in my introduction, considering recent work on maternal breast-feeding in terms of cultural concerns about gender, native origins, and national identity. Both in the socio-cultural work of redefining the household, and in the intellectual project of recovering native origins, structural tensions between savagery and domesticity informed early modern attempts to stabilize gender identities at the familial and national levels. The seventeenth-century domestication of the savage queen, that "woman at the bottom" of historically based national identity, was one of the cornerstones of this cultural stabilization.

I begin by surveying early modern treatments of Boadicea, noting the discrepancies between her universal condemnation by historians in the period and an incipient if limited literary tradition of praise. Pursuing the rare connections between Boadicea and Elizabeth articulated in this literature, I suggest why the two queens were so seldom compared in the early modern period. In the second section of the chapter, "The Savage Breast," I return to the Boadicean atrocity story in Holinshed, situating this graphic historical account of breast mutilation in the context of conflicted early modern attitudes to maternal nature and nurture, and raising theoretical questions about the period's troubled construction of the natural. The third section, "From Savage Mother to Subordinate Wife," explores seventeenth-century attempts to subordinate threatening aspects of maternal power to an ideal of subordinate wifehood.

Coming full circle in the last section, "The End of Dominion Maternal," I align Restoration adaptations of Boadicean dramas with the broader cultural exclusion of women from the public sphere by the late seventeenth century. Completing the arc of the early modern recovery of Boadicea, the domestication of the savage queen at the bottom of English identity both reveals and informs seventeenth-century struggles to dismiss maternal dominion from the national stage.

LET HISTORY JUDGE: EARLY MODERN RECEPTIONS OF BOADICEA

Recovered by Polydore Vergil in his humanist overhaul of the British chronicle tradition, Boadicea re-entered English historiography with the 1534 publication of his *Anglica Historica*. Polydore drew on classical accounts of the rebellion, which both acknowledged the legitimate patriotism of an ancient British queen and condemned the savagery of her rebellion. He may also have drawn on his own discovery, the sixth-century history of Roman Britain by the British monk Gildas. Writing more than a thousand years before Shakespeare, Gildas cast Boadicea in a role similar to that of the wicked queen who stood between Cymbeline and Rome. Like Cymbeline's Queen, Boadicea remained unnamed in Gildas's account, figuring only as a "deceitful lioness" who "put to death the rulers who had been left among them, to unfold more fully, and to confirm the enterprises of the Romans" (1878: 153).[2] The English historians who took up Boadicea's story in the sixteenth century shared this view of her role. As they struggled to found a national history based on Roman Britain, they focused their anxiety about unfolding and confirming the enterprises of the Romans on the figure of the savage British queen. Unlike the Roman-identified Gildas, however, early modern historiographers could not entirely dismiss the legitimacy of British nationalism.[3] Some concern of this nature seems even to have influenced the Italian Polydore. Perhaps from the difficulty of reconciling the ancient queen's savagery with her patriotism, as well as from the manifold versions of her name in classical sources, Polydore inferred the existence of two queens. The one, "Voadicia," he endowed with warlike spirit and patriotism, while the other, "Bonduica," he depicted as the savage perpetrator of war atrocities and barbaric resistance to the enterprises of the Romans.

From the beginning of her early modern recovery, then, Boadicea posed the problem of reconciling savagery and nationalism. Polydore dealt with the problem by splitting the queen who embodied these elements into two figures, one to be praised, and the other, abhorred. As late as Holinshed, a northern Queen Voada was included in histories of Scotland, where she was praised for the patriotic leadership of her people (Holinshed, "History of Scotland" 1587: 45–50). By the last quarter of the sixteenth century, the two elements of patriotism and savagery had been reunited in her southern counterpart, Voadicia, or Boadicea. The story of this British queen was included in Holinshed's "History of England" (1587: 42–6), which draws on the *Roman History* of Dio Cassius (1925: 62.1–12), and in Camden's *Britannia* (1610: 49–52), which follows accounts by Tacitus (1932: 15–16; 1937: 14.30–6). The historiographical tradition of moral judgment developed in Greco-Roman antiquity and adapted in medieval and early modern Europe consistently condemned Boadicea. Ruling against her across national and period divisions, historians from Tacitus to Gildas to Holinshed and Camden expressed their revulsion at both the fact and the conduct of her revolt. The unanimity of historians, their willingness to judge and to condemn the British queen, was somewhat mitigated by more complex literary representations of Boadicea in early modern England. The negative historiographical accounts nevertheless took precedence in the period, both in the priority of their composition and in the depth of their treatment of the ancient queen and her uprising. Before examining the more complex depiction of Boadicea in literary works, let me review the elements of her story available to their authors in classical and early modern histories.

Boadicea was a first-century queen of the Iceni, a British tribe occupying what would become East Anglia. Her husband, Prasutagus, was king, and after his death she ruled as regent for their two daughters. Prasutagus willed his kingdom jointly to his daughters and the Roman Emperor Nero. After the British king's death, however, the occupying Roman forces took full control, spoiling the kingdom, whipping Boadicea, and raping her daughters. In 60 or 61 CE, Boadicea led the Iceni in revolt against their Roman despoilers, gathering support from neighboring tribes. Classical estimates of her numbers ranged as high as 230,000. She moved her people to rebellion by the power of her oratory, in which she emphasized the historic freedom of the Britons and their island, and condemned their shameful submission to Rome. She also invoked the aid of the British goddess of victory, Andates or Adraste, who spurred her people on to bloodshed. By means of such leadership, Boadicea defeated the Ninth Roman Legion in the field and sacked the three settlements of Camalodunum, Londinium, and Verulam. The British lust for plunder was great, and they spared neither women nor children. As many as 70,000 Romans and their supporters fell at their hands. After the sack of Verulam, Boadicea was defeated in the field by 10,000 men from the Fourteenth Legion under the command of Suetonius. Eighty-thousand Britons died, as compared to 400 Romans. Boadicea died of grief or killed herself in order to avoid capture, and the revolt came to an end.

The ultimate verdict against Boadicea is clear in Camden and Holinshed. Although both initially acknowledge the legitimacy of her grievances against the Romans, they recoil from the nature and extent of her reaction. Savagely excessive in its cruelty and destructiveness, Boadicea's revolt revealed elements of the national character that needed to be subordinated to Roman principles of order. The most important of these principles was masculine control of government and the military. Camden and Holinshed interrupt their narratives to note that the ancient Britons made no distinction of sex in government, either in peace or war.[4] This reversal of the "natural order" eventually had its consequences for the British revolt. In the final battle, Boadicea's force of 230,000 – including many women – was defeated by 10,000 Roman men under the leadership of Suetonius. The contrast between the shapelessness of the unwieldy British host and the Romans' disciplined formation is emphasized by both English historians. Indeed, in its assessment of the battle's outcome, the *Britannia* takes the side of the Roman victors. It refers to the British host as "a multitude of barbarous people," and gives the final tally from the perspective of the Romans:

> This was a day of great honor and renown, comparable to the victories of old time: for, some report, that there were slain few less in number, than fourscore thousand Britons; but of our soldiers, there died not all out four hundred.
>
> (1610: 52)

The odd use of the first person to celebrate the Roman victory completes a process of disengagement from the British revolt begun in the earlier Latin editions of the *Britannia*. Expanding his account of the revolt in the 1600 edition, Camden also increased his condemnation of the savage queen who led it.[5] Philemon Holland, Camden's antiquarian colleague and the English translator of the *Britannia*, gave fullest expression to Camden's implicit identification with the Romans. Avoiding any attempt to supply an independent national account of the period, he simply spliced a long translation of Tacitus into the narrative of Roman Britain. The voice that speaks of the Romans as "our soldiers" in the first English edition of the *Britannia* was thus originally that of Tacitus. And yet the disorienting effect of the Roman first person at this juncture should not be dismissed as a simple effect of unadapted translation. In its long interpolation of Tacitus – an extended quotation of sixteen quarto pages covering precisely the period described by Gildas as the unfolding and confirmation of the enterprises of the Romans

– the *Britannia* becomes a Roman text, eschewing any identification with the native Britons (Camden 1610: 42–4; 48–62). Holland introduces this long interpolation of Tacitus with the words "The rest of the occurrences which happened in Britain afterward unto the very latter end of Domitian, Tacitus, who best can do it will declare by his own words to this effect" (42). By the time it concludes, any sense of a separate speaker or historiographical tradition has disappeared. Incorporating Gildas's aversion to the "deceitful lioness,"[6] the Roman–British voice of Tacitus/Camden/Holland narrates the noble history of the enterprises of the Romans in Britain.

In contrast to the historiographical condemnation of Boadicea, early modern literary works were more equivocal, allowing at least a provisional place for the ancient queen in nationalist celebrations. Most explicit literary references to Boadicea in the period were cursory, generally figuring in catalogues of notable ancient women, both British and classical. Glenda McLeod suggests that the catalogue comes into prominence in Europe during times of major cultural change characterized by a special interest in the past and a need to reinterpret older authorities. Straddling literature and history, the catalogue genre was revived by Renaissance humanists in their projects of historical recovery and reevaluation. More concerned to establish the historicity of illustrious men, however, these authors were less rigorous in their application of humanist canons of evidence to famous women (McLeod 1991: 1–9). Boadicea's moral status in early modern English catalogues was ambiguous. She was occasionally included in Elizabethan lists of the "Female Worthies," and Jonson placed her alongside the classical martial heroines Penthesilea and Camilla in his *Masque of Queenes*. The Female Worthies were also invoked as negative exempla in the period, however, and Boadicea was more often included among these counterexamples. Generally cited in the context of warlike valor or cruelty, she represented the dangers of female rule as much as she did any ideal of female heroism.[7] Whether laudatory or condemnatory, these brief invocations of Boadicea's name did not seriously challenge her more developed historiographical depiction, functioning more as nostalgic evocations of a legendary past that historians (however regretfully) no longer found tenable.

Only three pre-Restoration writers developed sustained accounts of Boadicea as a national heroine. In her polemic tract, "Esther hath hanged Haman," Esther Sowernam praised the British queen for having "defended the liberty of her Country against the strength of the Romans when they were at the greatest, and made them feel that a woman could conquer them who had conquered almost all the men of the then known world" (1985: 229). Sowernam's tract was published in 1617 during the Jacobean resurgence of what Linda Woodbridge calls "the formal controversy about women," an intermittent pamphlet war of attacks upon the defenses of women. Announcing her project as the revival of "the honorable records and Monuments for and of women," Sowernam included Boadicea with other examples of heroic female virtue. Polemicists typically adopted extreme positions in the formal controversy, and there is some evidence that a number of the purportedly feminist tracts were written ironically by men using female pseudonyms. "Esther Sowernam" was almost certainly a pseudonym coined in punning opposition to Joseph "Swetnam", author of the most notorious misogynist text in the controversy.[8] Sowernam's praise of Boadicea as a woman who "could conquer them who had conquered almost all the men of the then known world" is a good example of the hyperbole attached to gender conflict in these pamphlets. In the context of the extreme rhetoric and assumed gender identities of the formal controversy, it may have been ironic. Boadicea certainly received no praise for her initial victories over the Romans in Holinshed or Camden. The voice that commends her for having defended "the liberty of her Country" in Sowernam recalls rather the ancient queen's own oratory in Holinshed, where she presented herself as a defender of liberty and exhorted the Britons to return to the customs and laws of their "own country" (43). If a man did indeed write "Esther hath hanged Haman" ironically, he may have adopted his "feminine" voice of praise from Holinshed's (masculine) construction of Boadicea's oratory.

Whatever its polemical intent, Sowernam's invocation of Boadicea still presented her as a national heroine, defending her country against the masculine aggression of Roman conquerors. Thomas Heywood ascribes a similar role to the British queen in his *Exemplary Lives and Memorable Acts of Nine the Most Worthy Women of the World* (1640). Celebrating "Bunduca, the Heathen" in the first of three gentile lives in the collection, Heywood qualifies her suicide with the improbable claim that "all conclude that she was one of the best She Worthies in the whole universe" (1640: 91). The commendatory verses that introduce Bunduca's life history register some disappointment at the lack of English participation in the queen's otherwise universal acclaim:

> Of whom, although our modern Authors wrote
> But sparingly, least they should seem to dote
> Too much upon their Natives, foreign ink
> Hath been so lavish, it would make men think
> Her valor inexpressible; Tacitus
> Made her his ample theme, and to discuss
> Her gifts were Dio's labor.
>
> (1640: 68)

Heywood's puzzlement at native English reticence is matched by his confusion about the ultimate balance of judgment against the barbaric queen in Tacitus and Dio. Writing more than two generations after the peak of Elizabethan antiquarianism, he may have been the first to observe the conflicted attitudes toward "their Natives" in early modern English historiography.

Only one other pre-Restoration author developed a sustained heroic potrait of Boadicea. Spenser invoked Boadicea twice in *The Faerie Queene* and gave her uprising a central place in his lament *The Ruines of Time*.[9] Her depiction in both cases is heroic, and in the chronicle of "Britons Moniments" in Book Two of *The Faerie Queene* she emerges as a native example of courage and patriotism, comparable to other barbarian queens who resisted Rome. Yet Spenser's more elaborate treatment of Boadicea's uprising in *The Ruines of Time* ultimately arrives at the same rejection of the ancient queen that characterized early modern histories of her rebellion. *The Ruines of Time* is a lament spoken by the genius of Verulam, the last settlement sacked by Boadicea before her defeat by Suetonius. Verulam's chief cause of lament is her own consignment to oblivion, the result of many sackings, of which Boadicea's was only the first. She nevertheless describes Boadicea's attack in the context of praising the latter's brave transcendence of womanly weakness and Roman oppression:

> *Bunduca* Britonnesse
> Her mightie hoast against my bulwarkes brought,
> *Bunduca*, that victorious conqueresse,
> That lifting up her brave heroïck thought
> Bove womens weaknes, with the *Romanes* fought,
> Fought, and in field against them thrice prevailed:
> Yet was she foyld, when as she me assailed.
> (1989: 106–11)

The last line is puzzling, since Boadicea did indeed sack Verulam, as recorded in both classical and early modern histories of the uprising. Spenser later invokes Camden as his source, indicating that he knew the standard historiographical account of the rebellion. In this earlier reference, he may be conflating the sack of Verulam with Boadicea's defeat by Suetonius shortly thereafter, suggesting that she was "foyld" at the time she sacked Verulam, rather than in her desire to do so. If this is the correct rendering, the line constitutes the only reference to Boadicea's eventual defeat in Verulam's account of her uprising.

None of the revulsion at female sovereignty and excess that characterized early modern historiographical accounts of the rebellion is reflected in Verulam's description of her own sack. Both here and in his *Faerie Queene* genealogies, Spenser begins to develop a positive literary account of Boadicea, one in which she already embodies the patriotic heroism attributed to her more broadly in the eighteenth and nineteenth centuries. Yet a second reference to the ancient rebellion in *The Ruines of Time* acknowledges the historiographical tradition of condemnation, bringing its language of moral judgment to bear on the ferocity of the uprising. From lamenting her ancient sack by her own people, Verulam turns to celebrate the new native champion who has recently retrieved her from oblivion:

> *Cambden* the nourice of antiquitie,
> And lanterne unto late succeeding age,
> To see the light of simple veritie,
> Buried in ruines, through the great outrage
> Of her owne people, led with warlike rage.
> (169–73)

If Verulam seemed to excuse her own sack by Boadicea earlier, she condemns it here. In place of the "brave heroïck thought" of the earlier passage, Boadicea's martial exploits now represent "the great outrage/Of her owne people, led with warlike rage." The language and attitudes of historiographical accounts of Boadicea are recuperated in this emphasis on warlike rage. Similarly, the self-destructiveness of the historiographical Boadicea, both in personal and national terms, is reinstated in the image of Verulam sacked by her own people. The agent of these recuperations is Camden. Conjured by Verulam, he brings the historiographical language of ruin and outrage into the poem, transforming the "brave heroïck thought" of Boadicea into a warlike rage that destroys the Britons and their monuments. Once Spenser's historiographical source enters the text explicitly, the alternative literary vision of a noble Boadicea collapses under the weight of rigorous moral judgment.

The most developed example of the positive literary treatment of Boadicea thus acknowledged its divergence from the contemporary historiographical tradition, ultimately deferring to it.[10] The locus of greatest anxiety in the period, even within the limited literary tradition, was Boadicea's conduct in war.[11] Boadicea's war atrocities, the ultimate expression of her female excess, constituted the most damaging element of her portrait in early modern accounts. The modern sense of an atrocity as something unacceptable even in time of war was only beginning to be developed in late sixteenth-century England, largely as a result of the Irish campaigns. Stephen Greenblatt has argued that accounts of atrocities on both sides produced a growing need in late Elizabethan England to dissociate the exercise of power in Ireland from its violent means of enforcement (1980: 184–8). Nationalist scholars and poets who condemned the savage excess of Boadicea's uprising thus echoed contemporary concern about English military practices under Elizabeth.

James Aske's blank verse epic, "Elizabetha Triumphans," which celebrates Elizabeth's victory over the 1588 Armada, makes an explicit comparison between the two queens. In a passage developing the military iconography of Elizabeth's appearance before her troops, Aske likens her to "Voada, once England's happie Queene," and "Vodice her daughter [...] / Who urging wounds with constant courage died" (Nichols 1823: II.570–1). Both the form Voada and the mention of her daughter by name indicate that Aske was probably not working from the description of Boadicea's revolt in Holinshed's "History of England," but rather from the more laudatory account of Queen Voada in the "Description of Scotland" (Holinshed 1587: 45–50). Susan Frye describes Aske's account of the Tilbury episode as an attempt "to turn Elizabeth's visit into a court pageant presided over by a warrior-queen." Frye also notes the similarities between Aske's fanciful pedigree of the Queen and her Spenserean genealogy in Book II of *The Faerie Queene* (1992: 105). I would add that Aske's positive invocation of "Voada, once England's happie Queene" may well be at the base of Spenser's heroic portrait of Bunduca in the same chronicle of "Briton's Moniments" in Canto 10, as well as in Verulam's initial description of her in *The Ruines of Time*. The positive literary tradition of Boadicea evident in Spenser, some of the catalogues, and Jonson's *Masque of Queenes* may thus date from Aske's 1588 celebration of Elizabeth's Armada victory, as against the nearly contemporary historiographical condemnations in Holinshed (1577, 1587) and the first Latin edition of the *Britannia* (1586).

The positive literary tradition links Elizabethan and Boadicean iconography, from Aske's explicit comparison to Spenser's genealogies and even the post-Elizabethan celebration of the new queen "Bel-Anna" in Jonson's masque.[12] Frye argues persuasively for the creation of a "myth of Elizabeth at Tilbury" in the decades following the defeat of the 1588 Armada as a central part of the queen's contemporary and posthumous iconography. One of the internal discrepancies in this myth raises the question of whether Elizabeth in fact delivered a speech to the troops assembled at Tilbury, and if so, what she said. Frye indicates that the most commonly accepted version of Elizabeth's "Tilbury speech," reprinted in John Nichols's *Progresses and Public Processions of Queen Elizabeth* and generally referred to in scholarly accounts, dates from no earlier than 1623, and was not published until 1654. In Aske's description of the Tilbury episode – one of only three contemporary accounts and the only one to invoke Boadicea – the queen does not address her troops

13. Woodcut of Voadicia in Raphael Holinshed, *Chronicles* (1577), by permission of the Houghton Library, Harvard University.

directly. Rather, she speaks to her sergeant-major, calling on him to relay her words to her subjects after she departs from the camp (Nichols 1823: II.573–4). Elizabeth's speech thus has less the quality of an oration than of a personal communication in Aske's poem.

Relinquishing her queenly right to make public speeches was not typical of Elizabeth's royal style. Just as the center of Boadicea's power in historiographical accounts was her oratory, a power that historians from Camden to Milton sought to suppress, so Elizabeth insisted on her princely right to make formal addresses to her people.[13] Elizabeth's speeches were published in the 1587 edition of Holinshed, thus taking their place in the same historiographical corpus as Boadicea's oration, and a strikingly Elizabethan woodcut of Boadicea illustrates the ancient queen's oration in the 1577 edition (Figure 13).[14] Aske's confinement of Elizabeth's "Tilbury speech" to a private exchange with her sergeant-major thus both weakens the comparison to Boadicea and undercuts Elizabeth's own use of public oratory to establish her female sovereignty. Even the more famous 1623 version of the Tilbury speech, in which she does address her troops directly, stops short of having her claim military leadership on the field of battle. Although she initially promises that "I myself will be your general, judge, and rewarder of every one of your virtues in the field," it quickly becomes apparent that she means this in a symbolic sense only when she qualifies her promise with the statement that "my Lieutenant-General shall be in my stead," referring to him thereafter as the general (Nichols 1823: II.536). Just as she abdicates her queenly right to address the troops in her own person in Aske's poem, so in this later version of the Tilbury speech Elizabeth carefully distinguishes between her symbolic leadership and the exercise of military agency on the field of battle.

The distinction between symbolic and active leadership in battle opens a gap between the early modern queen and her ancient predecessor. Just as Spenser eventually joined Camden and other historians in condemning the "great outrage" and "warlike rage" to which Boadicea moved her people, Aske was careful to praise Elizabeth as one "who never thurst for blood" (Nichols 1823: II.552).[15] Aske's contemporary account of Elizabeth's Tilbury visit may well be historically accurate in having the queen relay her address via a male officer after her own departure from the camp. Careful to withdraw her royal person from the projected scene of battle, Elizabeth also protected her chaste persona from public military engagement, both active and rhetorical.[16] In contrast to Elizabeth's public observance of silence and chastity in Aske's poem – the two pillars of idealized womanhood in the period – Boadicea delivered at least two speeches in military contexts in Holinshed. Her wartime atrocities were particularly heinous because of her own female leadership in battle and the strong fighting presence of women in her army. Where Elizabeth withdrew, silent and chaste, from the scene of projected battle at Tilbury, Boadicea publicly revealed her savage incontinence in her bellicose rhetoric and in the shameful display of the bodies of her elite female captives.

In my introductory chapter, I argued that the parodic element of sewing her captives' severed breasts to their own mouths was a projection of Boadicea's own monstrosity, both in her grotesque inversion of the queenly role of mother to her people, and in the savage isolationism of her absolute resistance to Rome. The emphasis on public display in this atrocity would also have reflected negatively on its perpetrator, suggesting Boadicea's own shamelessness in publicly assuming military leadership of the revolt. Where Elizabeth delegated command of her troops and withdrew from the public military arena of Tilbury, Boadicea carried out her rhetorical promise to lead her people in battle. By claiming a (masculine) military role, she forfeited the initial moral advantage of avenging personal, familial, and national violation. Realizing the worst early modern fears about female savagery and native origins, her military conduct was as humiliating to the early modern nation as her display of their naked and mutilated bodies was to the women of great nobility and worthy fame. As typical of early modern misogyny in her wild savagery as Elizabeth was exceptional in her self-contained chastity, Boadicea was indeed the frightful "woman at the bottom" who revealed misogynist anxieties about "women on top" in early modern England. Informing native origins with her savage femininity, the ancient queen provided the negative complement to Elizabeth's chaste embodiment of national security.

THE SAVAGE BREAST

Let me return now to the atrocity story I discussed in my introduction, considering its relevance to a wider range of "women on top," namely, the mothers of families as well as of nations:

> They spared neither age nor sex: women of great nobility and worthy fame, they took and hanged up naked, and cutting off their paps, sewed them to their mouths, that they might seem as if they sucked and fed on them, and some of their bodies they stretched out in length, and thrust them on sharp stakes.
>
> (Holinshed 1587: 45)

The overwhelming femininity of the Boadicean story is exemplified in this episode. Boadicea, mother and queen, moved to defend the inheritance of her daughters, stirred her people to battle. She was in her turn incited to acts of violence by the British goddess of war and victory, Adraste, whose barbaric cult she perpetuated. Her worst atrocity, and the only one described in more than general terms, was visited upon women, and was indeed a form of mutilation that could be inflicted only on women. Its savage violence exists in a context that is entirely feminine, including the perpetrator and those she claims to avenge, the divine force she invokes, and the victims she mutilates. The insistent femininity of the atrocity suggests that the savage violence it represents is exclusively feminine, a product of that pre-Roman Britain constructed as female and savage in early modern accounts.

At the same time that Boadicea's atrocity foregrounds femininity, however, it also works to negate it. Breast mutilation was a punishment known from classical antiquity through the Middle Ages and into the early modern period, when it was recorded in the religious wars in France and the Low Countries, and in the public humiliation of condemned witches in Germany. In both written and pictorial representations, it seems to have figured as a corollary to castration. Just as castration symbolized the emasculation of the defeated men, so breast mutilation functioned as a symbolic defeminization of women.[17] The practice also had a significant role in legends of female Christian martyrs. More than eighteen female saints are recorded in medieval hagiographies as having been martyred by breast amputation (Witkowski 1907: 69–73). The hagiographical tradition implicitly aligns breast mutilation with female insubordination, recording its infliction on intransigent women who refused to acknowledge secular patriarchal authority. Despite the conventional celebration of the martyrs' fortitude and devotion, the manner of their martyrdom also suggests punishment for unfeminine behavior, that is, for their resistance to patriarchal authority. The early modern period would thus have been familiar with breast amputation in two contexts: as a contemporary war atrocity or public humiliation, and as a form of Christian martyrdom.[18] In both cases, the mutilation bears a symbolic relation to the construction of femininity, either as a forceful defeminization of conquered or unruly women, or as a concrete realization of the Christian martyr's own rejection of conventional female obedience.

Just as breast amputation symbolized both the utter humiliation and destruction of the female captive, and the triumph of the female martyr, so the breast mutilation in Holinshed represents female triumph in Boadicea's victory and female defeat and defeminization in the subjection of her victims. A grotesque image of feminine deformity, Boadicea's breast mutilation is also monstrous in combining opposing aspects of feminine power and impotence. This very combination provoked the outcry against women sovereigns in the sixteenth century. John Knox opened his notorious diatribe against female rule with the declaration that the practice was first and foremost "repugnant to nature." He went on to explain that nature "doth paint [women] forth to be weak, frail, impatient, feeble and foolish: and experience hath declared them to be unconstant, variable, cruel and lacking the spirit of counsel and regiment" (1972: 9–10). Responding to the mid-sixteenth-century European phenomenon of "women on top," Knox castigated these female rulers in his title as a "Monstruous Regiment of Women," elaborating in his text the degeneration of their very realms into monstrosity under this unnatural female dominion: "For who would not judge that body to be a monster, where there was no head eminent above the rest, but that the eyes were in the hands, the tongue and mouth beneath in the belly, and the ears in the feet. [...] And no less monstrous is the body of that commonwealth, where a woman beareth empire" (27).[19] Naturally unfit to rule, women become monstrous in their attempts to exercise sovereignty in Knox's formulation. His metaphor of the monstrous body politic evokes other misogynist commonplaces that emphasize grotesque female corporeality. Evident in scientific models of women's bodies as deviant or imperfect versions of the masculine norm, as well as in the broader revulsion at female reproductive functions in a developing culture of bodily shame, the feminine grotesque constructed women's bodies as naturally monstrous.[20]

These conflicting associations reveal one of the problems of definition in early modern depictions of Boadicea and other savage queens as denatured or monstrous. If women were naturally savage, self-destructive, and grotesque, what then was unnatural in their exercise of these qualities when in positions of unrestrained power? I have argued thus far that Boadicea embodied a savage femininity at native origins that was neither nurturing nor generative. The texts on which I draw emphasize the monstrous, the disfigured, and the unnatural in their depictions of her. And yet the same authors who produced, translated, and revised these accounts understood women to be "naturally" grotesque and deformed – in some sense, naturally unnatural. Like Knox's monstrous body politic, which evokes both the unnatural state of female rule and the "natural" monstrosity of the female body, Boadicea's breast atrocity is simultaneously natural and unnatural, depicting the expected abuse of power by a female ruler even as it grotesquely parodies her maternal role. The tensions and conflicts in this atrocity focus on its depiction of a perverse maternity. They point beyond the recovery of an ancient queen's rebellion to the shifting and troubled construction of motherhood in early modern England.

Feminist literary critics have identified the late sixteenth and early seventeenth centuries as a period when maternity began to be construed as problematic, citing the development of fantasies of maternal persecution and criminalized maternal agency in contemporary obsessions with witch-craft and infanticide, the competition for the maternal body evident in drama and social constructions of birthing and infant nurture, and the beginnings of the psychological Oedipal plot in which the best mother is absent or dead (Willis 1995: 6, Dolan 1994: 126, Paster 1993: 216, Rose 1991: 301). Early modern fears about maternal agency are also implicated in the anxieties provoked by female rule in nationalist historiography and iconography, particularly as represented in the Boadicean atrocity story, with its perverse emphasis on maternal nurture. The interdependence of constructions of motherhood and the emerging nation state has been well documented by feminist historians of the eighteenth century. In her fasci-nating account of the interlocked constructions of sexuality and maternity in eighteenth-century England, Ruth Perry ties the "invention of mother-hood" to the institutionalizing of the nation state. Describing motherhood as a colonial form, analogous to domestic land enclosure and overseas imperialism, she argues that maternity was constructed in similar terms to other industrial examples of the rational manipulation of natural forces for greater productivity (1991: 206).[21] Perry's persuasive analysis of the con-nections between modern concepts of nature, maternity, and communal identity receives additional support from Londa Schiebinger's considera-tion of why Linnaeus invented the term *mammalia* to designate a class of animals also distinguished by having hair, three ear bones, and a four-chambered heart. Far from privileging femininity or maternity, Schiebinger claims, Linnaeus's choice of female mammae as the "icon" of that class reinforced conventional associations of the female with nature, tying hu-mans to other animals in terms of a shared lactating function, as opposed to the masculine coinage *Homo sapiens*, which Linnaeus used to distin-guish human intellectual capacities from those of other primates (1993: 393–4). Noting Linnaeus's active partisanship of maternal breast-feeding, Schiebinger too frames her argument about the scientific construction of maternity in terms of nature and production: "Linnaeus's term *Mammalia* helped legitimize the sexual division of labor in European society by em-phasizing how natural it was for females – both human and nonhuman – to suckle and rear their own offspring" (409).

  As with eighteenth-century constructions of the nation and national-ism – phenomena linked by Perry, Mosse, and others to constructions of motherhood and sexuality – so eighteenth-century definitions of moth-erhood had their roots in the cultural contests of the late sixteenth and seventeenth centuries. Early modern theories and practices of infant nurture have been much discussed and documented over the last two decades by historians of the family, and more recently, breast-feeding has become an important topic in literary and cultural studies of the period.[22] Most accounts of early modern infant nurture focus on the elite practice of wet-nursing and its ramifications for class and individual (masculine) identity in the period. Although there was no option to breast-feeding as a means of nurturing infants, families that could afford to do so hired wet nurses from the lower social orders, thus freeing the mothers for other duties. Throughout most of the sixteenth century, wet-nursing was the rule in the elite and merchant classes, who placed a higher value on frequent childbearing and women's exercise of other duties in the family economy, both of which were disrupted by maternal breast-feeding.[23] By the end of the century, however, theologians and writers of domestic tracts had begun to encourage all mothers to nurse their own children. Their arguments were primarily moral and theological rather than medical, insisting on the mother's duty to breast-feed as part of her greater obligation to her husband and to God.[24]

Holinshed's recovery of the Boadicean atrocity story coincided with the beginnings of early modern anxiety and conflict over maternal breast-feeding. Ironically, Boadicea's mutilation of her elite female captives inflicts a mockery of maternal nurture upon the bodies of the very class of women who did not provide it in early modern England. As the salient example of Boadicea's own savage excess in leading the rebellion, it also associates the exercise of maternal dominion and female agency with the parodic rejection of the role of nurturing mother. The reluctance or refusal of elite women to nurse their own children in early modern England was increasingly represented as an act of rebellion against God, nature, and patriarchal authority. One domestic writer claimed that women who would not nurse their children for fear of soiling their clothes also stayed home from church in bad weather with an equal disdain for the nurture of their own souls (Clinton 1975: 19). Another acknowledged that maternal breast-feeding provoked the same worldly ridicule as other signs of godliness, claiming that "A lady that will condescend to be a nurse, though to her own child, is become as unfashionable and ungenteel as a gentleman that will not drink, swear and be profane."[25] So pronounced was the connection between wet-nursing and ungodliness in some households that more than one father inadvertently starved his newborn infant to death rather than engaging a wet nurse while the mother recovered from a difficult delivery (Fildes 1988: 90–2).

Maternal breast-feeding was thus first and foremost a sign of a woman's obedience to God. It also indicated her obedience to her husband, and in practical terms, it consolidated his authority over all members of the household. One of the points that have been emphasized about this episode in the history of the family is that maternal breast-feeding was a key element in the development of the nuclear family, with its strong patriarchal control. Wet nurses rarely lived in the family home in England, so that infants were generally sent out of the home for their first two years, particularly those born in urban areas. Because nurses often lived at some distance from the infant's family, there was little contact between parents and child during this period. Maternal breast-feeding, on the other hand, kept all children at home and under the direct control of the father. Fathers generally made the decisions about breast-feeding, whether maternal or otherwise.[26] In their influential household manual, Robert Cleaver and John Dod included their explanation of a mother's duty to nurse her own children in the chapter on a wife's duty to her husband, rather than with the duties of parents to their children. They emphasized that God gave women breasts not for show or ostentation, "but in the service of God, and to be a help to her husband in suckling the child common to them both" (1612: P5r). The placement of this discussion in the chapter outlining a wife's duty to her husband indicates the subordination of maternal authority within the patriarchal household. Cleaver and Dod's spiritual and social argument for maternal breast-feeding in fact provides the conclusion to their chapter on wifely subordination. Running to five pages and ending with a recapitulation of the three wifely duties of subordination, chastity, and staying in the home, their account presents maternal breast-feeding as the duty of a properly subordinate wife, rather than as the role of a potentially powerful mother vis-à-vis her infant children (P3v–5v).

Only one domestic writer in the period placed the primary moral emphasis on the mother–child relationship. Elizabeth Clinton, the only contemporary female author in the field, announced the subject of her *Nursery* as "the duty of nursing due by mothers to their own children" (1975: 1). The body of Clinton's work was more orthodox, however, upholding the conventional understanding of the nursing mother's first duties to God and her husband, and only then to her child.[27] The end of this theoretical trajectory toward full masculine control over childrearing and the nuclear family is best articulated in William Cadogan's *Essay on Nursing* (1748), in which he advocated paternal supervision of all aspects of childrearing with the words, "I earnestly recommend it to every Father to have his Child nursed under his own Eye."[28] This all-seeing paternal eye could regulate both childrearing and the behavior of the mother. Early modern attacks on wet-nursing stressed the moral delinquency of wet-nurses, and warned of the dangers of moral contamination from both their milk and their early example.[29] Spenser traced the degeneration of the English in Ireland to their practice of fostering their children with Irish wet nurses, whereby English infants drank in the Irish nature and disposition of their nurses with their milk, and learned their first words in Irish (1934: 88).[30] Almost two hundred years later, Linnaeus was still drawing on examples from Erasmus to caution elite fathers against the possible class contamination of sending infants out to nurse (Schiebinger 1993: 407). By keeping his infant at home, nursed by his wife under his own eye, a father could avoid such contamination, affirming his paternal dominion over all members of the household.

While thus supervising the nourishment of his infant children, the omniscient patriarch could also carry out his societal role of restraining his wife's natural excesses. The most influential domestic handbooks in early modern England equated a mother's refusal to nurse with savagery, indeed, with something worse than savagery, as even savages and beasts would nurse their offspring.[31] Boadicea's breast-mutilating atrocity, with its symbolic and violent refusal of the role of nurturing mother, gave expression to the worst early modern fears about the non-nurturing mother. In mutilating her female captives, the ancient queen exercised the female savagery presumed to erupt wherever maternal dominion held sway outside patriarchal control. And by sewing the women's severed breasts to their own mouths, she went beyond the early modern condemnation of mothers who refused to nurse, constructing a visual satire of breast-feeding itself (to which there was no reliable alternative in the period) as inherently violent and grotesque.

One might read this atrocity as the "natural" construction of an unnatural mother, her rebellious mockery of the nurturing role she rejects. And yet the savage attributes of Boadicea's parody also figure in the breast-feeding literature. Violence and the grotesque haunt early modern descriptions of suckling, even and perhaps especially those designed to encourage maternal breast-feeding. Gail Kern Paster has demonstrated that medical and homiletic advice about breast-feeding in the period was part of a general movement to construct certain bodily functions as shameful and therefore requiring discipline. Surveying social constructions of birthing and infant nurture, she associates their ambivalence with "the fear of maternal agency and competition for the maternal body so pervasive in Elizabethan–Jacobean drama" (1993: 216). Early modern attempts to discipline the shame of maternal nurture intersect with historiographical anxieties about the savage maternity of native origins in the grotesque humiliation Boadicea inflicts on her female captives. The same language and attitudes of moral judgment deployed against the ancient queen also informed discussions of breast-feeding in the period. Especially in their evocation of nature as a model, many domestic homilists implicitly associated breast-feeding with the grotesque and the savage. Citing the salutary example of "the brute beasts lying upon the ground, and granting not one nipple or two, but six or seven to their young ones," Cleaver and Dod decried the ungodly refusal of mothers to breast-feed at the same time that they aligned that maternal duty with the grotesque overabundance of bestial nurture "upon the ground" (1612: P5v).[32] Elaborating on scriptural authority that women who refuse to nurse their own children are more cruel than sea monsters (Lamentations 4:3), William Gouge compared such mothers unfavorably to "unreasonable creatures, and among them the most savage wild beasts, as tigers and dragons" as well as "heathen women, and very savages," who have "in all ages been moved to nurse their own children" (1622: 513).

These paradoxical evocations of heathen, savage, and bestial mothers to exhort Christian women to nurse their young recall the terms of female excess that constructed Boadicea and other ancient queens in early modern accounts. Indeed, the relation between blood and the breast so violently realized in the Boadicean atrocity story was also an element of the orthodox literature on maternal breast-feeding. The standard medical understanding of the role of blood in the nurture of infants was that the child was nourished on menstrual blood in the womb, which was transformed into breast milk after parturition, thus explaining the absence of menses during pregnancy and breast-feeding. The "natural" connection between breast milk and blood could take more violent forms in the homiletic literature. Gouge included an image of the bloodied maternal breast in his encouragement to nursing mothers to overcome the pain of sore nipples, writing that "Many mothers have given their children suck when blood hath run by the mouth of the child by reason of sore nipples" (1622: 517).[33] A counterexample also employing the image of the bloody breast to encourage maternal breast-feeding was that of the Emperor Caligula, whose cruelty as an adult was traced to a bloodthirsty wet nurse who daubed her nipples with blood (Fildes 1986: 189). This cautionary tale figured in breast-feeding tracts from the late sixteenth through the seventeenth centuries, precisely the period in which the parallel domestications of the savage queen and the nursing mother were being accomplished.

The domestic homilists also refused to acknowledge bloody or deformed breasts as excuses for not nursing, asserting that there were "means" for the correction of such conditions. "Means," or specially designed instruments to facilitate breast-feeding, were in use from the mid-sixteenth century forward. One of the most common conditions requiring correction was that of flat or inverted nipples, a condition possibly exacerbated by the elite practice of corseting girls from early childhood. The remedy was a device called the sucking glass, consisting of a cup to fit over the breast with a curved pipe attached, which allowed the nipple to be drawn out by suction. The sucking glass was in use as early as 1545, and is mentioned and/or illustrated by sixteen medical authors between that date and 1800. The great advantage of the curved pipe was that a woman could suck it herself, thus drawing her own nipples out. The self-sufficiency provided by this feature was emphasized throughout the medical literature and celebrated in the highest terms by its inventor, the influential Ambrose Paré, who claimed that "we have invented this instrument of glass, wherewith, when the broader orifice is fastened or placed on the breast or dug, and the pipe turned upwards towards her mouth, she may suck her own breasts herself."[34] Boadicea's sewing of her captives' breasts to their mouths "that they might seem as if they sucked and fed on them" thus had its analogue in the medical literature. Figuring as a standard and perfectly acceptable procedure to facilitate maternal breast-feeding, the sucking glass was particularly recommended as a means of offering nursing mothers a measure of the self-sufficiency claimed by the savage queen in her own right, and on behalf of her nation.

Even as they promoted the practice, then, orthodox accounts of maternal breast-feeding incorporated the elements of blood, savagery, the grotesque, and feminine self-sufficiency that characterize the Boadicean atrocity story. The paradox suggested by these unarticulated connections between the encouragement of maternal breast-feeding in the homiletic literature and the monstrous perversion of maternity in the Boadicean atrocity story is endemic to the discourse of breast-feeding in the period. It emerges most clearly in the conflicting ways that "nature" was evoked to condemn mothers who refused to nurse their own children. On the one hand, the non-nursing mother was seen as savagely refusing her God-given role as nurturer, indeed, refusing it in a way that exceeded the savagery of heathen women and beasts. On the other hand, images of maternal breast-feeding, both orthodox and parodic, connected it with bloodshed and the grotesque. The first formulation constructs the non-nursing mother as unnatural in her refusal to fulfill the function carried out even by savages and beasts; paradoxically, the second constructs the nursing mother in a way that also invokes savagery and the grotesque. And in cases of the mothers' own desire to avoid bloodshed or physical deformity, medical writers and domestic homilists called for the use of artificial means to facilitate the "natural" practice of maternal breast-feeding, overturning the godly model of nature as an illustration of divine law. In all these formulations, the mother as natural or closer to nature than the father was reconstructed as unnatural or grotesque, a creature who could not even maintain the standards of savages and beasts. Nature itself, in early modern accounts of maternal breast-feeding, emerges as monstrous or unnatural.

The collapse of distinctions between the natural and the unnatural in early modern discourses of maternal nurture puts into question the system of binary oppositions resting on the nature/culture dichotomy that is commonly believed to have structured western experience and understanding since at least the early modern period. The classic alignment of the female with the natural/wild/savage, and the male with the cultural/tame/civilized has been questioned by feminist social theorists since the early 1970s, most notably in Sherry Ortner's article "Is Female to Male as Nature Is to Culture?" Ortner cautioned that these parallel oppositions should not be invoked in absolute terms to describe gender relations, since upon closer analysis women will be seen to occupy an intermediate position between nature and culture in most formulations. She nevertheless concluded that the superiority of men over women was still underwritten by the nature/culture opposition in societies that give a higher value to culture, since women are universally perceived as being closer to nature than men.

Ortner's ground-breaking work was complicated in the 1980s by British sociologists also examining the gendering of the nature/culture opposition. Carol P. MacCormack integrated Ortner's feminism with the structuralist proposition that for Europeans, binary oppositions are dynamic rather than static, representing relations of becoming and transforming rather than fixed oppositions. The theoretical relation between nature and culture is thus one in which nature is in a constant state of becoming or being transformed into culture. Using this principle, MacCormack arranged the parallel sets of nature/culture oppositions on a grid where the wild becomes the tame and the savage the civilized, just as nature becomes culture. When the female/male opposition is added to this grid, however, it creates a non sequitur, for the female cannot be said to become the male without disturbing the conventional assumptions of gender distinction that govern such a model. The category of gender is thus revealed as a construction of culture in the very model that would define it as an immutable fact of nature. Within that cultural construction, it would be possible both for the female to evolve into the male, and for the male to devolve into the female (1980: 1–24).[35]

MacCormack's grid helps to explain the gender anxiety aroused by the recovery of native origins in early modern England. If one interprets this anxiety in terms of mutable gender polarities, then national regression to an originary state could be conceived as a degeneration from masculinity and culture into an exclusively feminine state of nature. It was precisely this fear of degenerating from a desired state of modern civilized masculinity into a feared precedent of ancient female savagery that haunted early modern English projects of historical recovery. The intersection of gender anxiety with concerns about the recovery of native origins lay behind historiographical efforts to establish a masculine foundation for the nation in antiquity. It informed Hobbes's association of maternal dominion with the state of nature, and helped to shape the propensity of ancient queens to savage excess in early modern drama and historiography.

Early modern anxieties about gender, national identity, and monstrosity come together in the parodic breast mutilation of the Boadicean atrocity story. Socio-anthropologists generally interpret the closer association of women with nature as a function of the mother's role in breast-feeding. And yet the mother's role as nurse, which Ortner takes to be an immutable fact of nature, was very much under discussion in early modern England. The construction of the natural as unnatural, of female nature as savage beyond the containment of a binary opposition, crystallized as an issue of maternal nature and nurture in this period. This crystallization emerged in projects of national recovery as a concern about feminine representations of the land and native origins, particularly as such representations, in their positing of an originary and engulfing femininity, inevitably involved a maternal relation of the land and its history to the early modern nation. Historiographical concerns about the savagery of native origins thus take their place in the wider social context of a crisis in familial relations, particularly regarding the nature and role of the mother. In their turn, the scholarly and literary manipulations that defused these anxieties about native origins throw light on broader cultural strategies for the containment and rechannelling of feminine forces perceived as dangerously uncontrollable in the sixteenth and early seventeenth centuries.

FROM SAVAGE MOTHER TO SUBORDINATE WIFE

The "unnatural nature" of the maternal is a recurrent trope in early modern English discourses of the family. In her study of elite familial records, Barbara J. Harris notes that "natural" and "unnatural" were the terms most frequently used to describe the relation of elite mothers to their sons in the sixteenth century (1990: 619).[36] By the second half of the century, maternal infanticide as the ultimate expression of unnatural motherhood had emerged as a major cultural preoccupation. From the 1560s forward, infanticide was regularly indicted in England, after a virtual absence from court records in the two preceding centuries.[37] Frances E. Dolan describes the development of "a particular kind of criminalized maternal agency" in legal representations of infanticide in the period (1994: 126). Noting the more complex agency in literary representations of the phenomenon, she posits a cultural obsession with child-murder that focused blame on murderous mothers even as it privileged the stories of murderous fathers (121–70). Dolan's finely textured account of the diverse discourses of infanticide in the period – from legal statutes and depositions to pamphlets, ballads, and plays – indicates the extent to which the ideology and practice of motherhood were riven with contradiction, repeatedly producing the oxymoron of the mother's "natural" tendency to unnatural acts of savage maternity.[38]

One of the most notorious infanticide pamphlets of the early seventeenth century condemned a mother's murder of two of her children in the same terms of horror employed by Gouge in reviling mothers who refused to breast-feed: "And shall woman, nay a Christian woman, God's own Image, be more unnatural than Pagan, Cannibal, Savage, Beast or Fowl?" (Henderson and McManus 1985: 367). Titled *A Pitilesse Mother* (1616), it demonstrates what Dolan calls "the violence and self-destruction inherent in the ideal of maternal nurturance" in the period (150). Dolan's articulation of this violent ideal of maternity recalls G. Wilson Knight's condemnation of Cymbeline's Queen as an extreme figure of motherhood, "a possessive maternal instinct impelling her savage life" (1947: 132). Although the Queen's murderous intent is directed at her step-daughter rather than her son, her ambition for Cloten does indeed bring about his death. In Knight's formulation, even her devotion to Cloten demonstrates a savage, instinctive maternity governed by primitive or bestial drives. Knox conceived of this savage maternity in explicitly murderous terms. As part of his assault on the "Monstruous Regiment of Women," he cited examples of queens who had killed their children or grandchildren in order to gain the throne as the strongest evidence against allowing women to rule (1972: 12v). The popular conflation of violence and maternity in the pamphlets thus had its elite analogues in early modern representations of female sovereignty, from the savage ancient queens "at the bottom" of national historiography to the "women on top" of contemporary Europe.

References to infanticide in English drama of the period abound, as in the celebrated boast of Lady Macbeth before the murder of Duncan, when she brings her husband to the sticking point of regicide with an image of tearing a child from her breast to murder it (1.7.54–9).[39] Lady Macbeth's violent conflation of her experience of breast-feeding with a willingness to murder her infant was shaped by English stereotypes about Scottish motherhood in the sixteenth century. Elite Scotswomen, unlike their English counterparts, were known to practice maternal breast-feeding as a means of fortifying kinship bonds and imbuing male infants with their own fighting spirit.[40] Lady Macbeth could thus speak from experience – "I have given suck, and know / How tender 'tis" – even as she renounced this tenderness by proclaiming her willingness to dash her infant's brains out. The English perceived the Scots as primitive in social organization and government, a view elaborated by Shakespeare in *Macbeth*, with its evocation of archaic Scottish institutions and emphases on bloodshed and the supernatural. The vision of medieval Scotland in *Macbeth* recalls similar evocations of the primitive in *Cymbeline*, suggesting a parallel between the arrested historical development of Scotland and native British origins. Just as the wicked Queen articulates the wild, isolationist nationalism of *Cymbeline*, so *Macbeth*'s future queen gives voice to conflicted early modern attitudes to maternal breast-feeding – calling on the spirits to unsex and denature her female body as she professes equal willingness to nurse and to murder her child.

The denatured and unnatural mothers of early modern drama, cheap print, and national historiography – from Lady Macbeth to the "Pitilesse Mother" to Boadicea – all fulfilled the natural imperative of women acting independently of patriarchal structures. In terms of early modern gender stereotypes, their unnatural maternity was a paradoxical expression of their female nature, that tendency to savage excess and (self)destruction restrained and uneasily monitored by the masculinist gender hierarchy. In contrast to these naturally unnatural mothers, the elaborate maternal iconography developed for the royal persons of Elizabeth I and James I was free from any taint of natural motherhood. Necessarily metaphorical in both cases, the maternal claims of these monarchs emphasized their superior alignment with culture over nature. James in particular was anxious to distance himself from examples of savage maternity, especially that of the infamous Scottish queen who was both his mother and the source of his claims to the thrones of England and Scotland. Jonathan Goldberg describes how James repositioned himself as the father of a line of kings rather than the son of a discredited queen. The first English monarch since Henry VIII who could claim to be a natural father to his family as well as a metaphorical father to his people, James derived his claim to the role of *parens patriae* from the fact of his having produced male heirs to the throne. Concern about the looming female presence of his notorious mother nevertheless shaped various late Elizabethan and Jacobean artistic works, from epic poetry to mythological paintings, and informed James's reactions to them (Goldberg 1983: 1–17).[41]

One way that James dealt with the problem of his filial identity was to assert equal sovereignty with his mother, as though they had ruled jointly over Scotland as husband and wife. He later adapted this spousal relationship in metaphors for his rule over England, claiming the magisterial authority of a husband over his kingdom–bride as frequently as the more conventional paternal role of the monarch. As with his paternal claims, James derived the authority for these spousal metaphors of kingship from his literal achievement of them in family life (Goldberg 1983: 30–1, 46; 1986: 3–5, 14–17). He also drew on the early modern understanding of marriage as a fundamental institution of the social order. By the early seventeenth century, the need to enforce this marriage-based order was being felt throughout England. Responding in part to deteriorating economic conditions at the turn of the seventeenth century that made it difficult for the poorest orders to marry and support children,[42] the new emphasis on marriage was also part of a general movement to restrict female power and agency.

Recent socio-historical work on the early modern English family has challenged the view that the advent of the so-called "companionate marriage" in the late seventeenth century heralded a more egalitarian attitude toward women.[43] Dismissing the idea that the romantic ideal of the companionate marriage articulated in the eighteenth century was less patriarchal than its predecessor, Anthony Fletcher contends that "there was a strong male imperative from the Elizabethan period onwards to reconstruct patriarchy on more effective foundations." Within that context, the companionate marriage enforced a new prescriptive code of personal characteristics and behavior that came to characterize subordinate femininity from the 1670s forward (Fletcher 1995: 395–6). Amy Louise Erickson's work on women's relation to property bears out Fletcher's view of marriage as an institution that increasingly acted to subordinate women in the seventeenth century. Despite a reluctance to generalize about trends in women's "status" (a word she routinely puts in quotation marks), Erickson does state categorically that "the shifting legal balance of power over a period of several hundred years – but particularly in the seventeenth century – cut serious inroads into women's already severely restricted entitlement to property." Citing the general climate of conservatism following the restoration of the monarchy, as well as the overt identification of the individual as masculine in contemporary political and property theory, she concludes that the "incremental 'rationalization' of the legal system succeeded simultaneously in creating a consistent theory of private ownership and in excluding women from that theory by virtue of their marriage" (Erickson 1993: 230).

The early modern restriction of the wife's role within marriage and the family economy, felt most acutely by the poorest women, has been compared to the parallel enclosure of land in the period, with its equally serious consequences for the poor (Perry 1991, Stallybrass 1986, Fabricant 1979).[44] Both phenomena enhanced the consolidation of power in the figure of the *paterfamilias* who controlled the new estates of marriage and the land. In the increasingly masculinist construction of the family, the mother's authority was greatly abridged. Her role in the family economy was restricted to childbearing and childrearing, and her power to convey and bestow family property was severely curtailed.[45] When James used marriage as a metaphor for his relationship to the kingdom, then, he invoked an arena in which the independent agency of women, and particularly mothers, was being written out in favor of an institution that emphasized wifely subordination. The maternal role, which allowed for considerable female power vis-à-vis male children, was increasingly defined as secondary to a wifely role, in which a woman carried out all her functions in subordination to her husband. Similarly, in the household analogies of contemporary political theory, English writers tended to distinguish domestic government as entirely determined by paternal authority, frequently eliding the ruler's roles of husband and father to the nation (Jordan 1993).

These processes of redefinition and subordination also inform the plot of *Cymbeline*. The wicked Queen, female embodiment and partisan of British nationalism in the political scenes of Act 3, disappears from the drama as Imogen takes the ascendancy in Acts 4 and 5, tracing the landscape of Wales in her faithful journey to rejoin her husband at Milford Haven. The Queen is herself a wife to Cymbeline, but her character is shaped primarily in terms of the maternal drives G. Wilson Knight found so disturbing. It is this figure of savage maternity and isolating nationalism that Imogen redeems with the role of devoted wife to Posthumus and servant to Lucius. Her rising from the ground of Wales and the body of "DuChamp," in reality the boorish offspring of the savage Queen, redefines both familial and national formulations of womanhood. Imogen's role throughout the play is one of wifely fidelity and submission, and it is her willingness to reaffirm this role in the last scene that allows for the play's romance conclusion. The most important redemption in this long scene is not the enlightenment of Posthumus or Cymbeline, who simply accept the facts as finally presented to them, but rather the dramatic subordination of the wicked Queen's savage maternity to the idealized wifely forgiveness of Imogen.[46]

The dramatic substitution of Imogen's wifely fidelity for the Queen's maternal savagery in *Cymbeline* represents a broader cultural desire to subordinate any independent source of female power to a wifely role. At the same time, the denouement of Shakespeare's romance also reveals the difficulties of redefining early seventeenth-century womanhood so as to banish all its threatening qualities. The number of women accused of insubordination in early modern courts and extralegal community actions testifies not simply to concern about wifely insubordination, but also to the difficulty of theorizing a wifely ideal in the face of widespread female resistance.[47] The stage work required to reveal the "true identities" of the Queen and Imogen – from the delivery of messages revealing the Queen's wicked intentions and announcing her death, to the blow Imogen willingly suffers from Posthumus while still in disguise – participates in this cultural problem of redefinition. Just as the complicated resolution of the political plot suggests the difficulties of articulating the relationship of Britain to Rome, so the complexities of the dramatic revelations about the characters of the Queen and Imogen indicate how hard it still was in the early seventeenth century to fulfill the cultural desire of replacing savage maternity with wifely fidelity. Imogen's retention of her boy's costume after her reunion with Posthumus suggests an inability to present a fully purged and subordinate womanhood. The romance conclusion of *Cymbeline*, dependent on Imogen's wifely forgiveness and public acceptance of her subordinate role in marriage, is still accomplished without her womanly re-emergence from behind the disguise of "Fidele."

THE END OF DOMINION MATERNAL

The full subordination of maternal authority to wifely dependence was still confined to theory in the early seventeenth century when Shakespeare attempted to dramatize it in the conclusion of his Roman–British romance. In the same long recognition scene, he also drew on another Jacobean device for rechanneling maternal power, namely, the appropriation of powerful maternal attributes by men.[48] When the identities of Imogen and the Princes are revealed to Cymbeline at the end of the play, he exclaims, "O, what am I? / A mother to the birth of three? Ne'er mother / Rejoic'd deliverance more" (5.5.369–71). This maternal analogy is an odd vehicle for the expression of Cymbeline's joy at being restored to his paternal role. It is further complicated by his status as the leader of a nation that accepts civil membership in the Roman Empire despite its recent military victory over the latter. For in his evocation of a mother's joy at delivery, Cymbeline claims the authority of giving birth that Hobbes identified as the basis of maternal dominion in the state of nature. The indisputable physical kinship between mother and child that privileged maternal dominion in Hobbes's account of the state of nature impinges metaphorically on the conclusion of the civil drama of *Cymbeline*. The implication of its appearance there is that only the invocation of the natural bond between mother and child can sufficiently express Cymbeline's extraordinary joy at being reunited with his children. Moved to question and redefine his own parental status, Cymbeline metaphorically reclaims his children in terms of maternal dominion.

Cymbeline's curious use of this maternal metaphor suggests an inability to dispense with motherhood entirely at the conclusion of *Cymbeline*, despite the wifely subordination of Imogen, the denunciation of the "wicked Queen," and the reintegration of Britain into the masculine embrace of Augustan Rome. And yet Cymbeline's comparative formulation of the analogy could also be construed as a claim that his joy exceeds that of most and perhaps all mothers – "Ne'er mother / Rejoic'd deliverance more" – that his metaphorical experience of maternity is in fact more profound than that of a natural mother. This claim rests rhetorically on the unexpectedness of his reunion with his children. The miraculous reunion that takes Cymbeline beyond the realm of probability also allows him to claim a role that lies outside the course of nature. In advancing his claim, Cymbeline articulates his masculine motherhood as something fuller than that of a natural mother precisely because it is removed from nature. And even as he affirms and appropriates the power of the maternal role, Cymbeline still subordinates it within the restored patriarchal structure of the kingdom. Noting the dynastic consequence to his daughter of the restoration of her brothers, Cymbeline concludes his speech of maternal recovery with the words "O Imogen, / Thou hast lost by this a kingdom" (5.5.373–4).

One might construe Imogen's loss more broadly in terms of other feminine icons of the nation. Just as she is displaced dynastically by the recovery of her royal brothers, so the prior feminine iconography of the nation was eventually replaced by masculinist images and theories of government in early modern England. Cymbeline's assumption of an artificial maternity that transcends natural motherhood anticipates Hobbes's invention of the Artificial Man. Just as the Artificial Man replaced the earlier feminine iconography of Mater Terra, so his resolutely masculine torso on the *Leviathan*'s title page replaced that nexus of gender anxiety and savage maternity that was Boadicea's legacy to historically based formulations of the nation. Emphatically artificial, Hobbes's masculine construct was attended by none of the confusion of nature and culture in Cymbeline's invocation of natural motherhood to express his joy at being restored to full paternity. The king on Hobbes's title page has no need to display the appropriated attributes of maternal nurture on his masculine breast. When metaphorical maternity does intrude into Hobbes's discussion of the nation, as in his conventional reference to "(the two breasts of our common Mother) Land and Sea" (1978: 2.24.295), it is so bracketed and incidental as to indicate that the earlier tradition of feminine national iconography no longer posed a threat to his masculine articulation of the state. In Hobbes's construct of the Artificial Man, the end of maternal dominion over national iconography and historiography has been reached.

Independent female sovereignty had also largely disappeared by the time Hobbes formulated his theory of the state. When the Stuarts were restored to the throne, queenly images of the land conformed to the domestic model of wifely subordination. Dryden described Charles II's barren Queen Catherine as "A Soyl ungratefull to the Tiller's Care" in *Absalom and Achitophel* (1969: 12). Mary II, the first queen regnant since

Elizabeth, was primarily defined in the nationalist literature by her role as wife to William of Orange. Although she ruled jointly with William and led the government during his military campaigns, her death was articulated as the private loss of her husband rather than the public passing of a monarch. The vesting of military leadership in William relieved Mary's reign of the most troublesome aspect of female sovereignty, and even her right to govern in his absence was carefully presented as having been ratified by Parliament ("J. S." 1695). Her sister Anne's sovereignty was similarly circumscribed, despite the fact that she ruled alone. Depicted by contemporaries as a weak monarch because of her gender and physical frailty, Anne was routinely described in terms of a daughterly dependence on her ministers, one of whom was said to have conducted her "with the care and tenderness of a father, or a guardian, through a state of helpless ignorance" (Gregg 1980: 136–8).

Female personifications of the nation are similarly dependent and domesticated in Restoration and eighteenth-century histories of Mary and Anne. A history of Mary's reign published after her death in 1695 describes the England of 1688 as a "startled nation" stretching out "her hand in earnest for help and succour" and casting "her languid eyes about" until they fix on William and Mary. Mary herself quickly drops out of this national image, leaving William to figure alone as the nation's military savior ("J. S." 1695: 40, 46–9).[49] William Dove's elegy "Albiana: A Poem Humbly Offered to the Memory of our Late Sovereign Lady, Mary, Queen of England" recalls the land-based nationalism of a century earlier, calling on the earth to heave her pensive breast and all of English topography to join in mourning Mary/Albiana. This section of the poem ends with a call to the "Beauties" of the Court, who most feel the corporate loss of Albiana, to appear "in wildest dress […] / With garments flowing, and dishevill'd hair" and raise "a hollow moan" for the death of their queen. Yet Dove's stylized invocations of native topography and courtly Maenads defuse the wild excesses of female grief in a storming natural world, and he ends by acknowledging to William that "We mourn a *Queen*, but thou, what's more, a *Wife*," abandoning his cosmic meditation on Mary's death to return to her primary domestic role as wife. His ability to include elements of topographical and female savagery, like Hobbes's references to ancient matriarchies, testifies to the historical containment of any real threat from the unruly feminine forces of nature to the masculine cultural order of the state. Unlike Boadicea and her daughters, Albiana and her mourning Maenads had no real agency in the construction of national identity.

Boadicea herself underwent a transformation in the Restoration that reduced her savagery and brought her more into line with late seventeenth-century ideals of subordinate womanhood. George Powell's adaptation of Fletcher's *Bonduca* for the Restoration stage shifts the emphasis of the play from Bonduca to her daughters on the one hand, and to Caratach on the other. The pivotal scene of 3.5 in Fletcher, where the daughters attempt to torture their Roman captives in revenge for their rapes, and where they and their mother meet the Romans in battle, is shortened and changed by Powell so as to distance all three women from the violence of war. The desire to torture the Roman prisoners is transferred to the male Briton Nennius, and the references to the Romans' rape of the British princesses disappear altogether. Powell also excised the battle, moving directly to the triple suicide of Bonduca and her daughters. Even there, he robbed Bonduca of her one moment of glory in Fletcher, giving her last words, "If you will keep your Laws and Empire whole, / Place in your Romane flesh a Britain soul" (Fletcher 1966: 4.4.152–3), to Caratach, who kills himself at the end of the play with the words "I wear a British Soul" (Sprague 1926: 165).

The appropriation of Boadicea's role by Caratach, which had begun in Act 5 of Fletcher's text, was thus strengthened by Powell, who made Caratach the representative Briton, killing himself to avoid Roman capture. Charles Hopkins's original drama, *Boadicea Queen of Britain*, goes even farther in reducing its heroine's independence. Improbably, Hopkins's queen is herself an initial champion of union with the Romans, proclaiming in the first act "Let every Voice, where Seas and Shore extend, / Aloud proclaim, that *Rome* is *Britain's* friend" (1697: 1.5). Despite Boadicea's articulation of this political sentiment, the love interests of her two daughters govern the plot of Hopkins's drama. The Britons are moved to resist the Romans only when one of the daughters, beloved of a British general, is sought in marriage by a Roman commander. Hopkins transfers the female savagery of British war atrocities to the Roman commander who threatens that unless he is given Boadicea's daughter, "Chaste Matrons, shall like common Strumpets burn, / And Infants from the Brests they suck, be torn" (1.5). In contrast, Boadicea's younger daughter articulates the proper behavior of a woman when addressed by her Roman lover: "Our Sex is govern'd by severest Laws, / Mutes only in our most important Cause" (2.3). In Hopkins's drama, a woman's "most important Cause" is no longer the public fate of the nation, but rather, her private success in winning a suitor.[50]

The domestication of Boadicea and her daughters in these Restoration dramas reflects the exclusion of women from the public sphere of the nation by the end of the seventeenth century. The dramas' emphasis on the familial concerns of the daughters' marriages is consistent with the disappearance of the threatening national role of women at a time when the regulation of the family was no longer the central concern of those seeking to maintain the social order. Boadicea and her daughters paradoxically became less dangerous in their willingness to subordinate matters of national importance to their private love interests. In contrast to the Boadicea of the early seventeenth century, whose female savagery was her primary disqualification as a leader, the modest daughters of Hopkins's drama are unfit to lead their people because of their inability to transcend the private sphere. The savage violence of the Renaissance Boadicea had thus been defused by the Restoration, when the emphasis was more on her younger and less threatening daughters, whose adherence to an ideal of private womanhood guaranteed their dependence on men and disqualified them from any public role in the construction of the nation.[51]

At the same time that Boadicea became less threatening, the specter of an independent ancient Britain, untamed by membership in the Roman Empire, disappeared. Hopkins's drama is particularly noteworthy in this respect. Not only does he subordinate any national or historical interest to the daughters' love plots, but he shares none of the Renaissance concern about ancient British savagery. The Romans articulate and enact the violence and atrocity of war in his drama. In addition to raping Boadicea's eldest daughter, the Roman commander Decius articulates the combined savagery of Holinshed's Boadicea and Shakespeare's Lady Macbeth when he threatens to desecrate British matrons and to tear British infants from the breasts they suck. Hopkins thus removed the taint of savagery from the ancient Britons even as he emphasized the domestic subordination of the female characters. Reversing the Roman/British polarities of gendered savagery in Renaissance accounts of the uprising, he laid the ground for the reception of "Boadicea Queen of Britain" as a national heroine in the eighteenth century.

The apparent lack of anxiety about native origins was not unrelated to the rechannelling of female savagery in Restoration adaptations of the Boadicean material. Indeed, the ability to dispense with the former was very much an effect of the latter. In the late sixteenth and early seventeenth centuries, the maintenance of hierarchical gender relations was a central concern in any construction of the nation, be it social, political, or historiographical. Symbolic representations of the nation inevitably participated in this discourse of gender relations, whether substituting the masculine embrace of Roman Britain for the savage femininity of native origins, or struggling to dislodge the iconography of Mater Terra in favor of the "reall Unitie" of the Artificial Man. By the end of the seventeenth century, both the shift to a masculine iconography and the relegation of women to the private sphere had been largely accomplished, banishing the figure of the unruly woman from the realm of public concern and the specter of ancient female savagery from national identity. Once women were no longer perceived to threaten the masculinist order of the state, their overwhelming symbolic and historical function in representations of the nation could also be dismissed. The efforts of local authorities and communities to discipline unruly women; the growing masculine absolutism of political philosophy; masculine appropriations of the maternal and the subordination of wives to husbands in moral and theological constructions of the household; and the scholarly and literary attempts to disown, deny, and finally domesticate the savage queen of native origins, all participated in a broad cultural anxiety about female power and agency.

The end of this trajectory was an exclusively masculine articulation of the state as a commonwealth of individual men represented by one artificial man who rises above and dominates the natural world beneath him. This theoretical model of the state replaced what had been a symbolic vision of the nation in the sixteenth century, based on the mutually constitutive bodies of the monarch and the land. Closer to nature, the earlier vision of the nation had foregrounded femininity in the symbolic gendering of the land and native origins as feminine. It had allowed a female monarch like Elizabeth to constitute herself as the embodiment of the nation, even as it gave expression to the anxiety about female rule felt by those who helped to fashion this iconography. The early modern apprehension of ancient British femininity – from Britannia to native topography to Boadicea and other savage queens – participated in a broad cultural movement to restrict and appropriate female agency, both in artistic and literary representations, and in the theory and practice of familial and national government. From Holinshed's and Camden's histories, to *Cymbeline* and *Bunduca*, Hobbes's *Leviathan*, and Restoration revisions of Boadicea's uprising, the recovery of native origins played a central role in the cultural stabilizing of national identity over the course of the seventeenth century. Working through the issues of gender, sexuality, and savage maternity that troubled Elizabethan nationalism, these texts ultimately effected the desired masculinization of native origins by their progressive domestication of the savage queen.

EPILOGUE

That great antiquity America lay buried for thousands of years,
and a large part of the earth is still in the urn unto us.

Thomas Browne, *Urn-Burial*

The historiographical and artistic recovery of native origins in early modern England seems to have come to a head in the decade 1606–1616, which saw the publication of the first part of *Poly-Olbion* (1612), the first English edition and expansion of the *Britannia* (1610), the first fully developed county atlas in Speed's *Theatre of the Empire of Great Britain* (1612), and a series of historical dramas set in pre-Roman and Roman–British antiquity, including *King Lear* (*c.*1605), *Cymbeline* (*c.*1609) and *Bonduca* (*c.*1616). The nationalist works produced in this decade distilled the tensions and anxieties of the first great period of English nationalism. Each of them marks in some way a point of no return in the development of early modern English nationalism. The empty stage of Speed's *Theatre* banished the conventional female embodiment of the nation at the eventual price of relinquishing the central place of native topography in the articulation of national identity. When that banished female figure was finally replaced on the title page of Hobbes's *Leviathan*, it had yielded to a constitution of the nation that was based on political rather than symbolic representation and that rigorously excluded women and feminine figuration from its theory of the state. *Lear*, *Cymbeline* and *Bonduca* dramatized the crisis in gender and family relations of the early modern period in terms of the relation of the nation as a whole to its origins and the role of the Romans in shaping its identity. After 1616, dramatizations of British antiquity virtually disappeared until the Restoration, when the gender conflict represented in the earlier plays as central to national identity had become a question of private or domestic concern only. Similarly, *Poly-Olbion* and the 1610 expansion and translation of the *Britannia* were the last original topographical surveys on a national scale to be attempted in verse or prose in the period. The very success of sixteenth-century nationalist scholars in compiling such vast works as the *Britannia* had finally produced a body of knowledge so unwieldy that it could not be shaped into a unified national form. New chorographical histories were henceforth restricted to single counties or monuments, and topographical verse abandoned Great Britain for the microcosms of country houses or single features such as "Cooper's Hill." The diminishing symbolic importance of topographical nationalism is evident not only in the reduced scale of later seventeenth-century projects, but also in their conscious evocation of *otium*. Where the great topographical celebrations produced between 1606 and 1616 actively participated in the shaping of national identity and the exploration of its social and political tensions, later works redefined topographical description as a specifically rural genre celebrating both a physical and moral retreat from the central concerns of the political nation.

Sir Thomas Browne's *Urn-Burial* is both an example of this transformation and a reflection upon it. Its publication date of 1658 makes it a useful point from which to survey the monuments of sixteenth- and early seventeenth-century English nationalism. Browne corresponded with the leading antiquarians of his own generation, many of whom had begun their work during Camden's lifetime and applied the *Britannia*'s principles of chorographical description to their more restricted and detailed county surveys. Browne was particularly involved in the work of William Dugdale, whose 1656 *Antiquities of Warwickshire Illustrated* represented the culmination of chorographical enumeration. Half again as long as the original 1586 edition of the *Britannia* (which surveyed Warwickshire in less than seven pages), Dugdale's *opus* is a quarto volume of 826 pages, illustrated with maps of each hundred and engravings of monuments, inscriptions, cityscapes, coats of arms and other notable features of the county and its history. Connected to conservative projects of chorographical description, Browne also pointed ahead to a more scientific approach to antiquities. He published accurate engravings of the urns that inspired *Urn-Burial*, producing what remain the first known archaeological illustrations of Anglo-Saxon pots, and the treatise itself has been called "the first English excavation report." Browne seems also to have been the first scholar to suggest making an actual dig to recover antiquities and learn the purpose of the monuments that contained them, rather than simply examining objects that had been disinterred inadvertently (Mendyk 1989: 159). Yet Browne did not act on his own suggestion, preferring speculative meditation to systematic empirical investigation. A country physician with a passion for antiquities, he may well have inaugurated the antiquarian persona of the local amateur as provincial eccentric.

Browne's slender treatise on the urns recovered in his native Norfolk testifies to the increasingly local focus of antiquarian scholarship in the seventeenth century and to its consequent marginalization as a branch of historiography. Although it points the way to the early development of archaeology in some respects, *Urn-Burial* also evokes earlier descriptive projects of English nationalism. The second chapter in particular, which focuses on the urns themselves, invokes all the topoi of investigations of native origins in the late sixteenth and early seventeenth centuries. Browne relies on the authority of Julius Caesar and other Roman sources, developing faulty etymologies of place names, lamenting the absence of ancient maps and the paucity of native artefacts, and locating his reconstruction of the urns' purpose within an account of Boadicea's revolt and the history of the Iceni in Norfolk. His relation of historical detail is curiously muted, however, and as he moves beyond the immediate examination of the urns, the antiquarian topoi become increasingly incidental to his broader meditation on death and human attempts to transcend it. The period of British antiquity that had so exercised earlier nationalist historians, with their need to recover native origins and to accommodate them to early modern principles of civility, is merely an established chronology in *Urn-Burial*, a documented historical framework in which Browne can situate his loftier reflections on universal human needs and practices.

In his last chapter, Browne adopts a spiritual perspective that reduces the recovery of the ancient past to an investigation of trivialities. Dismissing his initial approach to the urns, he articulates his new understanding of their significance as "a question above antiquarism, not to be resolved by man" (1972: 127). Indeed, Browne's concluding chapter is reminiscent of medieval retractions, taking the form of a pious renunciation of antiquarianism in favor of the timeless universality of God. Yet even as Browne renounces the investigation of antiquities that animated earlier projects of English nationalism, he pays tribute to their heroic magnitude by investing their remains in an antiquarian vision of God. Throughout his antiquarian-treatise-*cum*-spiritual-meditation, Browne acknowledges God as the divine originator of all antiquities. The eternal nature of this antiquary-God dwarfs the combined heroism of antiquity and the early modern nationalists who sought to recover it. In the dedication to Thomas Le Gros, Browne evokes a heroic age "when even living men were antiquities," urging his friend to fix his thoughts "upon the ancient of days, the antiquary's truest object, unto whom the eldest parcels are young, and earth itself an infant" (92). Browne's prefatory reference to the creation of the earth and living men as antiquities has its apocalyptic complement in his closing meditation on the Day of Judgment in Chapter 5. There, his antiquary-God effects the last disinterment and classification of creation, "when men shall wish the covering of mountains, not of monuments" (132).

Even as he renounces the worldly focus of the great early modern projects of national recovery, Browne articulates the cosmic drama of Christian history in their antiquarian terms. Christian cosmology was implicit in some of the earlier projects also, particularly (as in Browne's case) at difficult moments of closure. When Michael Drayton finally came to the end of England and *Poly-Olbion*, having abandoned his original plan to sing the glories of the whole island of Great Britain, he also abandoned his chorographical principles of empirical description. The major feature of Drayton's concluding "Song" was the northern river "Eden," a small river of no real topographical importance. Beginning and ending the Thirtieth Song with Eden, the Muse announces her attention to return to the river at the end of the poem with the words, "At *Eden* now arriv'd, whom we have left too long" (1933: 30.265). The implied return to a Christian paradise is made explicit in the Muse's first address to the river: "O my bright lovely Brooke, whose name doth beare the sound / Of Gods first Garden-plot, th'imparadized ground" (30.69–70).

Drayton's concluding turn to a spiritual topography of paradise signifies the collapse of his nationalist project in several ways. First, it abandons the chorographical principle of grounding national identity on the empirical description of native topography. Drayton marked the end of both the poem and England at the place where Eden meets the Scottish river Eske, and both fall into the sea: "Where I this *Canto* end, as also therewithall / My *England* doe conclude" (340–1). In striking contrast to the self-contained national icon of Elizabeth's virgin body, Drayton's England falls into a fluid mingling across its northern border at the conclusion of *Poly-Olbion*. The celebration of Eden also signifies a return to the symbolic landscape of medieval topographies like the *mappaemundi* or the stage plan for *The Castle of Perseverance*. The whole significance of the last river in Drayton's chorographical epic lies in its name and paradisal connotations, rather than in its topographical situation or its historical associations. Ending the poem with this emphasis on the river Eden, Drayton shifts his nationalist focus to a spiritual context that was both ahistorical and atopical. Song 30 begins with an invocation of God, the only such reference in a poem that celebrates the pantheistic world of nature deities (2–3). The treatment of Eden is the only other evocation of Christianity in the poem, and yet it constitutes Drayton's final attempt to fix the bounds of the nation. The protracted labor of delineating a topographical icon of the nation in *Poly-Olbion* thus collapses ultimately into a spiritual topography reminiscent of medieval *mappaemundi* and allegorical drama.

Drayton's chorographical epic looks forward to a greater poem that more famously collapses external place into the spiritualized heart. *Paradise Lost*, composed among other reasons as a substitute for Milton's projected epic of British history, also ends with the celebration of a new, spiritualized Eden in the famous formulation, "A paradise within thee, happier far" (1978: 12.587). Yet Milton did not return to a medieval spiritual topography in *Paradise Lost*. His opening description of Paradise in Book 4 testifies to the transformation of Christian universalism by more than a hundred years of English topographical nationalism:

> delicious Paradise,
> Now nearer, Crowns with her enclosure green,
> As with a rural mound the champaign head
> Of a steep wilderness, whose hairy sides
> With thicket overgrown, grotesque and wild,
> Access deni'd.
>
> (132–8)

The "champains riched" and "wide-skirted meads" of Goneril's portion return here, figuring the approach to Paradise in the language and imagery of English chorographical description. The swift transformation of this pleasant landscape into a grotesque wilderness "whose hairy sides […] grotesque and wild, / Access deni'd" testifies to persistent English anxiety about the untransmutable savagery of native topography and origins, particularly in the implications of an inescapable and terrifying femininity in the graphic image of hairy sides at the entrance to Paradise. The same concerns of gender, savagery and origins that animated earlier nationalist projects inform this first description of Paradise in Milton's belated epic, despite the poem's Christian universalism.

The English literary topography that testifies most strongly to the transformation of the national psyche by earlier nationalist projects is *Pilgrim's Progress*. Like the spiritual allegorists of medieval Europe, Bunyan portrays the progress of the soul through a metaphorical landscape on its way to salvation. In place of cosmic representations of Hell, Purgatory, and Heaven, however, he describes a journey through a peculiarly English landscape. *Pilgrim's Progress* nationalizes the Christian symbolism of metaphors such as the Valley of the Shadow of Death or the Strait Gate, embedding them in a local topography replete with the English detail of sloughs, meadows, walls, castles, and hills. Bunyan's ability to locate such insignificant features in a larger spiritual topography parallels the work of mid-seventeenth-century antiquarians such as Dugdale, who mapped the individual hundreds of their counties so that every detail of local topography might figure in a composite vision of the nation. The detailed evocation of the English countryside in *Pilgrim's Progress* would not have been possible before the development of English topographical nationalism, nor would it have been intelligible to a reading public that had not already internalized a chorographical vision of the nation. More than a century after English topography began to be mapped and celebrated in the construction of national identity, Bunyan allegorized local topography as a vehicle for the attainment of individual identity and spiritual transformation in *Pilgrim's Progress*. In his cosmic allegory of the English landscape, Bunyan exploited the earlier corporate icons of English nationalism to forge the individualist English spirituality of post-Restoration dissenting Protestantism.

Although national topography had by Bunyan's time lost its pre-eminence in the articulation of the state, it had acquired an even more significant role in the shaping of English national consciousness. Bunyan's transcendent allegory of local English topography, like Browne's antiquary-God and Milton's English Paradise, manifests a new English ability to reconceive the cosmic in terms of a national identity that had become so naturalized as to seem universal. Where earlier nationalists had labored to transform the barbarism of native origins by integrating Britain and its history into the larger world of Roman civility, the English of the late seventeenth century were already consolidating the foundations of an empire that would assert (and impose) English national consciousness as universally normative. The importance of early modern projects of national recovery in developing this consciousness is evident in the cosmic rearticulation of their nationalist topoi in contemporary works of English literature. Rather than abandoning the concerns of earlier English nationalism, *Urn-Burial*, *Paradise Lost*, and *Pilgrim's Progress* effectively embed a nationalist vision in their universalist meditations on the human spirit. The problems of gender, nature, and savagery encountered during the recovery of native origins in the late sixteenth and early seventeenth centuries leave their mark on universalized English nationalism, as in the "hairy sides [...] grotesque and wild" that deny access to Milton's English Paradise. Through the enduring influence of works such as *Paradise Lost*, Boadicea's legacy to early modern English nationalism continues to shape concepts of individual, national, and spiritual identity.

NOTES

INTRODUCTION

1 The epigraphs are taken from Greenfeld 1992: 23 and Anderson 1992: 205. For their respective theoretical positions, see Greenfeld 17–21 and Anderson 1–7. Anderson's preface to the second edition provides a useful summary (c.1991) of the 1980s transformation of the study of nationalism and the ironies of the impending world political transformations of the early 1990s.

2 Like the general terminology of nationhood, the specific terms "Britain," "British," and "Britons" – as well as their sometimes elided components "England" and "English" – have also received scrutiny from a wide range of historical, socio-political, and cultural critics (see especially Colley 1992; Samuel 1989; Nairn 1977, rev. 1981; and Pocock 1975). It is indeed *England* and *English* national identity that I explore in this period. English conceptions of Wales, Scotland, and Ireland, their inhabitants and their histories, are important in this discussion, but they function precisely as *English* conceptions. Unless otherwise noted, the terms "Britain," "British," and "Britons" refer to the antiquity of the island and its inhabitants as named by the Romans, rather than to a modern nation or national identity shared by the English, Welsh, Scots, and (some) Irish. To the extent that the English of the early modern period acknowledged any such shared identity, it was in reference to a common point of origins that led them to see Wales as the last refuge of the ancient Britons, to welcome a Scottish king as the first monarch to reign over the whole island of Britain since a legendary antiquity, and to guard against any return to primitive savagery from their contact with the Irish. Their nation was the English nation, and their attempts to articulate political and symbolic relations to the other British peoples were shaped by the complexities of their own national definitions and representations.

3 For Renaissance Italian antiquarianism, see especially Burke 1969; D'Amico 1984; Mandowsky and Mitchell 1963; Mazzocco 1975 and 1977; Mitchell 1960; Momigliano 1950; and Weiss 1969.

4 For Polydore Vergil's revisionist *Anglica Historia* and its reception in sixteenth-century England, see Gransden 1982: 425–43. MacDougall 1982: 7–27 traces the cultural influence of Geoffrey's *Historia Regum Britanniae* through the eighteenth century, but acknowledges its loss of authority among historians by the late sixteenth century. For English antiquarianism in the sixteenth and seventeenth centuries, see especially: Ferguson 1979 and 1993: 84–105;

Gransden 1980; Helgerson 1992: 1–62, 105–48; Levine 1987: 73–106; Levy 1964, 1965, and 1967: 124–66; Piggott 1956 and 1989: 7–35, 87–122; Kevin Sharpe 1979 and 1989; van Norden 1946; and Woolf 1987 and 1990.

5 I draw here on Stephen Greenblatt's use of "prehistory" in his essay, "Psychoanalysis and Renaissance Culture," where he articulates modern psychoanalysis's quest for the individual as "the historical outcome of certain characteristic Renaissance strategies" (1986: 224).

6 I share Claire McEachern's caution about ascribing to early modern England a "'proto' or 'emergent' form of some later, fully achieved nationhood"(1996: 5–6). I am less concerned to evaluate the developmental stage of the early modern English nation than I am to explore the difficulties it had in defining itself historically in relation to its native origins. As McEachern writes, "A grasp of its own temporal location is a self-conscious constituent of Tudor–Stuart national imaginings"(1996: 33).

7 The most notorious celebration of Elizabethan England in this regard is A. L. Rowse's "The Elizabethan Discovery of England" (1950: 31–65); Kendrick's *British Antiquity*, also published in the early post-war era, gives a more judicious account of medieval and Renaissance attitudes to his subject, including the important observation that late sixteenth-century illustrations of ancient Britons in antiquarian texts were modelled on drawings of native Americans (1950: 116–17, 123–5).

8 "The meaning of 'nation' is often unmistakably political. While the use of the word in relation to communities of kin and language could come from the Latin version of the Bible, its consistent application to polities, territory, and peoples (which makes of these distinct concepts synonyms) is, clearly, a peculiarity of the English translation" (Greenfeld 1992: 53).

9 *De l'esprit des lois*, quoted in Zernatto 1944: 361. Zernatto also cites Schopenhauer in this regard.

10 Bacon's full description of "antiquities" offers a good working definition of the practice and materials of Renaissance antiquarianism, as well as some of its frustrations in early modern England:

> Antiquities are the wrecks of history, wherein the memory of things is almost lost; or such particulars as industrious persons, with exact and scrupulous diligence, can any way collect from genealogies, calendars, titles, inscriptions, monuments, coins, names, etymologies, proverbs, traditions, archives, instruments, fragments of public and private history, scattered passages of books no way historical, etc.; by which means something is recovered from the deluge of time. This is a laborious work; yet acceptable to mankind, as carrying with it a kind of reverential awe, and deserves to come in the place of those fabulous and fictitious origins of nations we abound with; though it has the less authority, as but few have examined and exercised a liberty of thought about it.
>
> (53)

11 By the end of the seventeenth century, the same imagery was invoked in reference to England's ruined monasteries, as in John Aubrey's lament for the great religious houses of Wiltshire: "These Remaynes are 'tanquam tabulata naufragii' (*like fragments of a Shipwreck*) that after the Revolution of

so many yeares and governments have escaped the teeth of Time and the hands of mistaken zeale" (cited in Aston 1984: 333 from *Topographical Collections of Wiltshire*, left unfinished at Aubrey's death in 1697).

12 The antiquarian John Selden also upheld the Roman invaders' priority as the earliest reliable historical sources for British antiquity: "untill *Caesars Commentaries*, no piece of [Britain's] description was known, that is now left to posterity. For time therefore preceding *Caesar*, I dare trust none; but with Others adhere to *Conjecture*. In Ancient matter since, I relie on *Tacitus* and *Dio* especially" (Drayton 1933: x).

13 "*Britanniam qui mortales initio coluerint, indigenae an advecti, ut inter barbaros parum compertum.*"

14 For the place of Caesar's *Gallic War* in the grammar school curriculum and its antecedents see Baldwin 1944: 130–3, 272–88; and Nicholas Orme 1989: 271–90. I am grateful to Coppélia Kahn for suggesting this connection between the learning of Latin and the revelation of savage origins in early modern England. Helgerson also notes that "the Roman sense of Britain – *ultima Britannia*, they called it – as far removed from the center of civilization contributed significantly to English self-alienation in the sixteenth century" (1992: 308).

15 Anderson elaborates his discussion of "last wave" nationalism in one of the chapters added to the second edition of *Imagined Communities*, "Census, Map, Museum" (1992: 163–87). For the early modern English tendency to attribute monumental remains to the Romans, see especially Nearing's articles and Piggott 1956 and 1989: 102–4.

16 Holinshed's version of this prayer downplays potential claims to absolute female sovereignty by Boadicea, whose address to Adraste in the original Greek of his classical source is more properly rendered as "I thank thee [...] as woman speaking to woman," and whose ascription of government over the Britons is to herself rather than the goddess (Cassius 1925: LXII.6.2–3).

17 The addition of the nursing twins beneath the Capitoline Wolf is a case in point. It is now generally agreed that the Capitoline Wolf did not have twins in its antique state, as it faces forward, and the twins are generally only included when the wolf turns her head back toward them in other antique representations. Renaissance artists not only modified this icon of the Roman founding by adding casts of the twins to the Capitoline installation, but they also turned the she-wolf's head toward her nurslings in most two- and three-dimensional images of the trio (Bober and Rubinstein 1986: 218).

18 Other classical associations of nursing mothers with native origins were also recovered in the Italian Renaissance. Chief among these was Tellus, or Terra Mater, the divine image of the earth mother with her children playing about her. Adapted in medieval art as a *mater nutrix*, this figure became a common image of the native soil as a nursing mother in the Renaissance. Like the she-wolf, this figure of native maternal nurture was carefully subordinated to male figures of imperial dominion, thus symbolizing masculine control over the earth rather than female sovereignty (Strong 1937).

19 A set of celebratory verses opens by ascribing precisely this role to the ancient queen: "How much of Britain are we bound to thee / Mother and Nurse of magnanimity?" (Heywood 1640: 68). The poem is unusual for the period in its sustained praise for Boadicea's conduct and leadership of the uprising,

commending also the "masculine spirit" that led her to conspire "Against the Roman Monarchy" (1640: 68).

1 From mater terra to the artificial man

1 Morgan (1979: 151–2) notes the connection between Sir Henry Lee, Elizabeth's host at Ditchley Park on the 1592 visit the portrait commemorates, and the Sheldon family of Warwickshire, whose tapestry manufactory was producing images based on Saxton's maps at the time. Roy Strong describes the occasion of the portrait (1977: 151–6).

2 Historians of early modern England have enumerated various kinds of change – social, political, agrarian, economic – and developed various theories of gradual change, cumulative crises, overriding continuity or a crisis of order, to explain or deny a perceived revolution in the seventeenth century. The "Whig" position explicitly invoked by Helgerson has been challenged by two quite different groups of historians: (1) social historians, who argue against the narrowness of the Whig focus on the gentry and the reductive equation of Parliamentary support with "the people" and Royalist support with the aristocracy (e.g., Underdown 1987); and (2) the so-called "revisionists," or administrative historians, who argue against any significant social or administrative upheaval in the period, and regard the civil wars as largely the result of personal error and idiosyncrasy at the level of the aristocracy, or just another example of the internecine strife that had punctuated English history for centuries (e.g., Russell 1989).

3 Roy Strong emphasizes the interchangeability of the queen and the nation in his account of the Ditchley portrait (1987: 134–41).

4 Pastoureau 1984: 81–3. Of the atlas's iconographic purpose, Pastoureau writes: "Bouguereau voulut même que son atlas fût le symbole de l'unité nationale et l'«image» d'un royaume dans lequel toutes les provinces seraient dévouées à leur souverain."

5 Bibliographical references to this edition describe this page with the portrait above the sonnet, suggesting that its addition was standard and intended by Bouguereau. The map beneath it seems not before to have been uncovered or documented.

6 An earlier French example also suggests the importance of gender in topographical figures of the nation. Frances A. Yates describes a decoration for the entry of Charles IX into Paris in 1571, in which a figure representing the Queen Mother, Catherine de Medici, holds a map of GALLIA over her head. Comparing a drawing of this figure to the "Ditchley" portrait, Yates claims that Catherine and Elizabeth function similarly as royal religious symbols in conjunction with national maps (1975a: 133–5, fig. 20c). Natalie Zemon Davis also notes this figure of Catherine de Medici in her discussion of the "gender styles" adopted by Elizabeth I, Catherine, and Anne of England (1993: 170–3).

7 Helgerson glances briefly at gender in the afterword to *Forms of Nationhood* (1992: 295–301). Claire McEachern places it more centrally in *The Poetics of English Nationhood, 1590–1612*, emphasizing "the *absolutely fundamental quality of gender to national identity in this period*. The figure of our country as 'she' is a commonplace of national affect: it connotes filial and romantic love and solicits loyalty and protection, as well as betrayal. For the

Tudor–Stuart nation, it expresses the titillative simultaneity of difference and resemblance necessary to nationhood; the volatile contours of female figurality draw the permeable borders of the domestic" (1996: 29).

8 For Drayton's thirty-year composition of *Poly-Olbion* and his engagement with other historicist and topographical projects of national representation, see esp. Moore 1968; Hardin 1973; and Gourvitch 1930.

9 See especially the portrait of Elizabeth by Crispin van de Passe (1596), where she stands between imperial pillars holding a sword and an orb, against a similar background of the sea with ships. Roy Strong discusses this portrait as an example of Elizabethan imperialism (1973: 114–15).

10 In her reading of the interplay between Drayton's verses and John Selden's scholarly "Illustrations" to *Poly-Olbion*, Anne Lake Prescott also comments on the gendering of Drayton's landscape, reading into the poem's multiple voices and diffuse authorities a political resistance to Jacobean absolutism (1991: 307–28).

11 Much work on *Poly-Olbion* reads the emphasis on marriage as a celebration of political harmony, particularly the Jacobean union of England and Scotland under one crown. See esp. Revard 1977; Hilda Taylor 1926; and McEachern 1996: 138–91.

12 Hole's maps include features only briefly mentioned (and sometimes not), as well as those whose personifications are developed in the poem. Even maps that include large and detailed masculine personifications (e.g., Neptune in the map to Song 4; Goodwin Sands in the map of Kent [Song 18]; the ditches of Cambridgeshire and Newmarket Heath in the map to Song 21) are still numerically dominated by feminine figures. In the Warwickshire map, the Edge Hills, which in accordance with the poet's general practice for hills might have been represented as masculine, are simply drawn as hills, without any personification. Rolritch Stones receive this same impersonal representation. Dunsmore Heath and Newnham Well, however, which are not mentioned in the text, are both personified as female, on a slightly smaller scale than Arden, Redhorse, and the towns.

13 See esp. Hall 1995, chs 2 and 3; Jones and Stallybrass 1992; Montrose 1991; and Patricia Parker 1987: 126–54.

14 See esp. McEachern 1996: 129–37; Woodbridge 1991: 336–42; Montrose 1991: 7–14, 28–9; and Marcus 1990: 51–105.

15 Goldberg notes that the landscape against which females were painted was nevertheless often an ordered one, as in a formal garden, signifying patriarchal control over the land and the masculine ability to shape nature into property, even as the dominance of the *pater familias* in the portrait suggests his control over the women of the family. See also his earlier book-length study, *James I and the Politics of Literature* (1983: 85–112).

16 Roy Strong discusses the antiquarian recovery of this female personification from Roman British coins, and how engravers like Hole drew on it in illustrating *Poly-Olbion* and more scholarly texts like Camden's *Britannia* (Strong 1980: 28–32). See also Corbett and Lightbown 1979: 153–61 and Gourvitch 1930.

17 James's own *Works*, first published in 1616, uses the same format of triumphal arch flanked by allegorical figures. As in Speed's *Theatre*, however, the central space contains no figure, but rather the title and names of author and publisher. Raleigh's *History of the World*, published in 1614, preserves the

central female figure of the Saxton atlas and *Poly-Olbion*. In this case, she is the personification of *Magistra Vitae*, standing in the central niche of the pillared house of fame, flanked by female personifications of experience and truth, and supporting a cartographical globe above her head. Here too, then, the connection between the mapped world and the female body is illustrated. For descriptions of both these title pages, see Corbett and Lightbown 1979: 137–44; 129–36.

18 Sarah E. Wall has pointed out to me that the plane on which the title is printed appears to be suspended from a hook, suggesting a screened rather than an empty stage. This title screen is reminiscent of the glued-on portrait bust of Henri II that covers the map of France in Bouguereau's *Théâtre François*. Unlike the portrait of Henri, however, Speed's title cannot be lifted by the reader.

19 See Corbett and Lightbown 1979: 213–30 for a detailed description of the *Leviathan*'s title page. Keith Brown gives the fullest account of the development of this engraving from original drawings by Hobbes, one of which survives in the manuscript copy Hobbes presented to Charles II (Brown 1978). In Hobbes's own drawing (Brown: fig. 2), the arms and torso of the sovereign are made up of individual heads, rather than bodies. This multitude of heads and faces on the Leviathan's upper body recalls the tattooed heads of beasts and devils conventionally depicted on the chest, shoulders and other joints of ancient Britons, Scots and Picts in early modern engravings, and notably on the right shoulder of the ancient Briton who surmounts the title page of Speed's *Theatre* (fig. 7).

20 Vulgate, 41:24a; Authorized Version, 41:33a: "Upon earth there is not his like."

21 Deborah Baumgold argues that representation is merely a synonym for the sovereign in the *Leviathan*, a necessary analytic feature in the constitution of sovereign authority (1988: 38–46).

22 As with his articulation of the state of nature, Hobbes's concept of representation has been accorded foundational importance in the development of modern political theory. Although Hobbes derives his concept of representation from theatrical personation in Chapter 16 of the *Leviathan*, Hanna Fenichel Pitkin argues that he insists on a political rather than an aesthetic context for the term. For her account of Hobbes as the first representation theorist, see *Concept of Representation* (1967: 14–37). Christopher Pye argues against the inscription of Hobbes as the first fully modern political theorist by emphasizing the continuity of quasi-mystical or magical concepts of representation that inform Hobbes's theatrical analogy and are implicit throughout the *Leviathan* (1984: 84–106).

23 Stillman highlights "a peculiar doubleness in Hobbes's philosophy, the creation of the *Leviathan* as a monster text to do battle against the monsters of history – as a text whose doubleness consists, that is, in its reliance upon metaphor to constitute its crucial arguments, and in its warfare against metaphor as an abuse of language and thought" (1995: 793).

24 Stillman notes the *Leviathan*'s dependence on historical realization: "Only at the moment that the sovereign in the text becomes a sovereign in the world, when the figural becomes literal, does linguistic chaos and the political chaos it spawns in society come to a close. […] The historical Leviathan erases the metaphorical" (1995: 812).

25 In citing the authority of Deuteronomy at the end of this paragraph, Hobbes uses the scriptural locution "to assemble the people, man, woman, and child" (319).

26 Amy Louise Erickson re-evaluates Clark's evidence for the deterioration of the relative status of women in the seventeenth century in her introduction to the most recent edition of Clark's classic *Working Life of Women in the Seventeenth Century* (1992). Although Clark's chronology of economic change has generally been pushed forward into the eighteenth and early nineteenth centuries, many of her specific examples of decline in the relative status of women over the seventeenth century have been upheld by subsequent research, from the loss of common land and grazing rights, to the displacement of women from the brewing trade and a general decline in girls' apprenticeship to trades and agriculture (Erickson: 1992: xxii–xxxiv). Erickson's own study of property law and women's experience of inheritance, marriage, and widowhood in early modern England confirms the trajectory posited by Clark, although Erickson extends its arc to run from the fourteenth through the eighteenth centuries. In particular, she emphasizes the "rationalization" of the law between 1300 and 1800, a process that "had deleterious effects for the economic security of daughters, wives and widows." Rejecting the idea of a medieval "golden age" for women, Erickson describes the deterioration of women's economic position in terms of a restrictive system that tightened further in the early modern period. Pointing to statutory changes in the late seventeenth century that diminished women's already limited entitlements to property, she claims that their "ostensible purpose was to secure the exclusive control of the male head of household over his – that is, the family's – property" (Erickson 1993: 6). Susan Amussen's work on Locke supports Clark's vision of a shift from families to individuals in understandings of the state. Amussen stresses that Locke was able to define the family as private in the early eighteenth century because it had already ceased to be of public concern after the Restoration, when local authorities no longer felt the need to regulate familial relations in order to maintain the social order (1985, 1988: 182–9).

27 See especially the first two chapters of *The Sexual Contract*, "Contracting In," and "Patriarchal Confusions"(1988b: 1–38).

28 Filmer's *Patriarcha* is the major English treatise of seventeenth-century patriarchalism. Locke's *Second Treatise of Government*, explicitly directed against Filmer, was probably written in 1679–80, with some revision over the ensuing decade. For the issues in dating both these texts, see Filmer (1991: vii–viii, xxxii–xxxiv) and Locke (1993: 55–66, 123–6).

29 Stillman asserts that "Hobbes's sense of his place in cultural history is key to understanding the character and contradictions of *Leviathan*" (1995: 791), later locating the composition of that text in "the transformative era of seventeenth-century Europe in its passage from millennial fervor to enlightenment philosophy" (797). My own positioning of Hobbes emphasizes his crucial and self-conscious role in the masculinization of the state and political representation in mid-seventeenth-century England.

30 Deborah Kuller Shuger recognizes the importance of the *Leviathan* in articulating a cultural ideal of patriarchy in the seventeenth century, particularly with regard to fear as a means of holding the individual's desire for domination in check. Although she does not consistently distinguish the

two senses of patriarchalism, Shuger does develop a rich account of how the *Leviathan* figured in the positive and negative ideals of patriarchal love and coercion that informed seventeenth-century political thought (Shuger 1990: 239–49).

31 Stillman notes that contemporary responses to the *Leviathan* emphasized its metaphorical language (1995: 794–6). In addition to other literary studies by Pye 1984, Silver 1988, and Victoria Kahn 1985: 152–81, see also the following political studies of Hobbes's use of metaphor: Johnston 1986: esp. 66–91; Pocock 1971: 148–201; Skinner 1996: esp. 181–211; and Wolin 1970 and 1960: 239–85, esp. 244–62.

32 This latter instance is possibly the only occasion when Hobbes uses a feminine analogy for the work of a (presumably) masculine member of the state. Deploring the vulgar tendency to credit individuals rather than science itself for inventions, he likens the "Artificer" to "(the Midwife passing with the vulgar for the Mother)." As in the maternal analogies for matter and need, this mother/midwife reference appears in parentheses.

33 Hobbes first personifies nature in his early chapter "Of Speech:" "Nature it selfe cannot erre" (1.4.106). The intellectual virtues and their defects catalogued and defined in Chapter 8 are similarly ungendered (1.8.134–47).

34 Prudence appears in Ripa's *Iconologia* as a helmeted woman holding a caduceus in her right hand and a hand mirror, in which she beholds the reflection of her own face, in the other. Suggesting Amphitrite in this last detail, and generally conforming to Elizabethan and Jacobean conventions of feminine personification in the display of breasts and hips through her draped garment, she recalls early modern depictions of a martial Britannia or Great Britain (Ripa 1976: 441–3).

35 When Hobbes returns to the subject of Prudence in his chapters on Reason and Science and the intellectual virtues and their defects, he again surrounds the term with masculine pronouns, subordinating it within the thoughts and observation of a representative man (1.5.117; 1.8.137–8). In his chapter, "Of Religion," he names this representative man "*Prometheus*, (which interpreted, is, *The prudent man*,)" as he elaborates the defect of this virtue: "So that every man, especially those that are over provident, are in an estate like to that of *Prometheus*" (1.12.169).

36 "[W]hat woman having ten pieces of silver, if she lose one piece, doth not light a candle, and sweep the house, and seek diligently till she find it?" (Luke 15:8, King James, or Authorized Version).

37 Twenty-five years after the publication of *Leviathan*, John Bunyan used a similar analogy in *Pilgrim's Progress* to develop one of the series of allegorical scenes in the House of the Interpreter. Although Bunyan's sweeper is a man, the intervention of a damsel to sprinkle water on the dust before it can be swept is crucial to the allegory (1987: 73–4). Many feminine personifications figure in the extended allegory of *Pilgrim's Progress*, including that of Prudence, one of the damsels with whom Christian converses in Castle Beautiful (92–5).

38 Women also appear occasionally in association with children, either as comparably deficient beings or as caregivers. Hobbes notes in his discussion of Reason and Science that women make children believe "that their brothers and sisters are not born, but found in the garden" (1.5.116). In his chapter on the passions, he designates women and children together as most subject

to sudden dejection and weeping (1.6.125–6). In both cases, women are invoked in passing only as examples of beliefs or behaviors that resist the establishment of the commonwealth. Women also figure briefly with "strangers" as likely to be impressed by men's appearance or "Forme" (1.9.151); as wives in a list of those who cannot accuse a man under the law (1.14.199); among creatures (male, female, animal, and vegetable) susceptible to deification by gentiles; and among the various parental combinations producing monsters (1.12.173, 175).

39 Susan Moller Okin cites this passage to demonstrate how Hobbes's insistence on radical individualism leads him to include women in his argument for equality in the state of nature, an equality based on the equal ability to kill. She notes that Hobbes's assumptions about the necessity for male dominance led him to fall back on the patriarchal family, rather than the individual, as the smallest unit of government, thus refusing the logic of his own atomistic individualism (1979: 197–9).

40 Natalie Zemon Davis comments on Hobbes's willingness in this chapter to conceive of the possibility of matriarchal dominion in the state of nature, and his use of the historical example of the Amazons (1975: 143–4). While I put greater emphasis on the qualification of these invocations of female sovereignty, I do agree that their exceptional place in the *Leviathan* merits notice.

41 For a range of philosophical responses to Hobbes's seeming inconsistency about the place of the family in the state of nature, and the role of maternal dominion in particular, see Schochet 1975: 227–33.

42 J. P. Sommerville notes the possibility of a female sovereign in Filmer's patriarchal theory in his introduction to *Patriarcha* (Filmer 1991: xxi). Filmer's long review of legal precedent to establish the king's authority as independent of parliament in Chapter 3 includes frequent references to women (and children). He develops extended feminine personifications of republican and imperial Rome (25–9), and generally displays a lively sense of women's active if subordinate presence within the nation. Margaret Ezell notes the attention to and respect for women in Filmer's unpublished domestic and theological tracts, where he defines womanly virtue in terms of courage and strength rather than chastity, and accords the wife considerable rights as well as responsibilities in marriage (1987: 130–40).

43 Hobbes's only reference to women in the chapter where he defines the Church and its membership is to cite (in demonstration of an unrelated point about the meaning of *ecclesia*) the Pauline injunction of womanly silence therein (3.39.496). He refers briefly to Eve and the hypothetical woman who had married many brothers in his discussion of eternal life (3.38.481), and invokes Christ's raising of Jairus's daughter as a model for the healing office of the Sovereign (3.42.573). Two passing references to matrons and wives (3.42.565, 590) complete the meager roster of women in Hobbes's description of a Christian commonwealth.

44 Hobbes dismisses the woman of Endor's claims to prophetic power as follows: "The woman of Endor, who is said to have had a familiar spirit, and thereby to have raised a Phantasme of Samuel, and foretold Saul his death, was not therefore a Prophetesse; for neither had she any science, whereby she could raise such a Phantasme; nor does it appear that God commanded the raising of it; but onely guided that Imposture to be a means of Sauls terror and

discouragement; and by consequent, of the discomfiture, by which he fell" (3.36.458). In an earlier chapter, "Of Religion," Hobbes dismisses "the leaves of the Sibills" along with other examples of pagan superstition (1.12.175–6).

45 Mack notes that the language of dissenting women prophets was less emotional, "pretentious," and unbalanced than that of their male counterparts. She finds women prophets less likely to insist on their absolute freedom to separate from the family, to travel, and to preach – all activities (particularly the last) that Hobbes denounces in self-styled prophets (1992: 4–5).

46 In addition to Natalie Zemon Davis's classic essay, "Women on Top," (1975: 124–51), see Jankowski 1992: 54–76; Rackin 1990: 146–200; and Jordan 1987.

47 Stillman notes that "Hobbes repeatedly connects the mid-century's cultural discord with linguistic discord" (1995: 798), arguing that "Rhetorical inflation of diction […] is always a sign in Hobbes of pressing political anxieties" (802).

48 Hobbes uses the phrase "old wives tales" to express his contempt for pagan or Roman Catholic superstitions ranging from "the Daemonology of the Heathen Poets" (4.44.628–9) to "the Errors from Tradition" (4.46.702) to "the *Kingdome of Fairies*; that is, to the old wives *Fables* in England" (4.47.712–15).

49 See also Silver's conclusions about the sacrifice of linguistic subtlety and resonance in favor of rigorous intelligibility in Hobbes's discourse (1988: 371).

50 Hobbes generally invokes only classical or biblical figures in the *Leviathan*. Henry VIII and Elizabeth I are the only two named figures from recent history.

51 Margaret Spufford, in her survey of Samuel Pepys's vast collection of popular chapbooks, notes the high percentage of historical fiction, in which the English of the period seem to have had an even greater interest than their French contemporaries. The favorite figures in these stories are kings, particularly Henry VIII; Elizabeth does not appear except as an adjunct to a long story about Drake's explorations (1981: 219–25).

52 I am grateful to Mary B. Campbell for introducing me to Cavendish's work, and for orienting me in that intellectual cosmology with her talk, "Other World, Inner World, *Blazing-World*; or, What the Microscope Missed," Harvard Center for Literary and Cultural Studies, 29 February 1996.

53 Cavendish contrasts the absolute monarchy of the Blazing World with her own world, which she castigates in Hobbesian terms for its divided government: "wherein are more sovereigns than worlds, and more pretended governors than governments" (1992: 201).

54 For Hobbes's relations to the Cavendish family, and his philosophical influence on Margaret Cavendish in particular, see Grant (1957: 88–95) and Kathleen Jones (1988: 60–1, 85). For an illuminating account of the intellectual links between Cavendish's (proto)feminism and her absolutism, see Gallagher (1988).

55 Cavendish uses this phrase twice to describe the Empress in this episode (1992: 211, 215), echoing Genesis 1:2b "And the Spirit of God moved upon the face of the waters" (King James, or Authorized Version). In her further ability "to walk upon the waters," the Empress also demonstrates a likeness to Christ. If one takes her imperial robes and the power to destroy whatever she pleases as allusions to the majesty of god the father, the

Empress combines attributes of all three persons of the Christian trinity in this passage.

56 Hobbes explicitly acknowledges the mortality of his Leviathan when he glosses his adoption of the term from *Job* (2.29.362–3).

57 A striking contemporary example is Milton's confused description of the Holy Spirit as both "brooding on the vast Abyss" and making it pregnant in the invocation to Book 1 of *Paradise Lost* (1978: 19–22).

58 James Fitzmaurice (1990) notes that any one of three different frontispieces can be found in any of Cavendish's books. He argues that Cavendish herself conceived of these self-characterizations, representing herself in the frontispiece described above as a solitary genius.

59 Translated and quoted in Yates (1975a: 85–6) from Giordano Bruno, *La Cena de le Ceneri* (1584).

60 For a description of this portrait, and the tradition of giving Elizabeth jewelled ornaments in the shape of a rainbow, see Strong (1987: 156–61).

61 See Frye 1992 for a re-evaluation of this tradition. The tradition of Elizabeth's armored oration at Tilbury has its strongest analogue in the Empress's own address to her troops before a naval battle in Part 2 of *The Blazing World* (1992: 210). Again, she appears in seeming "garments of light, like an angel, or some deity," recalling Astraea descending on the rainbow as her military scientists illumine both the air above her and water below with their pyrotechnics (210). Armed for battle with buckler and spear, a half-moon of "star-stone" on her forehead, she directs her warriors "to effect her design" of firing the enemy ships with "fire-stone." The several navies of her enemies destroyed in this fashion, the Empress is hailed by her own people as "an angel sent from God to deliver them out of the hands of their enemies" (211). The parallels to the English defeat of the Spanish Armada in 1588 are striking here, from the firing of the ships to the Empress's pre-battle oration and subsequent veneration as a figure of divine deliverance. The pyrotechnics also recall the lightning in the background of the Ditchley portrait, and the Empress's oceanic dominion is comparable to the imperial claims of the "Armada" portrait of Elizabeth.

62 Copies and images derived from Elizabeth's portraits were widely disseminated in published materials in the seventeenth century. Cavendish also had family connections to Elizabeth, her grandfather having entertained the queen at the family seat of St John's Abbey in 1579, and her aunt having served as a lady-in-waiting to Elizabeth before her marriage (Grant 1957: 29).

63 "Of the statesmen she enquired, first, why they had so few laws? To which they answered, that many laws made many divisions, which most commonly did breed factions, and at last break out into open wars. Next, she asked, why they preferred the monarchical form of government before any other? They answered, that as it was natural for one body to have but one head, so it was also natural for a politic body to have but one governor; and that a commonwealth, which had many governors was like a monster with many heads: besides, said they, a monarchy is a divine form of government, and agrees most with our religion; for as there is but one God, whom we all unanimously worship and adore with one faith, so we are resolved to have but one Emperor, to whom we all submit with one obedience" (Cavendish 1992: 134).

64 Paragraphing is editorial rather than authorial in *The Blazing World*. Eighteen

printed lines separate the Duchess's delight in her imaginary world and the Empress's regret at having nothing to change in the Blazing World.

65 Hobbes cites fear as one of the passions that incline men to peace (and therefore to civil government) in Chapter 13 of *Leviathan*, where he first sets out his definition of the state of nature (1.13.183–8). In the opening paragraph of Part 2, he emphasizes the importance of a "visible Power" that produces the "awe" and "feare of punishment" necessary for the maintenance of the commonwealth (2.17.223), and in his chapter on crimes, he identifies fear as the passion "which enclineth men least to break the Lawes" (2.27.343).

2   *King Lear* and the tragedy of native origins

1 Claire McEachern articulates the oxymoronic timelessness of ideas of the nation in similarly Derridean terms: "the force of the nation lies in its fleetingness. It is either always about to be, or on the wane, nascent or ancient" (1996: 33).

2 Both Turner and Halpern found their discussions of *Lear*'s generic complexity on Maynard Mack's description of the play's romance elements in *King Lear in our Time* (1965).

3 Johnson's closing comment on having been so shocked by Cordelia's death as not to have reread the play's last scenes until he "undertook to revise them as an editor" suggests the keenness of his own personal need to distance himself from *Lear* (1968: 704).

4 Felix Schelling notes that nothing in this legendary vein seems to have been written for the stage between *Gorboduc* in 1562 and the old *Leir* play in 1594 (1902: 172–207, 276–86).

5 The earlier regency of Guendoline for her son Madan, third king in the line of Brute, is specifically disqualified in a marginal note ("She is not numbered amongst those that reigned as rulers in this land"), and indeed she does not receive a place in the numerical list of rulers in the line of Brute (Holinshed 1587: 11).

6 John Turner notes that in effecting the premature death of Cordelia, Shakespeare anticipated the extinction of the Brutan line by nine generations (1988: 97).

7 In his introduction to the *Patriarcha*, Johann P. Sommerville emphasizes Filmer's intellectual affinity with earlier theorists of the Elizabethan and Jacobean state; Sommerville also notes Filmer's frequent references to Holinshed, Camden, and other nationalist historians in elaborating his theory of patriarchal rule (Filmer 1991: xvi–xix, xli–xliv).

8 Filmer also cites Caesar's survey of British disunity in the *Gallic War* to undermine historical claims for the authority of parliament, arguing that where there was no unity of state or law, there could be no parliament (1991: 53).

9 But see Hawkes 1989: 136, who reads the conspirators' map as emblematic of a sacrilegious interference with and degradation of the divinely sanctioned order of being. Philip Armstrong also compares the map scenes in *1 Henry IV* and *Lear*, emphasizing the arbitrary quality of the divisions in both (1995: 40–2).

10 Elton notes the emphasis on elemental deities such as the sun and moon in early modern understanding of ancient British religion (1968: 173–6).

Boadicea's revolt is presaged by supernatural portents in both classical and early modern accounts, and she cites the superior British ability to endure the elements in her oration in Holinshed (1587: 44). For Lear's belief that he can control the elements and his loss of confidence in this power during the heath scenes, see Hoeniger (1974: 93–4). Schelling notes that the issue of ancient British control over the elements emerges in other plays of the period, particularly with regard to royal or priestly figures (1902: 174–81).

11 For the wide cultural dissemination of Saxton's maps, see Morgan 1979. Morgan argues in another essay (1983) that by the time Shakespeare composed *Lear*, he could have assumed his audience's abilities to recognize and imagine a map. Hawkes, while emphasizing the impact of the map on a mostly non-literate audience, does not address the specific appearance of the map as stage property in early modern productions, nor does he elaborate his sense of its implications for a period audience (1989: 136–7).

12 Although most of Saxton's maps show one county only, they also include adjoining regions of neighboring counties, divided by just such lines as Lear points to in his description. Ten of the maps do include more than one county, and five of the single-county maps show their division into hundreds (Evans and Lawrence 1979: 10).

13 Philip Armstrong also emphasizes the illusion that the map offers Lear of standing at a "stable, potent, and central symbolic position." Lear's division of the kingdom reveals the map's omniscient perspective to be illusory, resulting in the loss of personal as well as national integrity: "By dividing one, [Lear] inadvertently fragments both" (1995: 40).

14 For the western recovery of Ptolemy and the subsequent revolution in Renaissance cartography, see Bagrow 1965: 77–89 and Dilke 1985: 160–4. For a broader cultural analysis of the effects of Ptolemaic principles on western art, see Alpers 1983: 119–68. Woodward (1987) develops the most extensive discussion of medieval world maps.

15 Belsey elaborates this argument from staging in ch. 2 ("Unity"). I summarize here the section of that chapter entitled "The spectator" (19–33).

16 McEachern explores the elaboration of corporate national identity from the tropes of personal subjectivity in her reading of the "person-ality" of the King in Shakespeare's *Henry V* (1996: 83–137). For a well-developed analysis of the role of the drama in the development of a national myth of origins and sense of modern identity, see also Edwards, whose reading of *Henry V* in terms of the conflict between a sense of identity defined by English nationality and the greater emotional power of a sense of unity based on the whole island is particularly astute (1979: 74–86).

17 Goldberg notes that the Globe itself, with its evocative name and theatre-in-the-round format, was part of this older emblematic tradition of staging (1984: 546). The complementary instance of this perceived relation between theatrical and cartographical representation is, of course, the use of "theater" for early modern atlases, as in Ortelius's *Theatrum Orbis Terrarum* (1570) and Speed's *Theatre of the Empire of Great Britain* (1612).

18 Flahiff nicely describes the corresponding replacement of spatial by human relationships in the play, which are increasingly defined in terms of nearness and distance (1986: 18–19). Armstrong 1995 and Hunt 1987 also discuss the spatial terminology of perspective in *Lear*.

19 Turner uses similar language to express the historiographical tragedy of *Lear*,

arguing that the play "depicts the history of its nation as nightmare, the doom of its Jacobean present inscribed inescapably in the social formation of its determinant prehistory" (1988: 117).

20 Despite much debate, there is still no consensus on whether Rastell's geographical figure was a map or a globe. On the basis of its description in Rastell's text, scholars are agreed that the figure conformed to Ptolemaic principles, which Rastell was demonstrating to his audience (Borish 1938; Parr 1948). For the range of Rastell's intellectual and professional interests, see Axton's introduction to *The Four Elements* (Rastell 1979: 1–29).

21 These stage directions (noted in the Signet edition) are taken from the First Folio. The first indication of the storm is "Storm and tempest" following 2.4.282. The rest maintain the form "Storm still" and are noted six times in the heath scenes.

22 Dollimore describes this collapse in his critique of humanist readings of *Lear* (1984: 194–5).

23 For the development of map projections and their various uses, see National Geographic Society 1950 and Raisz 1962: 166–78. Armstrong emphasizes the importance of the Mercator Projection and its distortions in Shakespearean evocations of world geography and in the vision they present of England's relation to potential colonies and new areas for trade (1995: 42–50).

24 Cherrell Guilfoyle suggests an analogy between Shakespeare's emphasis on Dover and King Arthur's landing there when he comes to challenge the usurper Mordred in the 1485 *Morte Darthur*. Tracing the Arthurian references throughout *Lear* to the Christian text of Malory, she reads the journeys of Lear and Gloucester to Dover as holy pilgrimages anticipating the arrival of the Christ-like Cordelia (1987: 214–28).

25 Jonathan Goldberg also reads the iteration of Dover in the play's middle acts as the naming of a site of desire or the hope of recovery (1984: 537–8).

26 The *Britannia* (which also describes the "stately cliffs" lining the coast between Deal and Dover) supports this distinction by noting that Dover best answers to Caesar's description of a place between two hills that "letteth in and encloseth the sea" (Camden 1610: 343).

3 *Cymbeline* and the masculine romance of Roman Britain

1 See especially Goldberg 1992 and Jones and Stallybrass 1992.

2 G. Wilson Knight includes this Jacobean speech with the other Shakespearean examples of what he calls Elizabethan post-Armada sentiment: Hastings's short invocation of the impregnable isle in *3 Henry VI* 4.1.43–6; John of Gaunt's speech in *Richard II* 2.1.31–68; and Austria's description of the kingdom he promises to the young Lewis of France in *King John* 2.1.23–30 (1947: 136). The context of this last example suggests a rather equivocal appeal to nationalism.

3 Rackin notes a similar syntactic construction of the national past in John of Gaunt's nostalgic elegy for the "scepter'd isle" in *Richard II* (1990: 122–3).

4 Constance Jordan reads *Cymbeline* as a vindication of the principle that "a word given in good faith has a force in conscience," both in the political

question of Britain's obligation to Rome, and in the familial question of the marital obligation between Imogen and Posthumus (1994: 53–54).

5 See especially Leggatt 1977; Marcus 1988; Miola 1983: 206–35; Rossi 1978; and Smith 1952.

6 Geoffrey Hill argues that although Shakespeare rejects the "ferocious insularity" of 3.1, most of his original audience would have applauded it (1984: 55–66). J. P. Brockbank, while recognizing the ancient savagery epitomized by Cloten and the Queen, also claims that their "minimal virtue of defiant patriotism" never poses a serious threat to the natural integrity of the British court (1958: 44).

7 Claire McEachern notes a similar discomfort with outspoken territorial loyalty in Drayton's *Poly-Olbion*, where it is characterized as female vanity "or, at its most threatening, a harpie-like tumult"(1996: 189).

8 Knight regards the Queen as an extreme figure of motherhood, "a possessive maternal instinct impelling her violent life" (1947: 132).

9 Carroll Camden discusses Imogen's conformity to conventional Elizabethan womanhood (1951).

10 Goldberg acknowledges the pioneering work of Ann Kibbey on the collapse of Pequots and Anglo women in (masculine) Puritan accounts of the Pequot War (Kibbey 1986: 92–120).

11 Even before she assumes her boy's disguise, Imogen's status and authority as a married woman are not clear. Anne Barton points to numerous ambiguities in the play's references to the union of Imogen and Posthumus, suggesting that it might have been an unconsummated precontract rather than a solemnized marriage (1994: 19–30). But see Linda Woodbridge, who sees in Imogen's status as "Shakespeare's only transvestite heroine who is not a virgin" a Jacobean break with the invasion-threatened virginity that shapes his Elizabethan visions of England (1991: 347). Janet Adelman and Ann Thompson both note the degree to which Imogen's disguise disempowers her, in contradistinction to the ways it enabled the selfhood of Shakespeare's earlier comic heroines (Adelman 1992: 210; Thompson 1991: 84).

12 Cymbeline's first queen, mother to Imogen and the lost princes, leaves no other trace in the play than the diamond Imogen gives Posthumus (1.2.43). Belarius's wife, Euriphile, nurse to the young princes and mourned by them as a mother, also seems to have been dead for some time (3.3.103–5). Adelman comments on the need to efface the maternal in the all-male pastoral of Wales (1992: 202–4), and Thompson reads Cymbeline's self-description as a "mother to the birth of three" (5.5.370) as an expression of the play's systematic removal of power from women (1991: 86).

13 Patricia Parker notes the many parallels between Cymbeline's Queen and the Latin Queen Amata in the *Aeneid*, who also rules her husband temporarily, advocating a narrowly nationalistic resistance to Aeneas and championing his rival. Parker likens the feminine obstructionism of Cymbeline's Queen to that of the "complex of female figures in the *Aeneid* ranged against the fulfillment of the Jupiterian plot of eventual Augustan peace" (1989: 196). Reading Shakespeare's histories of medieval England, Phyllis Rackin elaborates how women, and especially mothers, function as "antihistorians" who resist patriarchal structures of masculine history writing (1990: 146–200, esp. 190–1).

14 See especially Brockbank 1958: 44–5; Bergeron 1980 and 1985: 136–57; and

Woodbridge 1991: 342–49. Charles Wells argues that *Cymbeline* represents a synthesis of Roman and Christian values, thus resolving Shakespeare's increasingly critical attitude to the Roman tradition in his later plays, as well as celebrating the Augustan analogy of James's "Pax Britannica" (1993: 173–85). For other accounts of the idealization of Augustus as a context for *Cymbeline*, see Barroll 1958; Spencer 1957; and Knight 1947: 166.

15 Miola articulates the most radical development of this position in his two essays on *Cymbeline* (1983: 206–35, 1984). See also Leggatt 1977 and Thorne 1969. Both "pro-British" and "pro-Roman" historiographical readings of *Cymbeline* have trouble placing Iachimo and the scenes in Rome in a first-century Roman–British context. The anachronistic intrusion of Renaissance Italy in all its degeneracy may provide an outlet for anti-Roman sentiment by invoking the contemporary context of Rome as the papacy rather than as the ancient seat of empire. I share the general view that the only sense one can make of Iachimo in the play's first-century context is as a figure for the Roman invasion of Britain in the bedchamber scene with the sleeping Imogen. Like the Romans at Milford Haven, Iachimo fails to achieve his conquest yet collects his "tribute."

16 Brockbank makes a cautious suggestion in this regard (1958: 49, n. 20).

17 Camden also omits Boadicea's oration from editions of the *Britannia*, perhaps for reasons similar to Milton's.

18 Rackin describes a similarly gendered antithesis between Talbot and Joan of Arc in *1 Henry VI* (1990: 151).

19 For Caratach, Fletcher drew on the account of the northern queen Voada, which includes a British leader named "Caratake," in Holinshed's "History of Scotland" (1587: 45–50).

20 Stork dates *Shoemaker* to 1609. Bergeron also notes the contemporaneity and relevance of this play to *Cymbeline* (1985: 140).

21 The masculine embrace of *Shoemaker* takes place in the third act rather than at the play's conclusion. Several outspoken female characters, British and Roman, take part in this conclusion, distinguishing it from the all-male reconciliations of the other Roman–British dramas. The embrace that closes *Shoemaker* is performed by the newly liberated British queen and her recently restored sons.

22 Just as the Roman and British ensigns "wave friendly together" at the conclusion of *Cymbeline*, so too is Cymbeline's emblem of the radiant sun said to merge with the Roman eagle in the Soothsayer's interpretation of his vision before the battle (5.5.468–77). In this interpretation, the meeting of the emblems becomes the symbol of the right relation between Britain and Rome, vested with the force of destiny, and presented as the key to understanding the play's peaceful resolution. The implicit embrace of national emblems in *Cymbeline* is made explicit at the conclusion of *The True Trojans*. There, another soothsayer, the Druid Lantonus, describes the new device of Roman Britain, in which the British lion and the Roman eagle are surrounded by two semi-circles, representing the double letter "C" from the names Caesar and Cassibelan: "the semicircles, / First letters of the leaders' names, we see, / Are join'd in true love's endless figure" (Fisher 1825: 5.6). In Lantonus's description of their meeting, "true love's endless figure" represents the embrace of the names Caesar and Cassibelan, even as "The world's fourth empire Britain doth embrace."

23 Even in this role of feminized or subjected nation, Britain is potentially aligned with Rome. In her account of Shakespeare's consistent association of England with ancient Rome, Linda Woodbridge describes the binary image of Rome that haunted the European imagination: "Rome the implacable invader, thrusting its masculine armies deep into the virgin territory of the Goths, its soldiers raping the queen of Britain's daughters; and Rome the invaded, the sacked city, ravaged by Goths" (1991: 329). Woodbridge stresses Britain's identification with the latter (Elizabethan) image throughout most of *Cymbeline* (333), but reads the play's romance conclusion in terms of a third image of Rome/England, the "perhaps hermaphroditic 'peaceful empire' concept, symbolized by Augustus Caesar and King James" (343).

24 Jones and Stallybrass comment on early modern antiquarian assumptions about national character that linked barbarism with effeminacy in descriptions of the "Scythian disease," a condition of masculine effeminization that included impotence and the assumption of women's work, clothing, speech, and other forms of behavior, represented in national terms by the supposed hereditary effeminacy of the Scythian royal family. Noting the derivation of Irish origins from the Scythians in some late sixteenth-century apologies for Irish colonialism, Jones and Stallybrass argue for the English need to distinguish their own national identity from this barbaric effeminacy (1992: 158–65). Lyndal Roper has commented on the increasing importance of marriage to masculine civic identity in early modern Germany, claiming that "What gave one access to the world of brothers was one's mastery of a woman which guaranteed one's sexual status. […] As a result, the unmarried young man might come to seem not securely male" (1994: 46).

25 Rackin discusses Wales as a place of geographical and sexual liminality in Shakespeare's histories, "a scene of emasculation and female power, […] the site of a repression in the historical narrative" (1990: 170–2).

26 Hengist was the architect of the Saxon heptarchy, or seven minor kingdoms, that introduced Saxon rule to Britain. Holinshed chronicles his ascendancy and how as a result "the Saxons come over by heaps to inhabit the land" (1587: 78). Hengist appears with Brute, Julius Caesar, and William the Conqueror on the title page of Drayton's *Poly-Olbion*. A similar figure entitled "A Saxon" appears with a Briton, a Roman, a Norman, and a Dane on the title page of Speed's *Theatre of the Empire of Great Britain*.

27 Mid-seventeenth-century celebrations of England's Saxon heritage stress the purity of race, martial valor, and extraordinary chastity of the Saxon (MacDougall 1982: 59–64). The Welsh interlude of Caratach and Hengo anticipates this nationalist emphasis on the feminine virtues of purity and chastity, and their association with the Saxons.

28 Sharon Macdonald also notes the emphasis on manliness and homoeroticism in *Bonduca* (1987: 49–50).

29 The Welsh retreat of the princes has in fact led some critics to conclude that the setting of *Cymbeline* has no historiographical importance, and merely enhances the play's romantic qualities. I would argue that the Welsh setting of these scenes is of historical importance precisely because it dramatizes the anxiety of being excluded from history. For the opposing readings, see Irving Ribner 1956 and Arthur C. Kirsch 1967: 288–306.

30 See Schwartz 1970: 250–9; Skura 1980: 209–14; Landry 1982: 68–79; Bergeron 1983: 159–68.

31 Although I disagree with her reading of Wales as an unproblematically masculine sphere, I find Adelman's general discussion of *Cymbeline* (1992: 200–19) insightful and persuasive, particularly in her insistence on the interrelatedness of masculine anxiety about gender and sexuality in both the marriage plot and what she calls "the Cymbeline plot" (the question of British autonomy and the relation to Rome).

32 Rackin notes the nostalgic longing in *Richard II* for an all-male past where heroic deeds of warfare conferred meaning and value (1990: 191). Her historicist reading of masculine longing in this play complements and reinforces psychoanalytic readings of the princes' entry into adult masculine identity in *Cymbeline*.

33 Imogen's identity with Britain has been commented on from a variety of critical perspectives, especially regarding the analogy between the Roman invasion of Britain and Iachimo's invasion of Imogen's bedchamber (Leggatt 1977: 194; Schwartz 1970: 221; Skura 1980: 210; Woodbridge 1991: 334–5). Drawing on the play's pervasive engagement with *translatio imperii*, Parker suggests a further analogy between Iachimo's concealment in the trunk and the ruse of the Trojan horse. Robin Phillips's 1986 production at Stratford, Ontario, indicates the staging possibilities of this scene within the culminating period of Mosse's argument. Phillips set the play in twentieth-century England between the two world wars, with Iachimo as an Italian fascist whose invasion of Imogen's bedchamber enacted fascist intrusion into and regulation of private relations. His monologue was delivered in an amplified whisper, recalling the role of radio in bringing fascist "morality" literally into the home. I am indebted to Elizabeth D. Harvey for suggesting the radio analogy.

34 Some recent editors (following the Oxford Text) have reverted to "Innogen" as Shakespeare's intended form of the name (Shakespeare 1989: viii and 1997: 2964).

35 But see Nosworthy's note to this image in the Arden edition, where he surveys critical concern about the image as undignified or degrading (Shakespeare 1988: 96).

36 The line is from the First Eclogue, translated in the Loeb edition as "wholly sundered from all the world" (Virgil 1950: 36).

37 Simon Forman, who saw a performance of *Cymbeline* in 1611, mentions Milford Haven several times in his account as the place toward which all the action tends. Nosworthy cites Forman's account in full in the introduction to the Arden edition (Shakespeare 1988: xiv–xv).

38 For discussions of the power of Milford developed from Jones's argument, see Landry 1982: 71–3; Leggatt 1977; Marcus 1988; and Yates 1975b: 47–52.

39 The confusion is heightened by Imogen's invocation of Hecuba's "madded curses" as antetypes of her own grief and rage shortly before Lucius's entrance (4.2.313). Citing Imogen's explicit allusion and the description of Priam as "a nameless corpse" in Book II of the *Aeneid*, Patricia Parker remarks on the curious links forged between the narrow British nationalist Cloten, the fallen king of Troy, and the complicatedly British and Roman Posthumus in Shakespeare's romance of empire (1989: 196).

40 The Roman commander's name connects him with the very line of ancient kings celebrated by Cymbeline's Queen and Tudor mythographers alike. In Geoffrey of Monmouth's *Historia Regum Britanniae*, Lucius is the great-

grandson of Cassibelan, who resisted the invasion of Julius Caesar, and also of the Roman Emperor Claudius, whose daughter married a British king. In Geoffrey's account, Lucius converted Britain to Christianity, making it the first nation to publicly confess the new faith (MacDougall 1982: 9).

41 Jean E. Howard's discussion of Bess Bridges as an emblem of England in Heywood's *The Fair Maid of the West* raises many of these same issues of female subordination (Howard 1994). The similarities between Bess and Imogen are remarkable, including not only their symbolic roles *vis-à-vis* the nation, but also their parallel searches for husbands too easily alarmed over wifely fidelity, in which both women believe themselves widows for a time, only to be reunited with their husbands and (in Howard's terms) re-enclosed within the heterosexual marriage that comes to define Englishness. Howard insists on the bourgeois class valence of Heywood's construction of nationalism, noting that it could sometimes "conflict with aristocratic discourses, such as those of chivalric romance, which saw men of the same rank forming a community that cut across national lines" (1994: 101–2). The masculine romance of Roman Britain that I examine here does indeed imagine such a transnational community of men, allowing for further analysis of the complicated issues of sexuality as well as gender in the forging of early modern English nationalism.

42 In the medieval ballads her lament of masterlessness invokes, her role would have been to remain by her dead master's body until she herself died (e.g., like the "fallow doe/lemman" in "The Three Ravens").

43 Karen Cunningham notes the aggressiveness of the assaults on Imogen's fidelity throughout *Cymbeline*, arguing that by taking the form of rhetorical rather than physical acts, they construct "a new Imogen identical with the idea of infidelity" (1994: 19–20).

44 One might even suggest that Posthumus provides a needed vent for the collective masculine anxiety about Imogen's fidelity when he unwittingly strikes his disguised wife on stage (5.5.228–9).

45 Cymbeline's earlier recollection (3.2.69–73) of having served as a page in Augustus's household (a courtly anachronism culled from Holinshed 1587: 32) strengthens this parallel.

46 Nosworthy takes the name Fidele as French, arguing that Imogen makes a similar choice when she invents "Richard du Champ" in 4.2, and citing Samuel Johnson's disgust at "the confusion of names, and manners of different times" in *Cymbeline* (Shakespeare 1988: 112). Yet "Fidele" is also the feminine form of the Latin adjective *fidelis*, and Imogen first uses it in 3.7, long before she invokes "Richard du Champ." I am inclined to associate "Fidele" with the play's other Latinate names (Posthumus, Guiderius, Arviragus, Belarius), despite its femininity. To be sure, the latter quality makes it an odd choice for a masculine persona, but the display of explicitly feminine virtues is central to the gender confusion of the identity Imogen assumes under the name of Fidele.

47 Claire McEachern associates the "deliberately fragile national difference" of English nationalism with the fluid boundaries of femininity in the early modern period: "Tudor–Stuart England needed to be different from other polities, whether Roman or reformed, but not so different as to be beyond the pale of a recognizable political identity altogether. Femininity expresses both singularity and commonality" (1996: 31). I think the case of Imogen/

Fidele demonstrates the complexity and instability of such national constructs and their attempts to situate England or Britain in relation to other polities.

48 Adelman reads the Soothsayer's linguistic transformation of Imogen as an unmaking of her sexual body that "does away with the problematic female body and achieves a family and a masculine identity founded exclusively on male bonds" (1992: 218). Rackin, noting the importance of Elizabeth of York, Katherine of France, and the infant Elizabeth at the end of Shakespeare's two Henriads and *Henry 8*, argues that "the incorporation of the feminine represents the end of the historical process [… and] can only take place at the point where history stops. A world that truly includes the feminine is a world in which history cannot be written" (1990: 176). I would agree, adding the converse that in the romance of native origins, the dis-incorporation of the feminine is the place where history starts.

4   The domestication of the savage queen

1 Sharon Macdonald gives an excellent survey of references to Boadicea from classical accounts to the 1980s, touching on some of the same issues of gender, sexuality, maternity, and nationalism I address in this chapter. Antonia Fraser's similarly broad survey in *The Warrior Queens* is less reliable, particularly in the chapter "Elizabetha Triumphans," where she argues for a pervasive Elizabethan identification of the reigning sovereign with the ancient queen (1989: 203–25). Marina Warner documents more recent evocations of Boadicea in British cultural and political life, a set of references that indicates how closely the ancient queen is now bound up with the nationalist allegory Britannia (1985: 38–60).

2 "*rectores sibi relictos ad enuntianda plenius vel confirmanda Romani regni molimina leaena trucidavit dolosa*" (Gildas 1978: 6.1)

3 Gildas's anti-British stance has occasioned much comment in modern readings of his history, even to the point of prompting questions about his British "nationality." For a summary and refutation of such claims, see O'Sullivan (1978: 5–32).

4 Holinshed glosses Boadicea's leadership of the Britons as follows: "they chose her to be captain (for they in rule and government made no difference then of sex, whether they committed the same to man or woman)" (1587: 42). The *Britannia* follows the same form, noting that "they take arms under the conduct of Boadicia a Lady of the royal blood (for in matter of government in chief the Britons make no distinction of Sex)" (Camden 1610: 49). Both early modern accounts derived their parenthetical axioms from Tacitus's assertion that the Britons made no distinction of sex in government: "*neque enim sexum in imperiis discernunt*" (1932: 16.2–3).

5 Aside from an introductory historical survey, the *Britannia* is organized topographically rather than chronologically. In the first Latin edition of 1586, Camden mentioned Boadicea in conjunction with the Iceni tribe in his discussion of Suffolk, and with Camalodunum, London, and Verulam, the three settlements she sacked (1586: 251–2, 244–5, 228, 219–20). In the 1600 edition, he added a brief mention of her revolt to his history of Roman Britain (1600: 45), referring the reader to the fuller account in the section on the Iceni. The first English translation of 1610 expanded and combined

these references into a major episode in the historical narrative of Roman Britain (1610: 49–52).

6 Camden had introduced Gildas's phrase when he began expanding his account of the uprising in the 1600 edition: "*Boadicia illa, quam Leaenam dolosam vocat Gildas*" (Camden 1600: 404).

7 For Boadicea's place in early modern catalogues of illustrious women, see Wright 1946. Margaret Maurer argues that even Jonson's invocation of her as "The *Britanne* honor, *Voadicea*" (Jonson 1952: 406) is undercut by typological associations with the "Dance of the Witches" that introduces *The Masque of Queenes*, an anti-masque that she interprets as giving play to a suppressed revulsion at heroical femininity on behalf of Jonson and the elite males in the audience (including the king) (Maurer 1989).

8 Only one woman author in the controversy, Rachel Speght, has been satisfactorily identified. Other authors' names on the feminist side, such as "Jane Anger," also suggest the adoption of a pseudonym that implicitly discredits the supposed female author. For accounts of the Jacobean pamphlet controversy and its issues of gender and authorship, see especially Lewalski 1993: 152–75 and Woodbridge 1984: 74–113.

9 Boadicea figures in *The Faerie Queene* as a positive exemplum of female martial valor, invoked briefly in Book Three as one of several ancient British types of Britomart (1985: 3.3.54), and at greater length in three stanzas of "Britons Moniments" in Book Two (10.54–6).

10 A similar dichotomy of literary and historiographical treatments is evident in *Poly-Olbion*. Although repeatedly commending the resolve of her fighting *men*, Drayton develops a heroic portrait of Boadicea, culminating in her Cleopatra-like suicide to avoid figuring in a Roman triumph (1933: 8.269–88). The antiquarian John Selden reins in this literary fervor in his "Illustrations," describing the revolt in terms of the tribes involved rather than their female leader, referring to Boadicea principally as the wife of Prasutagus, and glossing Drayton's version of her heroic suicide as follows: "So *Tacitus*; but *Dio*, that she died of sickenes" (Drayton 1933: 160). For the complex (and interdependent) relation between Drayton's "female, fictionalized, and personified geography" and Selden's "masculine realm of difficult tell-troth," see Prescott 1991: 311. McEachern also notes Selden's tendency to demystify legendary examples of British female virtue, from Boadicea's suicide to the 11,000 virgins attending St Ursula (1996: 174–5).

11 Robert Burton invokes her martial prowess ironically to illustrate how a lover will turn the faults of his beloved into virtues. In contrast to the designation of a "dwarfish and little" woman as "pretty," he suggests that an inappropriately tall woman be hailed as "proper and man-like, our brave British Bonduica" (1964: 158).

12 Louis Montrose notes that Penthesilea, with whom Boadicea is ranked in Jonson's masque, was one of the few acceptable Amazon comparisons to Elizabeth because of her ties to Troy and thus to the legendary line of Brute (1991: 27).

13 Recent accounts of Elizabeth's oratory emphasize the queen's own role in framing and delivering her speeches, suggesting a greater control over her public self-presentation than scholars had previously accorded her. See especially Levin 1994: 39–65, 121–48; Frye 1993: 3–21; King 1990; and Heisch 1975 and 1980.

14 Heisch notes the addition of Elizabeth's speeches to the 1587 edition by John Stow, who also included them in his *Annals* (1980: 45). The 1577 woodcut does not appear in the 1587 edition of Holinshed, which had no illustrations.

15 Aske's commendation follows a description of the victory of Norfolk and Grey of Wilton over the French in Scotland, in which heaps of bodies and the tears of women, children, and servants figure largely. Far from condemning the English commanders for conduct that was routinely deplored in contemporary accounts of Boadicea, Aske celebrates the queen's masculine agents for their martial valor and defense of the realm (Nichols 1823: II.552).

16 Aske's account of the distance Elizabeth maintained from this engagement is consistent with the general resistance to Amazonian comparisons in her iconography (Montrose 1983: 76–8). But see Schleiner 1978 for exceptional Amazonian analogies for Elizabeth in celebrations of the defeat of the 1588 Armada.

17 For contemporary printed accounts of breast mutilation, including a woodcut entitled "Massacres d'Anvers," which may have been printed in the 1583 *Leo Belgicus* of Michel Aitsinger, illustrated by Hogenberg, see Witkowski 1903: 3–4, fig. 1, and 1907: 77–80. In early seventeenth-century Bavaria, the breasts of a convicted witch were cut off and placed in her own mouth and then in the mouths of her two grown sons, a form of public humiliation that one historian has described as "a hideous parody of her role as mother and nurse"(Barstow 1994: 144). The Welshwomen whose barbarism and "shameful villainy" Holinshed emphasizes in his reign of Henry IV inflict a similar gender humiliation on the male bodies of the English dead: "yet did the women of Wales cut off their privities, and put one part thereof into the mouths of every dead man, in such sort that the cullions hung down to their chins" (Holinshed 1587: 528).

18 Images of breast removal would also have been available in some medical treatises of the early to mid seventeenth century, when amputation was beginning to be advised for what would now be recognized as breast cancer (Zimmerman and Vieth 1967: 245–6). I have not included the medical literature in my discussion because the medical procedure was very new in the period and known only to a small number of professionals. For treatments of breasts and breast amputation in eighteenth-century medical literature see Jordanova 1989: 29–32 and Epstein 1986: 157–60.

19 Some apologists for Mary and Elizabeth Tudor did challenge the conflation of political and physical bodies that grounded opposition to female rule, citing the medieval concept of the monarch's two bodies, and arguing that the imperfections of a ruler's female body were overcome by the divine authority of her anointed political body. Yet despite local challenges to the idea of a natural gender hierarchy, these defenses of female rule largely emphasized the irrelevance rather than the worthiness of the queens' sex, arguing not so much for the right of the sovereign to be female as for the rights of Mary or Elizabeth to be considered male (Jordan 1987). The distinction between those willing to countenance female rule and those implacably opposed to it may also have been theological, with Anglicans drawing on humanist thinkers who posited women's near-equality with men, and Calvinists (like Knox) holding to their founder's view that women were inherently inferior to men, whom God had ordained to be their masters (Benson 1985).

20 Thomas Laqueur sets out most fully the deficiencies of female anatomy with respect to a male norm in early modern Galenic medicine (1990: 25–62). For the growing need to discipline the grotesque female body in this period, see Paster 1993: 163–280 and Stallybrass 1986.

21 While I would caution that constructions of motherhood should not be elided with arguments for the "invention of childhood" in the eighteenth century, since maternity was already an important symbolic and social category in classical and medieval European cultures, I would agree with Perry in locating the full expression of a modern concept of motherhood in the eighteenth century.

22 For socio-historical accounts of infant nurture in sixteenth- and seventeenth-century England, see Fildes 1986: 98–173 and 1988: 68–100; Crawford 1986; Schnucker 1974; and Stone 1979: 269–73. For literary and cultural studies, see especially Paster 1993: 163–280; Adelman 1992: 4–8, 130–64; Shuger 1990: 218–49; and Kahn 1986.

23 Barbara J. Harris offers some counterexamples to the thesis that elite women did not begin nursing their own children before the end of the sixteenth century (1990: 612–13).

24 Although earlier studies of this phenomenon tended to identify this new zeal for maternal breast-feeding with Puritanism, more recent work suggests that changing attitudes to infant nurture and childrearing practices generally were as common among religious conformists as radicals (Leverenz 1980: 1–8, 91, and Crawford 1986: 31–2.

25 Henry Newcome, *The Complete Mother or, An Earnest Persuasive to all Mothers (especially those of Rank and Quality) to Nurse their own Children* (London, 1695), cited in Fildes 1988: 85.

26 In countries where wet-nursing was not challenged in this period, it had generally evolved into a well-organized system controlled entirely by men; i.e., the fathers of the infants, the husbands of the wet nurses, and sometimes male intermediaries (Fildes 1988: 49–67).

27 Clinton was also one of the few writers in the period to give any attention to the deprivation of the wet nurse and her own infant, presenting the intervention of the elite employer as an unnatural disruption of the nurse's natural love for her own child (1975: 18–19).

28 Cited in Jordanova 1989: 31. Jordanova quotes Cadogan's advice as an example of the transferral of power from the "natural" wisdom of women to the scientifically codified knowledge of men, a process in which the male gaze provides the chief metaphor for paternal authority (30–32).

29 Crawford 1986: 31–34 and Fildes 1988: 72–8 both document early modern fears about wet nurses as sources of moral contamination. In the primary sources, see Gouge 1622: 513 and Cleaver and Dod, who put forth the theory that "maidens that have made a scape are commonly called to be Nurses" (1612: P4v).

30 W. L. Renwick notes in his commentary on the *View* that the danger of fostering English infants with Irish wet nurses was a common concern about the English presence in Ireland, and was in fact prohibited by act of Parliament, 11 Eliz.c.6 (Spenser 1934: 274).

31 This argument also survived into the eighteenth century, figuring in Linnaeus's 1752 pamphlet against wet-nursing in an unfavorable comparison of those barbaric women who refused to nurse their own

children with the natural tenderness of beasts to their young (Schiebinger 1993: 406).

32 A later seventeenth-century treatise on children's diseases argued that "the souls of infants differ little from beasts" precisely because they were drowned in so much moisture by breast-feeding (John Starsmere, *Children's Diseases* (London, 1664), cited in Crawford 1986: 29).

33 In exploring the connections between witches and mothers in the early modern imagination, Deborah Willis notes a variety of ways in which a mother's own milk (as well as her blood in the womb) might be perceived as potentially dangerous to her child (1995: 65–81).

34 *The works of that famous chirurgion Ambrose Parey*, tr. T. Johnson (London, 1634), cited in Fildes (1986: 141–2). See 141–4 for the prevalence of this device and its use in the early modern period.

35 Jordanova also qualifies any absolute application of the nature/culture dichotomy to gender, emphasizing the extent to which each human body was understood to be "a tangled composite of nature and culture" (26) in her review of women/nature and men/culture associations in eighteenth- and nineteenth-century biomedical writing (1989: 19–42).

36 Harris defines natural as "affectionate, kindly, grateful, and generous with one's resources and connections," and notes that the terms were used both descriptively and prescriptively. Elite mothers who were perceived to fall short of this definition felt constrained to defend themselves against charges of being "unnatural."

37 J. A. Sharpe refers to an "infanticide craze" throughout western Europe in this period, which may have resulted in more executions than the contemporaneous witch craze (1984: 30). Susan Amussen considers attitudes to infanticide in the context of women's position in early modern England (1988: 113–15). For a statistical study of English infanticide records in the period, see Wrightson 1975.

38 Willis's account of the many parallels between constructions of witchcraft and maternity also suggests the criminalization of the mother as an extreme example of early modern anxiety about female power and agency (1995: 65–81).

39 Lady Macbeth's sexuality has received much attention. For recent accounts addressing the intersections of motherhood, domesticity, and savagery, see Dolan 1994: 224–30; Adelman 1992: 130–48; and Newman 1991: 50–71.

40 Hector Boece's "Description of Scotland" (translated from the Latin by William Harrison and included in the 1587 Holinshed) claims that

> it was a cause of suspicion of the mother's fidelity toward her husband, to seek a strange nurse for her children [...]. They thought them furthermore not to be kindly fostered, except they were so well nourished after their births with the milk of their breasts, as they were before they were born with the blood of their own bellies, nay they feared lest they should degenerate and grow out of kind, except they gave them suck themselves, and eschewed strange milk, therefore in labor and painfulness they were equal, and neither sex regarded the heat in summer or cold in winter, but travelled barefooted, and in time of wars the men had their carriages and victuals trussed behind them on their horses, or else upon

their own shoulders without refusal of any labor enjoined unto them by their captains.

(Holinshed 1587: 21)

This account of Scottish insistence on maternal breast-feeding suggests not only the greater role of the mother in shaping the nature of male children in that nation, but also a kind of sexual equality ("therefore in labor and painfulness they were equal, and neither sex regarded the heat in summer or cold in winter") resulting from the practice. I am grateful to Eric Nicholson for bringing this passage to my attention.

41 Goldberg's later interpretation of Van Dyck's *Daedalus and Icarus* (*c*.1620) as a father–son pair modeled on Leonardo's magna mater and Christ child in the St Anne cartoon concludes: "If so, this antique family group has a Christian precedent, and behind patriarchal and filial assertions loom vast maternal powers" (1986: 30). Willis also notes James's need to defend himself against maternal agency, suggesting that his hostile attitude toward witches was "significantly shaped by his difficult relationships with his two powerful 'mothers,' Mary Queen of Scots and Elizabeth I, who frequently 'betrayed' him in his confrontations with an unruly Scottish aristocracy" (1995: 94–5).

42 For local responses to the increasing social effects of economic distress, see Levine and Wrightson 1980; Wrightson 1980; and Clark 1982: 42–149.

43 This view was developed and propagated in the work of Lawrence Stone and Randall Trumbach in the late 1970s (Stone 1979; Trumbach 1978), and has held sway (despite some feminist challenges) until very recently in socio-historical work on the family. It has also been enormously (and enduringly) influential among literary critics.

44 Erickson notes a legal parallel between the gradual enclosure of land in the sixteenth through eighteenth centuries and a series of late seventeenth- and early eighteenth-century statutes that pared down the inheritance rights of widows and daughters (1993: 29).

45 Harris documents the power of elite mothers to bestow their own property, and the high incidence (74 per cent) of their being named sole executrices or co-executors by their husbands in a sample of 411 wills made between 1450–1550 (1990: 625). By contrast, Amussen notes the decline throughout the seventeenth century of the practice of making wives executrices or of leaving them in charge of family businesses until a son came of age (1988: 91–3). For resistance to the increasing legal and cultural restrictions on early modern wives, see Erickson 1993: 139–43, 147–51, 204–22; Amussen 1988: 42–7, 119–22; and Underdown 1985, and 1987: 36–7.

46 Mary Beth Rose describes the displacement of political conflicts by the problematics of private life, often embodied in a female hero, in Elizabethan and Jacobean tragedy (1991: 298). In Imogen's quest to rejoin Posthumus, the problematics of marital betrayal and misunderstanding displace the political drama of tribute and resistance to Rome so forcefully articulated by the Queen. The reintegration of the domestic and political plots in the last scene resolves the drama as romance, expelling the maternal agency of the Queen and subordinating Imogen not only as the wife of Posthumus, but also as the sister of two brothers who once again take precedence over her as royal heirs. Ann Thompson also notes that Shakespeare takes pains to distance Imogen from her official role as princess and heir to the throne,

emphasizing her docile, wifely qualities over her leadership and strategic ability (1991).

47 Amussen argues that Englishwomen themselves were not brought to a general acceptance of wifely subordination as defined in domestic tracts until the late seventeenth century (1988: 118–23).

48 James's self-description as "a loving nourish-father to the church" in *Basilikon Doron* is the most notorious example, enhanced by his more conventional acknowledgment of the treatise itself as "this birth of mine" (1918: 24, 11). Scholars also troped on nursing, as in Camden's antiquarian epithet "nourice of antiquity" (Spenser 1989: 169; Drayton 1933: xii), and the personification of Cambridge and the other universities as "the nources, of our noble Realme" (Gascoigne 1910: 168). The fantasy of a nursing father was widespread in contemporary Puritan literature in New England, where it functioned as the key image in the metaphorical enhancement of male authority (Leverenz 1980: 1–22, 72–9, 138–67).

49 The illustration to a broadside ode on the death of Anne shows a similarly subdued feminine personification of the nation, portrayed as a veiled woman who reclines weeping beside neglected arms with her face downcast ("On the much lamented death").

50 Aylett Sammes's account of Boadicea's uprising in *Britannia Antiqua Illustrata* (1676) also diminishes her active martial role, emphasizing instead the collective agency of the Iceni tribesmen who "took arms to revenge the wrongs done to their Queen and the dishonor of his [*sic*] daughters" (224). A full-length engraving of Boadicea (facing a summary of her description in Dio Cassius and emphasizing her long tresses) surmounts verses proclaiming the feminine virtues and charm of the queen and her daughters: "To war this QUEEN doth with her Daughters move, / She for her Wisdom, followed They for Love; / What Roman force, Such joined powers could quell; / Before so murdering Charms whole Legions fell"(Sammes 1670: 228). Hopkins's *Boadicea* was published and first performed in 1697, and was said by Dryden to have been well liked in particular by "fair ladies." Boadicea's eldest daughter is indeed raped during the course of its action, but the corresponding desire for revenge and other violent qualities of the women in *Bonduca* are omitted. Hopkins seems to have had no recourse to primary historical materials in the preparation of his drama, drawing rather on Powell's adaptation of Fletcher (Maxwell 1928).

51 The limited agency of Boadicea in Restoration drama may also reflect statutory measures to restrict the economic independence of widows. Erickson notes that a series of late seventeenth-century Acts abolishing or severely restricting widows' ancient entitlements to portions of their late husbands' goods and properties "were meant to trim the financial independence of wealthy widows down to merely an adequate subsistence. [...] Widows poor enough to require parish relief were the objects of pity (and they were safely under control). But the self-sufficient widow – and particularly the well-to-do widow – was sufficiently feared to be popularly mythologized as rapacious and threatening" (1993: 227). The latter stereotype aptly describes Elizabethan and Jacobean visions of Boadicea and other ancient widowed queens, including the twice-married "wicked Queen" in *Cymbeline*. In the increased domesticity, passivity, and dependence of the Restoration Boadicea, the maternal dominion of the ancient queen and widow is brought into line with the statutory restrictions of a later age.

BIBLIOGRAPHY

A., R. (1902) *The Valiant Welshman, or The True Chronicle History of the life and valiant deeds of Caradoc the Great, King of Cambria, now called Wales*, ed. Valentin Kreb, Leipzig: Georg Bohme.

Adelman, J. (1992) *Suffocating Mothers: Fantasies of Maternal Origin in Shakespeare's Plays, Hamlet to* The Tempest, London: Routledge.

Alpers, S. (1983) *The Art of Describing: Dutch Art in the Seventeenth Century*, Chicago: University of Chicago Press.

Amussen, S. D. (1985) "Gender, Family and the Social Order, 1560–1725," in A. Fletcher and J. Stevenson (eds), *Order and Disorder in Early Modern England*, Cambridge: Cambridge University Press.

—— (1988) *An Ordered Society: Gender and Class in Early Modern England*, Oxford: Basil Blackwell.

Anderson, B. (1992) *Imagined Communities: Reflections on the Origin and Spread of Nationalism* (rev. edn), London and New York: Verso.

Anon. [n.d] "On the much lamented death of the most pious and illustrious Princess, her late Majesty Queen Anne, who died Aug. 1714," Broadside: [n.p.].

Armstrong, P. (1995) "Spheres of Influence: Cartography and the Gaze in Shakespearean Tragedy and History," *Shakespeare Studies* 23: 39–70.

Aston, M. (1984) *Lollards and Reformers: Images and Literacy in Late Medieval Religion*, London: The Hambledon Press.

Bacon, F. (1900) *Advancement of Learning*, New York: Willey Book Co.

Bagrow, L. (1965) *History of Cartography* (rev. edn), ed. R. A. Skelton, London: L. C. Watts & Co.

Baldwin, T. W. (1944) *William Shakespeare's Small Latine & Lesse Greeke*, vol. 1, Urbana: University of Illinois Press.

Barroll, J. L. (1958) "Shakespeare and Roman History," *Modern Language Review* 53: 327–43.

Barstow, A. L. (1994) *Witchcraze: A New History of the European Witchhunts*, San Francisco: Pandora.

Barton, A. (1994) *Essays, Mainly Shakespearean*, Cambridge: Cambridge University Press.

Baumgold, D. (1988) *Hobbes's Political Theory*, Cambridge: Cambridge University Press.

Belsey, A., and Belsey, C. (1990) "Icons of Divinity: Portraits of Elizabeth I," in L. Gent and N. Llewellyn (eds), *Renaissance Bodies: The Human Figure in English Culture, c. 1540–1660*, London: Reaktion Books.

Belsey, C. (1985) *The Subject of Tragedy: Identity and Difference in Renaissance Drama*, London: Methuen.

Benhabib, S. (1992) *Situating the Self: Gender, Community and Postmodernism in Contemporary Ethics*, New York: Routledge.

Benson, P. J. (1985) "Rule, Virginia: Protestant Theories of Female Regiment in *The Faerie Queene*," *English Literary Renaissance* 15: 277–92.

Bergeron, D. M. (1980) "*Cymbeline*: Shakespeare's Last Roman Play," *Shakespeare Quarterly* 31: 32–41.

—— (1983) "Sexuality in *Cymbeline*," *Essays in Literature* 10: 159–68.

—— (1985) *Shakespeare's Romances and the Royal Family*, Lawrence: University Press of Kansas.

Bober, P. P. and Rubinstein, R. (1986) *Renaissance Artists and Antique Sculpture: A Handbook of Sources*, Oxford: Oxford University Press.

Borish, M. E. (1938) "Source and Intention of *The Four Elements*," *Studies in Philology* 35: 149–63.

Bouguereau, M. (1594) *Le Théâtre François, où sont comprises les chartes générales et particulières de la France*, Tour: Maurice Bouguereau.

Brockbank, J. P. (1958) "History and Histrionics in *Cymbeline*," *Shakespeare Survey* 11: 42–9.

Brown, K. (1978) "The Artist of the *Leviathan* Title-Page," *British Library Journal* 4: 24–36.

Browne, T. (1972) "Hydriotaphia [Urn-Burial]," ed. R. H. A. Robbins. Oxford: The Clarendon Press.

Bunyan, J. (1987) *The Pilgrim's Progress*, ed. Roger Sharrock, Harmondsworth: Penguin.

Burke, P. (1969) *The Renaissance Sense of the Past*, London: Edward Arnold.

Burton, R. (1964) *The Anatomy of Melancholy*, ed. H. Jackson, London: Dent.

Caesar, J. (1986) *The Gallic War*, trans. H. J. Edwards, Cambridge, MA: Harvard University Press.

Camden, C. (1951) "The Elizabethan Imogen," *The Rice Institute Pamphlet* 38: 1–17.

Camden, W. (1586) *Britannia*, London: Ralph Newbery.

—— (1600) *Britannia*, London: George Bishop.

—— (1610) *Britain*, trans. P. Holland. London: George Bishop.

—— (1615) *Annales rerum anglicarum et hibernicarum regnante Elizabetha, ad annum salutis MDLXXXIX*, London: William Stansby.

—— (1625) "The True and royal history of the famous empress Elizabeth, queen of England, France and Ireland, etc. true faith's defendress of divine renoun and happy memory," in *Annales*, London: B. Fisher.

—— (1984) *Remains Concerning Britain*, ed. R. D. Dunn, Toronto: University of Toronto Press.

Campbell, M. B. (1996) "Other World, Inner World, *Blazing-World*; or, What the Microscope Missed," Women in Early Modern Europe Seminar, Harvard Center for Literary and Cultural Studies, Cambridge, MA, 29 February.

Cassius, D. C. (1925) *Dio's Roman History*, trans. Earnest Cary, London: William Heinemann.

Cavendish, M., Duchess of Newcastle. (1992) "The Description of a New World Called the Blazing World," in K. Lilley (ed.), *The Description of a New World Called the Blazing World and Other Writings*, New York: New York University Press.

Clark, A. (1982) *Working Life of Women in the Seventeenth Century*, London: Routledge & Kegan Paul.

Cleaver, R. [and J. Dod] (1612) *A Godly Form of Household Government, carefully to be practised of all Christian Householders*, London: Thomas Man.

Clinton, E. (1975) *The Countess of Lincoln's Nursery*, Amsterdam: Walter J. Johnson.

Colley, L. (1992) *Britons: Forging the Nation 1707–1837*, New Haven, CT: Yale University Press.

Corbett, M. and Lightbown, R. (1979) *The Comely Frontispiece: The Emblematic Title-Page in England 1550–1660*, London: Routledge & Kegan Paul.

Crawford, P. (1981) "Attitudes to Menstruation in Seventeenth-Century England," *Past and Present* 91: 47–73.

—— (1986) "'The Suckling Child': Adult Attitudes to Childcare in the First Year of Life in Seventeenth-Century England," *Continuity and Change* 1: 23–52.

—— (1990) "The Construction and Experience of Maternity in Seventeenth-Century England," in *Women as Mothers in Pre-Industrial England*. London: Routledge.

Cunningham, K. (1994) "Female Fidelities on Trial: Proof in the Howard Attainder and *Cymbeline*," *Renaissance Drama* 25: 1–31.

D'Amico, J. (1984) *Renaissance Humanism in Papal Rome*, Baltimore: Johns Hopkins University Press.

Davis, N. Z. (1975) *Society and Culture in Early Modern France*, Stanford, CA: Stanford University Press.

—— (1993) "Women in Politics," in N. Z. Davis and A. Farge (eds), *Renaissance and Enlightenment Paradoxes*, vol III of *A History of Women in the West*, Cambridge, MA: Harvard University Press.

Derrida, J. (1992) *The Other Heading: Reflections on Today's Europe*, trans. P.-A. Brault and M. B. Naas, Bloomington: Indiana University Press.

Dilke, O. A. W. (1985) *Greek and Roman Maps*, London: Thames & Hudson.

Dolan, F. E. (1994) *Dangerous Familiars: Representations of Domestic Crime in England, 1550–1700*, Ithaca: Cornell University Press.

Dollimore, J. (1984) *Radical Tragedy: Religion, Ideology, and Power in the Drama of Shakespeare and His Contemporaries*, Chicago: University of Chicago Press.

Dove, W. (1695) *Albiana: A Poem Humbly Offered to the Memory of our Late Sovereign Lady, Mary, Queen of England, etc.*, London: Daniel Dring.

Drayton, M. (1933) "Poly-Olbion," in J. W. Hebel (ed.), *The Works of Michael Drayton*, vol. 4, Oxford: Shakespeare Head Press.

Dryden, J. (1969) "Absalom and Achitophel," in G. Tillotson, P. Fussell, Jr., and M. Waingrow (eds), *Eighteenth Century English Literature*, New York: Harcourt Brace Jovanovitch.

Dugdale, W. (1656) *The Antiquities of Warwickshire Illustrated*, London: Thomas Warren.

Edwards, P. (1979) *Threshold of a Nation: A Study in English and Irish Drama*, Cambridge: Cambridge University Press.

Elshtain, J. B. (1981) *Public Man, Private Woman: Women in Social and Political Thought*, Princeton: Princeton University Press.

Elton, W. R. (1968) King Lear *and the Gods*, San Marino, CA: The Huntington Library.

Epstein, J. L. (1986) "Writing the Unspeakable: Fanny Burney's Mastectomy and the Fictive Body," *Representations* 16: 131–66.

Erickson, A. L. (1992) Introduction, in A. Clark, *Working Life of Women in the Seventeenth Century*, London: Routledge.

—— (1993) *Women and Property in Early Modern England*, London: Routledge.

Evans, I. M., and Lawrence, H. (1979) *Christopher Saxton: Elizabethan Map-Maker*, London: The Holland Press.

Ewell, B. C. (1978) "Drayton's *Poly-Olbion*: England's Body Immortalized," *Studies in Philology* 75: 297–315.

Ezell, M. J. M. (1987) *The Patriarch's Wife: Literary Evidence and the History of the Family*, Chapel Hill: University of North Carolina Press.

Fabricant, C. (1979) "Binding and Dressing Nature's Loose Tresses: The Ideology of Augustan Landscape Design," *Studies in Eighteenth-Century Culture* 8: 109–35.

Ferguson, A. B. (1979) *Clio Unbound: Perception of the Social and Cultural Past in Renaissance England*, Durham, NC: Duke University Press.

—— (1993) *Utter Antiquity: Perceptions of Prehistory in Renaissance England*, Durham, NC: Duke University Press.

Fildes, V. A. (1986) *Breasts, Bottles and Babies: A History of Infant Feeding*, Edinburgh: Edinburgh University Press.

—— (1988) *Wet Nursing: A History from Antiquity to the Present*, Oxford: Basil Blackwell.

Filmer, R. (1991) "Patriarcha," in J. P. Sommerville (ed.), *Patriarcha and Other Writings*, Cambridge: Cambridge University Press.

Fisher, J. (1825) "Fuimus Troes or the True Trojans," in R. Dodsley (ed.), *A Selection of Old Plays*, vol. 7, London: Septimus Prowett.

Fitzmaurice, J. (1990) "Fancy and the Family: Self-characterizations of Margaret Cavendish," *Huntington Library Quarterly* 53: 199–209.

Flahiff, F. T. (1986) "Lear's Map," *Cahiers Elisabéthains* 30: 17–33.

Fletcher, A. (1995) *Gender, Sex and Subordination in England, 1500–1800*, New Haven: Yale University Press.

Fletcher, J. (1966) "Bonduca," in F. Bowers (ed.), *The Dramatic Works in the Beaumont and Fletcher Canon*, vol. IV, Cambridge: Cambridge University Press.

Fraser, A. (1989) *The Warrior Queens*, New York: Alfred A. Knopf.

Frye, E. (1992) "The Myth of Elizabeth at Tilbury," *The Sixteenth Century Journal* 23: 95–114.

—— (1993) *Elizabeth I: The Competition for Representation*, New York: Oxford University Press.

Gallagher, C. (1988) "Embracing the Absolute: The Politics of the Female Subject in Seventeenth-Century England," *Genders* 1: 24–39.

Gascoigne, G. (1910), *The Complete Works of George Gascoigne*, vol. 2, ed. J. W. Cunliffe, Cambridge: Cambridge University Press.

Gildas (1878) "The Works of Gildas," in J.A. Giles (ed.), *Six Old English Chronicles*, London.

—— (1978) *The Ruin of Britain and Other Works*, trans. M. Winterbottom, London: Phillimore & Co.

Goldberg, J. (1983) *James I and the Politics of Literature*, Baltimore, MD: The Johns Hopkins University Press.

—— (1984) "Dover Cliff and the Conditions of Representation: *King Lear* 4:6 in Perspective," *Poetics Today* 5: 537–47.

—— (1986) "Fatherly Authority: The Politics of Stuart Family Images," in M. W. Ferguson, M. Quilligan, and N. J. Vickers (eds), *Rewriting the Renaissance: The Discourses of Sexual Difference in Early Modern Europe*, Chicago: University of Chicago Press.

—— (1992) "Bradford's 'Ancient Members' and 'A Case of Buggery ... Amongst Them'," in M. Russo, A. Parker, D. Sommer, and P. Yaeger (eds), *Nationalisms and Sexualities*, New York: Routledge.

Gouge, W. (1622) *Of Domestical Duties*, London: John Haviland.

Gourvitch, I. (1930) "A Note on Drayton and Philemon Holland," *Modern Language Review* 25: 332–6.

Gransden, A. (1980) "Antiquarian Studies in Fifteenth-Century England," *Antiquarian Journal* 60: 75–97.

—— (1982) *Historical Writing in England II: c. 1307 to the Early Sixteenth Century*, Ithaca: Cornell University Press.

Grant, D. (1957) *Margaret the First: A Biography of Margaret Cavendish, Duchess of Newcastle, 1623–73*, London: Rupert Hart-Davis.

Greenblatt, S. (1980) *Renaissance Self-Fashioning From More to Shakespeare*, Chicago: University of Chicago Press.

—— (1986) "Psychoanalysis and Renaissance Culture" in P. Parker and D. Quint (eds), *Literary Theory/Renaissance Texts*, Baltimore: The Johns Hopkins University Press.

Greenfeld, L. (1992) *Nationalism: Five Roads to Modernity*, Cambridge, MA: Harvard University Press.

Gregg, E. (1980) *Queen Anne*, London: Routledge & Kegan Paul.

Guilfoyle, C. (1987) "The Way to Dover: Arthurian Imagery in *King Lear*," *Comparative Drama* 21: 214–28.

Hall, K. F. (1995) *Things of Darkness: Economies of Race and Gender in Early Modern England*, Ithaca: Cornell University Press.

Halpern, R. (1991) *The Poetics of Primitive Accumulation: English Renaissance Culture and the Genealogy of Capital*, Ithaca: Cornell University Press.

Hampton, J. (1986) *Hobbes and the Social Contract Tradition*, Cambridge: Cambridge University Press.

Hardin, R. F. (1973) *Michael Drayton and the Passing of Elizabethan England*, Lawrence: University of Kansas Press.

Harley, J. B. (1983) "Meaning and Ambiguity in Tudor Cartography," in S. Tyacke (ed.) *English Map-Making 1500–1650*. London: The British Library Board.

Harris, B. J. (1990) "Property, Power, and Personal Relations: Elite Mothers and Sons in Yorkist and Early Tudor England," *Signs* 15: 606–32.

Harvey, P. D. A. (1980) *The History of Topographical Maps*, London: Thames & Hudson.

Hawkes, T. (1989) "Lear's Maps: A General Survey," *Deutsche Jahrbuch*: 134–47.

Heisch, A. (1975) "Queen Elizabeth I: Parliamentary Rhetoric and the Exercise of Power," *Signs* 1: 31–56.

—— (1980) "Queen Elizabeth and the Persistence of Patriarchy," *Feminist Review* 4: 45–56.

Helgerson, R. (1992) *Forms of Nationhood: The Elizabethan Writing of England*, Chicago: University of Chicago Press.

Henderson, K. U., and McManus, B. F. (1985) *Half Humankind: Contexts and Texts of the Controversy about Women in England, 1540–1640*, Urbana: University of Illinois Press.

Heywood, T. (1640) *The Exemplary Lives and Memorable Acts of Nine the Most Worthy Women of the World*, London: Richard Royston.

Hill, G. (1984) *The Lords of Limit*, London: André Deutsch.

Hobbes, T. (1978) *Leviathan*, ed. C. B. Macpherson, Harmondsworth: Penguin.

Hoeniger, F. D. (1974) "The Artist Exploring the Primitive: King Lear," in R. L. Colie and F. T. Flahiff (eds), *Some Facets of King Lear: Essays in Prismatic Criticism*, Toronto: University of Toronto Press.

Holinshed, R. (1577) *The Chronicles of England, Scotland and Ireland*, London: Lucas Harrison.

—— (1587) *The Chronicles of England, Scotland, and Ireland*, London: [n.p.].

Hopkins, C. (1697) *Boadicea Queen of Britain*, London: Jacob Tonson.

Howard, J. E. (1994) "An English Lass Amid the Moors: Gender, Race, Sexuality, and National Identity in Heywood's *The Fair Maid of the West*," in M. Hendricks and P. Parker (eds), *Women, "Race," & Writing in the Early Modern Period*, London: Routledge.

Hunt, M. (1987) "Perspectivism in *King Lear* and *Cymbeline*," *Studies in the Humanities* 14: 18–31.

James I (1918) *Basilikon Doron*, in C. H. McIlwain (ed.), *The Political Works of James I*, Cambridge, MA, Harvard University Press.

Jankowski, T. A. (1992) *Women in Power in the Early Modern Drama*, Urbana: University of Illinois Press.

Johnson, S. (1968) "Johnson on Shakespeare," in *The Yale Edition of the Works of Samuel Johnson*, vol. VIII, New Haven: Yale University Press.

Johnston, D. (1986) *The Rhetoric of Leviathan*, Princeton: Princeton University Press.

Jones, A. R., and Stallybrass, P. (1992) "Dismantling Irena: The Sexualizing of Ireland in Early Modern England," in M. Russo, A. Parker, D. Sommer, and P. Yaeger (eds), *Nationalisms and Sexualities*, New York: Routledge.

Jones, E. (1961) "Stuart Cymbeline," *Essays in Criticism* 11: 84–99.

Jones, K. (1988) *A Glorious Fame: The Life of Margaret Cavendish, Duchess of Newcastle, 1623–73*, London: Bloomsbury.

Jonson, B. (1952) "The Masque of Queens," in C. H. Hereford, P. Simpson, and E. Simpson (eds), *Ben Jonson*, vol. VII, Oxford: Clarendon Press.

Jordan, C. (1987) "Women's Rule in Sixteenth-Century British Political Thought," *Renaissance Quarterly* 49: 421–51.

—— (1993) "The Household and the State: Transformations in the Representation of an Analogy from Aristotle to James I," *Modern Language Quarterly* 54: 307–26.

—— (1994) "Contract and Conscience in *Cymbeline*," *Renaissance Drama* 25: 33–58.

Jordanova, L. J. (1989) *Sexual Visions: Images of Gender in Science and Medicine between the Eighteenth and Twentieth Centuries*, Madison: University of Wisconsin Press.

Kahn, C. (1986) "The Absent Mother in *King Lear*," in M. W. Ferguson, M. Quilligan, and N. J. Vickers (eds), *Rewriting the Renaissance: The Discourses of Sexual Difference in Early Modern Europe*, Chicago: University of Chicago Press.

Kahn, V. (1985) *Rhetoric, Prudence, and Skepticism in the Renaissance*, Ithaca: Cornell University Press.

Kendrick, T. D. (1950) *British Antiquity*, London: Methuen.

Kibbey, A. (1986) *The Interpretation of Material Shapes in Puritanism: A Study of Rhetoric, Prejudice, and Violence*, Cambridge: Cambridge University Press.

King, J. N. (1990) "Queen Elizabeth I: Representations of the Virgin Queen," *Renaissance Quarterly* 43: 30–74.

Kirsch, A. C. (1967) "*Cymbeline* and Coterie Dramaturgy," *English Literary History* 34: 285–306.

Knight, G. W. (1947) *The Crown of Life*, London: Oxford University Press.

Knox, J. (1972) *The First Blast of the Trumpet against the Monstrous Regiment of Women*, Amsterdam: Theatrum Orbis Terrarum.

Kolodny, A. (1975) *The Lay of the Land: Metaphors as Experience and History in American Life and Letters*, Chapel Hill: University of North Carolina Press.

Landry, D. E. (1982) "Dreams as History: The Strange Unity of *Cymbeline*," *Shakespeare Quarterly* 33: 68–79.

Laqueur, T. (1990) *Making Sex: Body and Gender from the Greeks to Freud*, Cambridge: Harvard University Press.

Leggatt, A. (1977) "The Island of Miracles: An Approach to *Cymbeline*," *Shakespeare Studies* 10: 191–209.

Leverenz, D. (1980) *The Language of Puritan Feeling: An Exploration in Literature, Psychology and Social History*, New Brunswick, NJ: Rutgers University Press.

Levin, C. (1994) *The Heart and Stomach of a King: Elizabeth I and the Politics of Sex and Power*, Philadelphia: University of Pennsylvania Press.

Levin, H. (1963) "The Heights and the Depths: A Scene from *King Lear*," in R.

Fraser (ed.), *The Tragedy of King Lear*, New York: The Signet Classic Shakespeare.

Levine, D., and Wrightson, K. (1980) "The Social Context of Illegitimacy in Early Modern England," in P. Laslett, K. Oosterveen and R. M. Smith (eds), *Bastardy and its Comparative History*, Cambridge, MA: Harvard University Press.

Levine, J. M. (1987) *Humanism and History: Origins of Modern English Historiography*, Ithaca: Cornell University Press.

Levy, F. J. (1964) "The Making of Camden's Britannia," *Bibliothèque d'Humanisme et Renaissance* 26: 70–97.

—— (1965) "Daniel Rogers as Antiquary," *Bibliothèque d'Humanisme et Renaissance* 27: 444–62.

—— (1967) *Tudor Historical Thought*, San Marino, CA: The Huntington Library.

Lewalski, B. K. (1993) *Writing Women in Jacobean England*, Cambridge, MA: Harvard University Press.

Locke, J. (1993) *Two Treatises of Government*, ed. Peter Laslett, Cambridge: Cambridge University Press.

Lynam, E. (1934) *The Map of the British Isles of 1546*, Jenkintown: The George H. Beans Library.

MacCormack, C. P. (1980) "Nature, Culture and Gender: A Critique," in C. P. MacCormack and M. Strathern (eds), *Nature, Culture, and Gender*, Cambridge: Cambridge University Press.

Macdonald, S. (1987) "Boadicea: Warrior, Mother and Myth," in P. Holden, S. Macdonald, and S. Ardener (eds), *Images of Women in Peace and War: Cross-Cultural and Historical Perspectives*, London: Macmillan.

MacDougall, H. A. (1982) *Racial Myth in English History: Trojans, Teutons, and Anglo-Saxons*, Montreal: Harvest House.

McEachern, C. (1996) *The Poetics of English Nationhood, 1590–1612*, Cambridge: Cambridge University Press.

McLeod, G. (1991) *Virtue and Venom: Catalogs of Women from Antiquity to the Renaissance*, Ann Arbor: University of Michigan Press.

McLuhan, M. (1962) *The Gutenberg Galaxy*, Toronto: University of Toronto Press.

Mack, M. (1965) King Lear *in Our Time*, Berkeley: University of California Press.

Mack, P. (1992) *Visionary Women: Ecstatic Prophecy in Seventeenth-Century England*, Berkeley: University of California Press.

Mandowsky, E., and Mitchell, C. (1963) *Pirro Ligorio's Roman Antiquities*, London: Warburg Institute.

Marcus, L. S. (1988) "*Cymbeline* and the Unease of Topicality," in H. Dubrow and R. Strier (eds), *The Historical Renaissance: New Essays on Tudor and Stuart Literature and Culture*, Chicago: University of Chicago Press.

—— (1990) *Puzzling Shakespeare: Local Reading and Its Discontents*, Berkeley: University of California Press.

Maurer, M. (1989) "Reading Ben Jonson's *Queens*," in S. Fisher and J. E. Hailey (eds), *Seeking the Woman in Late Medieval and Renaissance Writings: Essays in Feminist Contextual Criticism*, Knoxville: University of Tennessee Press.

Maxwell, B. (1928) "Notes on Charles Hopkins' Boadicea," *Review of English Studies* 4: 79–83.

Mazzocco, A. (1975) "Petrarcha, Poggio and Biondo: Humanism's Foremost Interpreters of Roman Ruins," in A. Scaglione (ed.), *Francis Petrarch, Six Centuries Later*, Durham, NC: Duke University Press.

—— (1977) "The Antiquarianism of Francesco Petrarch," *Journal of Medieval and Renaissance Studies* 7: 203–24.

Mendyk, S. A. E. (1989) *"Speculum Britanniae": Regional Study, Antiquarianism and Science in Britain to 1700*, Toronto: University of Toronto Press.

Milton, J. (1971) "History of Britain," in F. Fogle (ed.), *Complete Prose Works of John Milton*, vol 5:1, New Haven, CT: Yale University Press.

—— (1978) *Complete Poems and Major Prose*, ed. Merritt Y. Hughes, Indianapolis: The Odyssey Press.

Miola, R. S. (1983) *Shakespeare's Rome*, Cambridge: Cambridge University Press.

—— (1984) "*Cymbeline*: Shakespeare's Valediction to Rome," in A. Patterson (ed.), *Roman Images*, Baltimore, MD: The Johns Hopkins University Press.

Mitchell, C. (1960) "Archaeology and Romance in Renaissance Italy," in E. F. Jacob (ed.), *Italian Renaissance Studies*, London: Faber.

Momigliano, A. (1950) "Ancient History and the Antiquarian," *Journal of the Warburg and Courtauld Institutes* 13: 285–315.

Montrose, L. A. (1983) " 'Shaping Fantasies': Figurations of Gender and Power in Elizabethan Culture," *Representations* 1: 61–94.

—— (1991) "The Work of Gender in the Discourse of Discovery," *Representations* 33: 1–41.

Moore, W. H. (1968) "Sources of Drayton's Conception of *Poly-Olbion*," *Studies in Philology* 65: 783–803.

Morgan, V. (1979) "The Cartographic Image of 'The Country' in Early Modern England," *Transactions of the Royal Historical Society* 5th ser. 29: 129–54.

—— (1983) "The Literary Image of Globes and Maps in Early Modern England," in S. Tyacke (ed.), *English Map-Making 1500–1650*, London: The British Library.

Mosse, G. L. (1985) *Nationalism and Sexuality: Respectability and Abnormal Sexuality in Modern Europe*, New York: Howard Fertig.

Nairn, T. (1981) *The Break-Up of Britain: Crisis and Neonationalism* (2nd edn), London: NLB and Verso Editions.

National Geographic Society (1950) *The Round Earth on Flat Paper: Map Projections*, Washington, DC: National Geographic Society.

Nearing, H. J., Jr (1949a) "The Legend of Julius Caesar's British Conquest," *Publications of the Modern Language Association* 64: 889–929.

—— (1949b) "Local Caesar Traditions in Britain," *Speculum* 24: 218–27.

Newman, K. (1991) *Fashioning Femininity and English Renaissance Drama*, Chicago: University of Chicago Press.

Nichols, J. (1823) *The Progresses and Public Processions of Queen Elizabeth*, vol. 2, London: John Nichols and Son.

O'Sullivan, T. (1978) *The De Excidio of Gildas: Its Authenticity and Date*, Leiden: E. J. Brill.

Okin, S. M. (1979) *Women in Western Political Thought*, Princeton: Princeton University Press.

Orgel, S. (1984) "Shakespeare Imagines a Theater," *Poetics Today* 5: 549–61.

Orme, N. (1989) *Education and Society in Medieval and Renaissance England*, London: The Hambledon Press.

Ortner, S. B. (1974) "Is Female to Male as Nature Is to Culture?" in M. Z. Rosaldo and L. Lamphere (eds), *Woman, Culture and Society*, Stanford, CA: Stanford University Press.

Parker, A., Russo, M., Sommer, D., and Yaeger, P. (eds) (1992) *Nationalisms and Sexualities*, New York: Routledge.

Parker, P. (1987) *Literary Fat Ladies: Rhetoric, Gender, Property*, London: Methuen.

—— (1989) "Romance and Empire: Anachronistic *Cymbeline*," in G. M. Logan and G. Teskey (eds) *Unfolded Tales: Essays on Renaissance Romance*, Ithaca: Cornell University Press. *Essays on Renaissance Romance,*

Parr, J. (1948) "John Rastell's Geographical Knowledge of America," *Philological Quarterly* 27: 229–40.

Paster, G. K. (1993) *The Body Embarrassed: Drama and the Disciplines of Shame in Early Modern English Culture*. Ithaca: Cornell University Press, 1993.

Pastoureau, M. (1984) *Les Atlas Français XVI–XVII Siècles*, Paris: Bibliothèque Nationale.

Pateman, C. (1988a) "The Fraternal Social Contract," in J. Keane (ed.), *Civil Society and the State: New European Perspectives*, New York: Verso.

—— (1988b) *The Sexual Contract*, Stanford: Stanford University Press.

Perry, R. (1991) "Colonizing the Breast: Sexuality and Maternity in Eighteenth-Century England," *Journal of the History of Sexuality* 2: 204–34.

Piggott, S. (1956) "Antiquarian Thought in the Sixteenth and Seventeenth Centuries," in L. Fox (ed.), *English Historical Scholarship in the Sixteenth and Seventeenth Centuries*, London: Oxford University Press.

—— (1989) *Ancient Britons and the Antiquarian Imagination: Ideas from the Renaissance to the Regency*, New York: Thames & Hudson.

Pitkin, H. F. (1967) *The Concept of Representation*, Berkeley: University of California Press.

Pocock, J. G. A. (1971) *Politics, Language, and Time: Essays on Political Thought and History*, New York: Atheneum.

—— (1975) "England," in O. Ranum (ed.), *National Consciousness, History, and Political Culture in Early-Modern Europe*, Baltimore: The Johns Hopkins University Press.

Prescott, A. L. (1991) "Marginal Discourse: Drayton's Muse and Selden's 'Story,'" *Studies in Philology* 88: 307–28.

Pye, C. (1984) "The Sovereign, the Theater, and the Kingdome of Darknesse: Hobbes and the Spectacle of Power," *Representations* 8: 84–106.

Rackin, P. (1990) *Stages of History: Shakespeare's English Chronicles*, Ithaca: Cornell University Press.

Raisz, E. (1962) *Principles of Cartography*, New York: McGraw-Hill.

Rastell, J. (1979) *Three Rastell Plays*, ed. Richard Axton, Cambridge: D. S. Brewer.

Revard, S. P. (1977) "The Design of Nature in Drayton's *Poly-Olbion*," *Studies in English Literature 1500–1900* 17: 105–17.

Ribner, I. (1956) "Shakespeare and Legendary History: *Lear* and *Cymbeline*," *Shakespeare Quarterly* 7: 47–52.

Ripa, C. (1976) *Iconologia*. New York: Garland.

Roper, L. (1994) *Oedipus and the Devil: Witchcraft, Sexuality and Religion in Early Modern Europe*, London: Routledge.

Rose, M. B. (1991) "Where Are the Mothers in Shakespeare? Options for Gender Representation in the English Renaissance," *Shakespeare Quarterly* 42: 291–314.

Rossi, J. W. (1978) "*Cymbeline*'s Debt to Holinshed: The Richness of III.i.," in C. M. Kay and H. E. Jacobs (eds), *Shakespeare's Romances Reconsidered*, Lincoln: University of Nebraska Press.

Rowley, W. (1910) *A Shoemaker, a Gentleman*, ed. Charles Wharton Stork, Philadelphia: John C. Winston.

Rowse, A. L. (1950) "The Elizabethan Discovery of England," in *The England of Elizabeth*, London: Macmillan.

Russell, C. (1989) *Unrevolutionary England, 1603–1642*, London: Hambledon Press.

S., J. (1695) *A Brief History of the Pious and Glorious Life and Actions of the Most Illustrious Princess, Mary Queen of England, Scotland, France and Ireland*, London: John Gwillim.

Sammes, A. (1676) *Britannia Antiqua Illustrata*, London: Thomas Roycroft.

Samuel, R. (ed.) (1989) *Patriotism: The Making and Unmaking of British National Identity*, 3 vols, London: Routledge.

Saxton, C. (1579) *[An Atlas of England and Wales]*. London: [n.p.].

Schelling, F. (1902) *The English Chronicle Play*, New York: Burt Franklin.

Schiebinger, L. (1993) "Why Mammals Are Called Mammals: Gender Politics in Eighteenth-Century Natural History," *The American Historical Review* 98: 382–411.

Schleiner, W. (1978) "Divina Virago: Queen Elizabeth as an Amazon," *Studies in Philology* 75: 163–80.

Schnucker, R. V. (1974) "The English Puritans and Pregnancy, Delivery and Breastfeeding," *History of Childhood Quarterly* 1: 637–58.

Schochet, G. J. (1975) *Patriarchalism in Political Thought*, New York: Basic Books.

Schwartz, M. M. (1970) "Between Fantasy and Imagination: A Psychological Exploration of *Cymbeline*," in F. Crews (ed.), *Psychoanalysis and Literary Process*, Cambridge, MA: Winthrop Publishers.

Shakespeare, W. (1963) *King Lear*, ed. Russell Fraser, New York: New American Library.

—— (1965) *1 Henry IV*, ed. Maynard Mack, New York: New American Library.

—— (1985) *Macbeth*, ed. Alfred Harbage, Harmondsworth: Penguin.

—— (1989) *Cymbeline*, ed. J. M. Nosworthy, London: Routledge.

—— (1989) *Cymbeline*, ed. Roger Warren, Manchester: Manchester University Press.

—— (1997) *The Norton Shakespeare*, ed. S. Greenblatt, W. Cohen, J. E. Howard, K. E. Maus, New York: Norton.

Sharpe, J. A. (1984) *Crime in Early Modern England, 1550–1750*, New York: Longman.

Sharpe, K. (1979) *Sir Robert Cotton, 1586–1631: History and Politics in Early Modern England*, Oxford: Oxford University Press.

—— (1989) *Politics and Ideas in Early Stuart England: Essays and Studies*, London: Pinter Publishers.

Shuger, D. K. (1990) *Habits of Thought in the English Renaissance: Religion, Politics, and the Dominant Culture*, Berkeley: University of California Press.

Siculus, D. (1939) *Diodorus of Sicily*, trans. C. H. Oldfather, vol. III, Cambridge, MA: Harvard University Press.

Silver, V. (1988) "The Fiction of Self-Evidence in Hobbes's *Leviathan*," *English Literary History* 55: 351–79.

Skinner, Q. (1996) *Reason and Rhetoric in the Philosophy of Hobbes*, Cambridge: Cambridge University Press.

Skura, M. (1980) "Interpreting Posthumus' Dream from Above and Below: Families, Psychoanalysts, and Literary Critics," in M. M. Schwartz and C. Kahn (eds), *Representing Shakespeare*, Baltimore, MD: The Johns Hopkins University Press.

Smith, W. D. (1952) "Cloten with Caius Lucius," *Studies in Philology* 49: 185–94.

Sowernam, E. (1985) "Esther Hath Hanged Haman," in K. U. Henderson and B. F. McManus (eds), *Half Humankind: Contexts and Texts of the Controversy about Women in England, 1540–1640*, Urbana: University of Illinois Press.

Spencer, T. J. B. (1957) "Shakespeare and the Elizabethan Romans," *Shakespeare Survey* 10: 27–38.

Spenser, E. (1934) "A View of the Present State of Ireland," ed. W. L. Renwick, London: Eric Partridge.

—— (1985) "The Faerie Queene," in J. C. Smith and E. de Selincourt (eds), *Poetical Works*, Oxford: Oxford University Press.

—— (1989) "The Ruines of Time," in William A. Oram, *et al.* (eds), *The Yale Edition of the Shorter Poems of Edmund Spenser*, New Haven, CT: Yale University Press.

Sprague, A. C. (1926) *Beaumont and Fletcher on the Restoration Stage*, Cambridge, MA: Harvard University Press.

Spufford, M. (1981) *Small Books and Pleasant Histories: Popular Fiction and its Readership in Seventeenth-Century England*, Cambridge: Cambridge University Press.

Stallybrass, P. (1986) "Patriarchal Territories: The Body Enclosed," in M. W. Ferguson, M. Quilligan, and N. J. Vickers (eds), *Rewriting the Renaissance: The Discourses of Sexual Difference in Early Modern Europe*, Chicago: University of Chicago Press.

Stillman, R. E. (1995) "Hobbes's *Leviathan*: Monsters, Metaphors, and Magic," *English Literary History* 62: 791–819.

Stone, L. (1979) *The Family, Sex and Marriage in England 1500–1800*, New York: Harper & Row.

Strong, E. (1937) "Terra Mater or Italia?" *Journal of Roman Studies* 27: 114–26.

Strong, R. (1973) *Splendor at Court: Renaissance Spectacle and the Theater of Power*, Boston, MA: Houghton Mifflin.

—— (1977) *The Cult of Elizabeth: Elizabethan Portraiture and Pageantry*, New York: Thames & Hudson.

—— (1980) *Britannia Triumphans: Inigo Jones, Rubens, and Whitehall Palace*, New York: Thames & Hudson.

—— (1987) *Gloriana: The Portraits of Queen Elizabeth I*, New York: Thames & Hudson.

Tacitus, C. (1932) *Agricola*, trans. Sir W. Peterson, London: W. B. Heinemann.

—— (1937) *The Annals*, trans. J. Jackson, Cambridge, MA: Harvard University Press.

Taylor, E. G. R. (1930) *Tudor Geography 1485–1583*, London: Methuen.

Taylor, H. (1926) "Topographical Poetry in England During the Renaissance," PhD dissertation, University of Chicago.

Thomas, K. (1983) "The Perception of the Past in Early Modern England," in *The Creighton Trust Lecture*, London: University of London.

Thompson, A. (1991) "Person and Office: The Case of Imogen, Princess of Britain," in V. Newey and A. Thompson (eds), *Literature and Nationalism*, Savage, Maryland: Barnes & Noble.

Thorne, W. B. (1969) "*Cymbeline*: 'Lopp'd Branches' and the Concept of Regeneration," *Shakespeare Quarterly* 20: 143–59.

Trumbach, R. (1978) *The Rise of the Egalitarian Family: Aristocratic Kinship and Domestic Relations in Eighteenth-Century England*, New York: Academic Press.

Turner, J. (1988) "The Tragic Romances of Feudalism," in G. Holderness, N. Potter, and J. Turner (eds), *Shakespeare: the Play of History*, Iowa City: University of Iowa Press.

Underdown, D. (1985) "The Taming of the Scold: the Enforcement of Patriarchal Authority in Early Modern England," in A. Fletcher and J. Stevenson (eds), *Order and Disorder in Early Modern England*, Cambridge: Cambridge University Press.

—— (1987) *Revel, Riot and Rebellion: Popular Politics and Culture in England, 1603–1660*, Oxford: Oxford University Press.

van Norden, L. (1946) "The Elizabethan College of Antiquaries," PhD dissertation, UCLA.

Vergil, P. (1950) *Anglica Historica, A.D. 1485–1537*, ed. and trans. D. Hay, London: Royal Historical Society.

Virgil (1950) *Eclogues*, trans. H. R. Fairclough, vol. 1, Cambridge: Cambridge University Press.

Warner, M. (1985) *Monuments and Maidens: The Allegory of the Female Form*, New York: Atheneum.

Weiss, R. (1969) *The Renaissance Discovery of Classical Antiquity*, New York: Humanities Press.

Wells, C. (1993) *The Wide Arch: Roman Values in Shakespeare*, New York: St Martin's Press.

Willis, D. (1995) *Malevolent Nurture: Witch-Hunting and Maternal Power in Early Modern England*, Ithaca, Cornell University Press.

Witkowski, G. J. (1903) *Les Seins dans l'histoire*, Paris: A. Maloine.

—— (1907) *Les Seins à l'Eglise*, Paris: A. Maloine.

Wolin, S. S. (1960) *Politics and Vision: Continuity and Innovation in Western Political Thought*, Boston: Little, Brown.

—— (1970) *Hobbes and the Epic Tradition of Political Theory*, Los Angeles: William Andrews Clark Memorial Library.

Woodbridge, L. (1984) *Women and the English Renaissance: Literature and the Nature of Womankind, 1540–1620*, Urbana: University of Illinois Press.

—— (1991) "Palisading the Elizabethan Body Politic," *Texas Studies in Literature and Language* 33, no. 3: 327–54.

Woodward, D. (1987) "Medieval *Mappaemundi*," in J. B. Harley and D. Woodward (eds), *History of Cartography*, vol. 1, Chicago: University of Chicago Press.

Woolf, D. R. (1987) "Erudition and the Idea of History in Renaissance England," *Renaissance Quarterly* 40: 11–48.

—— (1990) *The Idea of History in Early Stuart England: Erudition, Ideology, and "The Light of Truth" from the Accession of James I to the Civil War*, Toronto: University of Toronto Press.

Wright, C. T. (1946) "The Elizabethan Female Worthies," *Studies in Philology* 43: 628–43.

Wrightson, K. (1975) "Infanticide in Earlier Seventeenth-Century England," *Local Population Studies* 15: 10–22.

—— (1980) "The Nadir of English Illegitimacy in the Seventeenth Century," in P. Laslett, K. Oosterveen, and R. M. Smith (eds), *Bastardy and its Comparative History*, Cambridge, MA: Harvard University Press.

Yates, F. A. (1975a) *Astraea: The Imperial Theme in the Sixteenth Century*. London: Routledge & Kegan Paul.

—— (1975b) *Shakespeare's Last Plays: A New Approach*, London: Routledge & Kegan Paul.

Zernatto, G. (1944) "Nation: The History of a Word," *Review of Politics* 6: 351–66.

Zimmerman, L. M., and Vieth, I. (1967) *Great Ideas in the History of Surgery*, New York: Dover Publications.

INDEX

Note: *Page references in italics indicate illustrations.*